PLAINS HISTORIES

John R. Wunder, *Series Editor*

WHERE THE WEST BEGINS

DEBATING TEXAS IDENTITY

WHERE THE WEST BEGINS

GLEN SAMPLE ELY

FOREWORD BY ALWYN BARR

TEXAS TECH UNIVERSITY PRESS

This book is typeset in Monotype Haarlemmer. The paper used in this book
meets the minimum requirements of ANSI/NISO Z39.48–1992 (R1997).

Designed by Lindsay Starr

LIBRARY OF CONGRESS CATALOGING-IN-PUBLICATION DATA
Ely, Glen Sample.
Where the West begins : debating Texas identity / Glen Sample Ely ;
foreword by Alwyn Barr.
p. cm. — (Plains histories)
Summary: "Examines the historical debate surrounding Texas's identity: investi-
gates whether Texas, with its heritage of slavery, segregation, and cotton
production, is 'Southern' or, with its cowboys, cattle drives, mountains,
and desert, is 'Western'"—Provided by publisher.
Includes bibliographical references and index.
ISBN 978-0-89672-724-3 (hardcover : alk. paper) 1. Texas—Civilization. 2. Texas—
Social life and customs. 3. Group identity—Texas. 4. Texas—Relations—
Southern States. 5. Texas—Relations—West (U.S.) 6. Southern
States—Relations—Texas. 7. West (U.S.)—
Relations—Texas. I. Title.
F386.E57 2011
976.4—dc22   2010051912

PRINTED IN THE UNITED STATES OF AMERICA
11   12   13   14   15   16   17   18   19   /   9   8   7   6   5   4   3   2   1

TEXAS TECH UNIVERSITY PRESS
Box 41037, Lubbock, Texas 79409–1037 USA
800.832.4042 | ttup@ttu.edu | www.ttupress.org

To Harwood Perry Hinton, Jr., and Diana Davids Hinton,
with much admiration and appreciation.

CONTENTS

ILLUSTRATIONS

ACKNOWLEDGMENTS

Numerous people and institutions generously assisted the author over the last seven years. Without their help, this work would not have been possible. The author extends his gratitude to Plains Histories Series Editor John R. Wunder; Todd M. Kerstetter; Ben Johnson; Gregg Cantrell; Pecos County Clerk's Office; Noel Parsons, Robert Mandel, Judith Keeling, Karen Medlin, and Joanna Conrad at Texas Tech University Press; Fort Stockton Public Library; Pat McDaniel and Jim Bradshaw at the Haley Library; John Anderson and Donaly Brice at the Texas State Library and Archives; Joan Kilpatrick, Doug Howard, John Molleston, Bobby Santiesteban, and Susan Dorsey at the Texas General Land Office Archives; Kit Goodwin, Cathy Spitzenberger, and Brenda McClurkin at University of Texas–Arlington Special Collections Library; Kay Edmonson and Jill Kendle at TCU Interlibrary Loan Department; Jim Ed Miller; Joe Primera; M. R. González; Betty Hargus; Colonel Thomas "Ty" Smith; Fort Stockton ISD; City Manager's Office, City of Fort Stockton; Suzanne Campbell and the West Texas Collection Staff at Angelo State University; Dave Kuhne, Cynthia Shearer, and Harry Antrim at the TCU Writing Center; Janet Neugebauer and Randy Vance at the Southwest Collection, Texas Tech University; University of Texas–El Paso Special Collections Library; Patrick March Dearen; Donald Worster; and Texas A&M Agricultural Extension Service, Fort Stockton.

Appreciation also goes to Tom Beard, Jesús F. de la Teja, Clara Duran, Bruce Glasrud, Charles Hart, Skeet Lee Jones, Robert J. Kinucan, Bill Leftwich, Bill Moody, Pete Terrazas, Jerry D. Thompson, Rick McCaslin, Robert Wooster, Mike Foster, Gary Williams, Mike Mecke, Gordon Morris Bakken, Paul Carlson, Alwyn Barr, Byron Price, Arnoldo De León, Oscar Martínez, Sherry Smith, Bob Righter, Quendrid and Ralph Veatch, David Weber, Martha King, Holle Humphries, Bill Phillips, Glynda Reynolds, Cathie and Len Jackson, Dan Penner, Sally Sample, Roland Taylor Ely, Melinda Ann Veatch, Janice Whittington, and Howard Lamar.

PLAINSWORD

Western images came to dominate the popular memory and mythology of Texas and Texans in the twentieth century, and continue to hold sway in the twenty-first. For a striking example, one need look no further than the names of most professional sports teams created in the state during the late 1900s—Cowboys, Texas Rangers, Spurs, and Mavericks. Movies, and later television shows, about cattle drives and ranching helped create, then reinforce, popular perception of Texas as part of the West. Even as film and television portrayals of the Battle of the Alamo seemed to generate Anglo American and Anglo Texan nationalism or exceptionalism, the battle's frontier setting lent its story a western theme.

In part those dramatizations rested upon the works of nineteenth-century historical writers, who often combined a romantic style with the concept of manifest destiny. Professional historians of the late 1800s and early 1900s provided more research as a basis for their studies, while continuing to reinforce ideas of Anglo dominance. Some prominent historians of the early to mid-twentieth century, including Eugene C. Barker and Walter Prescott Webb, emphasized Texas in its nineteenth-century frontier period. Popular writers even in the early 2000s continue to devote much of their attention to lively tales of that era.

Other Texas historical writers in the late 1800s and early 1900s focused attention on the southern and Confederate heritage of most Anglo

Texans. These views led to romantic images about the antebellum South and the Confederacy, reflected in numerous statues and memorials in East and Central Texas. One monument, however, in Comfort, in the Hill Country west of Austin, honors Texans of that area who died fighting for the Union. Beginning with Charles Ramsdell, professional historians began to examine the cultural and economic interest of Anglo Texans in cotton production based on slavery and later sharecropping.

According to historian Walter Buenger, that southern and Civil War mythology of a Lost Cause began to be replaced in Texas during the early to mid-twentieth century by more positive accounts of the Texas Revolution and a frontier that advanced westward. Texas Senator Lyndon B. Johnson provided a practical example when he emphasized his western ranching background, allowing him to more easily establish an appealing national image as a presidential candidate in the 1960s.

Still other historians and historical geographers sought to solve conflicting southern and western images of Texas by analyzing which regions of Texas might fall more clearly into one category or the other. Interest in regionalism also led to the creation of historical organizations that focused on West, East, or South Texas. Furthermore, several historians have contributed specialized studies of subregions. Books about areas in West Texas have focused on the Panhandle, the South Plains, Northwest Texas, and the Big Bend, while almost none have encompassed the entire region.

Glen Sample Ely offers thoughtful and thought-provoking new approaches to these debates. First he challenges the view that all of Texas has been dominated by southern attitudes. To support that conclusion he presents evidence that such concepts break down in a transitional region across west central Texas where the natural environment altered economic activity and cultural ideas. There he finds mixed views of the Confederacy and problems with frontier defense during the Civil War. Thus he offers further perspective on discussions of whether the frontier receded while that conflict raged. His most important revelation is the development of trade between Confederates in Texas and the Union forces in New Mexico.

Ely is not content to defend old, popular images of West Texas. Instead he presents new views of the region that are more complex and analytical as he explores issues and questions raised by the new Western historians including Patricia Limerick and Richard White. Nevertheless, he chides them for not devoting more attention to West Texas in their studies.

Two valuable elements that distinguish this study from earlier histories of West Texas are Ely's emphasis on the Trans-Pecos border region and his long-term view of western Texas history. Both lead to an expanded awareness of Tejano history as well as ethnic and religious diversity in West Texas. The lengthy presence of Mexican Americans also narrows the concept of Anglo domination in West Texas to a limited period. While Anglo assumptions of superiority led to discrimination, cultural exchange and cooperation also occurred. Patterns of racial violence are undeniable, but far less extensive than in other parts of the state, which more closely mirrored the American South.

Ely's inclusion of the Trans Pecos in his long view of West Texas contributes also to his analysis of how natural resources have been managed. He finds problems with conservation of water and grasslands that foreshadow declines in farming and ranching.

Clearly this is a challenging new interpretation of which areas form West Texas, why it is different from other regions of the state, and how these differences will play into its future. Even careful questioning of popular historical images is sure to stir debate. Without doubt, however, Ely has altered the shape of several discussions about Lone Star myths and realities, especially as they relate West Texas to larger patterns of western, southern, and national history.

ALWYN BARR

WHERE THE WEST BEGINS

Detail from a Fort Worth Police car with the Cowtown logo and the city's motto, coined by Amon Carter in the 1920s. Photo by author.

WHERE THE WEST BEGINS

The motto on the side of the parked police cruiser reads "Fort Worth: Where the West Begins." Since the 1920s, the City of Fort Worth has actively promoted this slogan, after local newspaper publisher Amon Carter, Sr., inserted it into his paper's masthead. Over the ensuing decades, Carter and the city persistently endeavored to brand Fort Worth as "western." For example, in 1936 Carter spearheaded the Texas Frontier Centennial in Fort Worth to promote the "culture and atmosphere of the old frontier."[1]

Over the last century, the city also acquired the nickname "Cowtown." With its old frontier fort, Stock Show, Stockyards, Wild West shows, Sundance Square (after Butch Cassidy and the Sundance Kid), cattle drives, cowboys, and shootouts, Fort Worth certainly seems to exude a western identity. During a more recent image makeover, city promoters coined the motto "Cowboys and Culture," projecting a refined and cultured western identity. With its world-class Museum District (Amon Carter, Sid Richardson, Kimbell, and The Modern art museums), "Cowtown" provides just the right blend of Wild West and genteel sophistication.[2]

Fort Worth promotes a western image and markets itself as "Where the West Begins," but is this really the case? Is Cowtown part of the American West? Consider the following. On July 17, 1860, a vigilante mob in Fort Worth lynched alleged abolitionist William H. Crawford from a pecan tree. Supposedly, Crawford was stockpiling a cache of weapons to aid in a slave insurrection. On September 13, 1860, another Fort Worth mob hung Methodist Episcopal Church minister Anthony Bewley from the same pecan limb used to dispatch Crawford two months earlier. Like Crawford, Bewley was allegedly "involved in a murderous abolitionist plot." Citizens of Fort Worth were petrified that abolitionist allies of John Brown, who led the October 16, 1859, raid on Harpers Ferry, Virginia, would try and foment a similar slave revolt in North Texas.[3]

Finally, consider Tarrant County (where Fort Worth is the county seat) and its vote in the statewide secession referendum of February 23, 1861. On that date residents of Fort Worth and Tarrant County voted overwhelmingly for secession by an almost four to one margin. Clearly, Fort Worth residents were concerned with protecting slavery, stopping abolitionists, and preventing slave rebellions. While Cowtown may promote itself today as western, on the eve of the Civil War its mindset appeared decidedly southern. Fort Worth's identity, then, is both confusing and contradictory. Chapter Five further explores the city's characteristics.[4]

Fort Worth's example is representative of Texas as a whole. Like Cowtown, Texas is wrestling with an identity crisis; unsure which of its legacies are accurate and uneasy about which ones to embrace. Today, the Lone Star State sometimes resembles a lumbering Atlas shouldering the unwieldy burden of multiple personalities, and the state is in the midst of a culture war for control of its identity and history. Some Lone Star scholars insist that Texas, with its heritage of slavery, segregation, and historic dependence upon cotton, is southern. Another group of historians argue that Texas is western, as evidenced by its cowboys, cattle drives, mountains, and desert. Still others say that the Lone Star State is unique, winning its independence from Mexico during the Texas Revolution and existing as an independent republic for ten years prior to joining the Union.[5]

Texans may want to consider carefully before augmenting their Lone Star lineage with either a southern or western identity because both of these regions, like Texas, have their own confusing and conflicted legacies and plenty of historical baggage. The South is still grappling with its identity and coming to terms with its past, as C. Vann Woodward notes in his work, *The Burden of Southern History*. Woodward says that the southern legacy has not always been in sync with the national narrative. For example, throughout much of their history, Americans believed in a national "legend of success and invincibility." Americans also saw themselves as living in a land of plenty and as a people blessed with freedoms that many in Europe could not enjoy.[6]

In the South, however, many were not living in abundance, and poverty was widespread. In addition, a number of its residents, most notably African Americans, were not free but held in slavery or oppressed by a Jim Crow–Ku Klux Klan society that deprived them of their basic constitutional rights. Finally, unlike the rest of America, the South did not share the same national legend of success and inevitability. Southern history included "not only an overwhelming military defeat" during the Civil War but also the humiliation of Reconstruction and occupation and "long decades of defeat in the provinces of economic, social, and political life."[7]

For those seeking to escape the South's problems by heading out West, it should be noted that the western frontier offered no safe haven. The region had its own incommodious legacy that was also often at odds with the national narrative. As Patricia Limerick notes in her chapter "The Burdens of Western American History," those who invoke the western frontier and its rugged, individualistic Anglo pioneers as the embodiment of America's finest ideals and national character do so at "considerable risk." For when one invokes an idealistic memory of the Old West, "the brutal massacres come back along with the cheerful barn raisings, the shysters come back with the saints," and the treaties "broken come back with contracts fulfilled." Like the South, the American West has its own embarrassing share of violence, racism, and mistreatment of minorities.[8]

Ultimately, as Texas resolves its own unique historical encumbrances, it must also address these southern and western elements of the Lone Star heritage. Throughout its existence, Texas has juggled a complicated assortment of identities. Consequently, the state's multiple characteristics often confuse historians. Because many southern and western scholars do not know what to make of Texas, they ignore it altogether.

Interestingly, some western historians, while acknowledging Texas's rightful place in the Old West, now exclude it from today's New American West. Perhaps the Lone Star State and its multiple identities are just too confusing to unravel. With its immense land size, its notable environmental, geographical, and cultural differences, its status as a onetime independent republic, its colorful history and larger-than-life legends, Texas does indeed seem "like a whole other country." Piled on top of all this confusion is the state's sometimes comic book mythology that brashly claims "everything is bigger and better in Texas."[9]

All of this, then, raises the question. Is Texas, and more specifically West Texas, southern, western, or unique? The present study resolves this thorny question. Texas's identity issue is one that the state has often wrestled with since joining the Union on February 19, 1846. At various times during its history, people have viewed the Lone Star State as western, southern, and one of a kind. Over the last several decades, however, scholars of Texas's Southern School have increasingly promoted "the oneness of Texas and the rest of the South." Several issues drive this new southern orientation. The first is what Paul Lack calls "the Long Shadow of Eugene C. Barker." Lack might well have added Barker's fellow historian Walter Prescott Webb to that long shadow. Both men were greatly influenced by Frederick Jackson Turner and his frontier thesis that was much in vogue during the first half of the twentieth century.[10]

For many years Barker and Webb exerted significant influence on the scope of Lone Star history. Central to the writings of these men was the theme of superior Anglo American stock, divinely ordained to fulfill its manifest destiny and bring civilization and order to the savage frontier. These authors believed that the western frontier experience imbued citizens with the essential national characteristics necessary for sustaining a modern American democracy. This chauvinistic glorification of Anglo Americans marching inexorably westward and conquering the frontier dominated Texas publications for decades.[11] (Throughout this book the words *Anglo* and *white* are often used interchangeably.)

The wide acclaim and success that Barker and Webb enjoyed from their books only served to stifle alternative viewpoints and voices. Minorities, women, and another part of Texas, the southern Texas, received scant recognition during this period. For decades Texas writers of both southern history and literature chafed under the pair's "western frontier shadow." With the passing of Barker and Webb by the mid-1960s, their concept of Texas and its history was open to challenge.

Since the late 1980s, Texas's Southern School has actively reshaped the discussion of Lone Star history to fit its perspective, a southern perspective. These historians argue that Texas is actually southern in nature, and they dismiss West Texas's rich heritage as brief and limited and of only marginal import to the state's overall history. Ironically, by seeing Lone Star history as primarily southern, members of Texas's Southern School have in turn cast their own, "long southern shadow," a vision every bit as stifling as Barker and Webb's western frontier orientation.[12]

As to which is the more significant field of study, western or southern, one needs to remember that what is deemed "important" at any given time in Texas history depends on what school of thought is ascendant at that particular moment. Whoever controls Texas history also influences Texas identity. In shaping their vision of Lone Star history and memory, Texas's Southern School portrays the eastern half of Texas and its southern heritage as the "real" Texas, or the "most important part" of Texas, while marginalizing a Texan West. Their "Texas is southern" vision falls apart, however, when one looks closely at the long duré of West Texas. Attempts to superimpose a predominant southern culture, Old South slavery, and a southern agrarian model upon the western region of Texas, from its Spanish period to the twenty-first century and beyond, are simply not sustainable.

For several decades, arguments by Texas's Southern School have largely gone unanswered. It is time, then, to take a fresh look at what exactly Texas is and what it is not. Is Texas southern? Is it western? Does the American West begin in the western part of Texas, and if so, how can one accurately discern this? Environment, culture, and race relations all prove useful in determining the various aspects of Texas identity.

Starting with the environment, West Texas features two major ecosystems. The first is the Great Plains. Within the Great Plains are two subsections: the High Plains, and the Edwards Plateau. The High Plains encompasses the Texas Panhandle southward to Midland. The Edwards Plateau lies south of Midland to Ozona, Uvalde, Del Rio, and the Rio Grande. Major cities in this ecosytem include Amarillo, Lubbock,

Midland, Odessa, Abilene, and San Angelo. West Texas's second major physiographic region is the Intermontane Plateau, or Basin and Range Province. This region includes the Trans-Pecos, that area lying west of the Pecos River to El Paso, the region's largest city.[13]

In 1905 Vernon Bailey, Chief Field Naturalist for the U.S. Department of Agriculture, conducted a biological survey of Texas. Bailey observed that "the eastern part of Texas, west to approximately the 98th meridian, agrees very closely in climate, physiography, and the bulk of its species of plants and animals with the lower Mississippi Valley." At the 98th meridian, he discerned "a well-defined division" between East and West. The naturalist found that "by combining the limits of range of eastern and western species of mammals, birds, reptiles, and plants, an average line of change can be traced across the State." At the 98th meridian, Vernon Bailey had discovered the eastern edge of Texas's environmental transition zone.[14]

Studies by other naturalists and geographers conclude that in the western half of Texas, the arid Chihuahuan Desert, 8,700-foot mountain ranges (Guadalupe Mountains), and the semiarid Great Plains converge to form a distinctly western environment. Today, a drive across the Llano Estacado Caprock near Dickens, or along the Devils and Pecos rivers, reveals an authentic glimpse of the American West. One might also hike to the top of 7,800-foot Emory Peak, located in the Big Bend's portion of the vast Chihuahuan Desert, where the view of the Rio Grande below with Mexico on the other side remains a truly magnificent southwestern panorama. Prickly, harsh, dry, dusty, and rugged, this is typical desert terrain and every bit as southwestern as that found in New Mexico, Arizona, and California. Clearly, then, West Texas's geography is quite distinct from that of East Texas and the South.[15]

The East-West transition zone described by Vernon Bailey in 1905 can still be seen fifty miles north/northwest of Fort Worth. Lying next to Clear Creek in far southwestern Cooke County is a massive 900-foot-high natural barrier called The Backbone. This rocky, rugged ridge is located on the eastern edge of Texas's Western Cross Timbers (also known as Upper Cross Timbers), a hilly, broken country covered with dense forests of post oak and blackjack.[16]

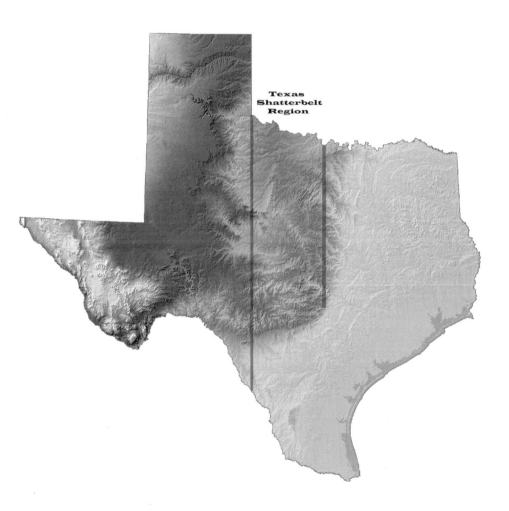

Texas Shatterbelt Region

Texas's unique western terrain, including Texas's ecological transition zone, the Shatterbelt Region, which lies between the 98th and 100th meridians. Map courtesy of Texas Water Development Board. Details added by author.

The Backbone, located in the Upper or Western Cross Timbers. The Upper Cross Timbers are on the eastern edge of Texas's Shatterbelt Region, which extends 200 miles westward to the 100th meridian. Map detail from *S.A. Mitchell's No. 12 Map of the State of Texas, 1859*. Courtesy of the Virginia Garrett Cartographic History Library, Special Collections, University of Texas at Arlington Library, Arlington, Texas. Backbone detail added by author.

The Western Cross Timbers comprise part of Texas's environmental and cultural netherworld, forming essentially a shatterbelt or transition zone. This 200-mile-wide shatterbelt extends westward from Decatur, east of the 98th meridian, to Sweetwater, Texas, west of the 100th meridian. Within this transition zone, America's Old South collides with the Old West, scattering and commingling fragments of each over a broad area. Ecologically and culturally, Texas's shatterbelt has a mixed identity, possessing both southern and western characteristics. By the time one reaches Sweetwater beyond the 100th meridian, however, this part of Texas westward to El Paso clearly has far more in common with the American West than it does with the Old South.[17]

At The Backbone on Clear Creek, the average annual rainfall is thirty inches. Beyond Sweetwater at the western edge of the shatterbelt, precipitation drops to twenty inches a year. It is at this twenty-inch rainfall line that the nineteenth-century South petered out into the arid West. West Texas's drought-prone environment and lack of modern irrigation technology meant that East Texas had encountered what Walter Prescott Webb calls an "institutional fault" zone where "the ways of life and of living changed." Geoff Cunfer refers to this zone as "natural limits" of rainfall, temperature, and soil limitations that nature places upon people living in the region.[18]

Aridity has shaped much of the history and culture of the American West since man first came to the region. Walter Buenger observes that prior to the Civil War, "agricultural patterns determined by the environment . . . distinguished the frontier from the rest of Texas." John Wesley Powell's 1878 congressional report on aridity in the western United States revealed that successful agriculture in the West required rainfall of at least twenty inches a year. Any crops receiving less than that amount required irrigation. In Texas's High Plains and South Plains regions, the twenty-inch rainfall line falls between the 101st and the 102nd meridians near Amarillo and Lubbock, Texas. In the Rolling Plains and Edwards Plateau sections of West Texas, the twenty-inch rainfall line is between the 100th and the 101st meridians, near Colorado City.[19]

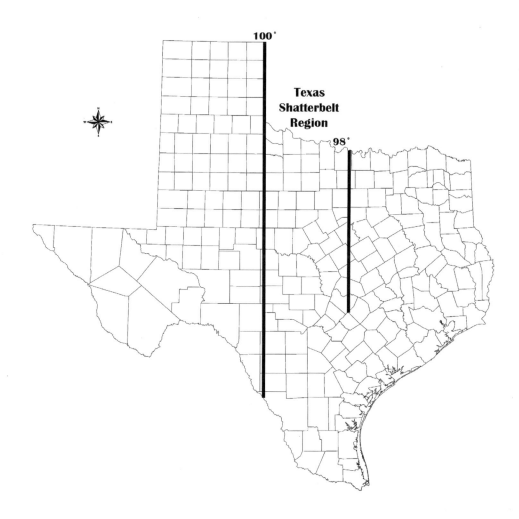

Texas's ecological and cultural Shatterbelt Region, lying between the 98th and
100th meridians, where the South slams into the West and begins to fragment.
Texas Counties Map courtesy of Texas Parks and Wildlife Department.
Details added by author.

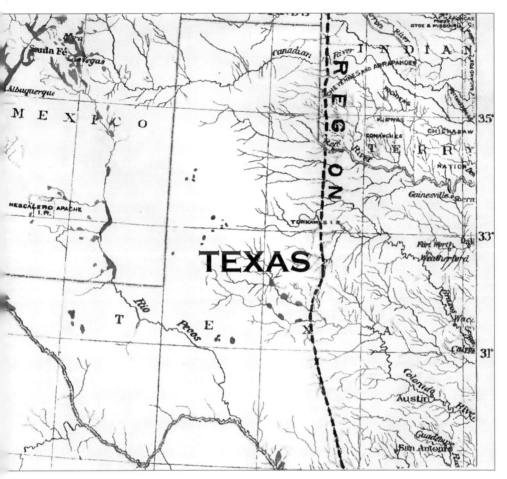

Close-up detail of John Wesley Powell's Arid Region Twenty-Inch Rainfall
Line in West Texas. From *11th Annual Report*, 1891, USGS, Part II,
Irrigation, by John Wesley Powell.

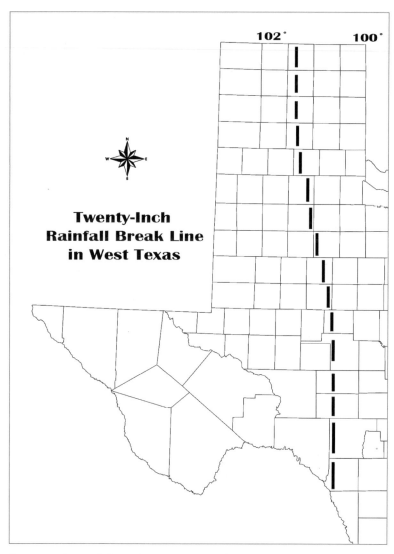

Twenty-Inch Rainfall Break Line in Texas today. This line, from south to north, is just east of the 101st meridian near Del Rio and Colorado City, Texas, to just east of the 102nd meridian, near Lubbock and Amarillo, Texas. Texas Counties Map courtesy of Texas Parks and Wildlife Department. Details added by author.

It is highly unlikely that in the nineteenth century, widespread cotton agriculture typical of the South could have ever taken hold west of the 100th meridian. As Donald Green and Geoff Cunfer have shown, West Texas lacked adequate irrigation methods until the late 1930s and the development of affordable well-drilling technology. The 1930s Dust Bowl disaster amply illustrated the pitfalls of dry-land farming beyond the 100th meridian. Because of these technological and natural limitations, irrigation and cotton farming did not proliferate in the region until after World War II.[20]

Interestingly, the Nueces River in Texas served as the western boundary for the Spanish province of Tejas during the late eighteenth and early nineteenth centuries. The Nueces, located at the 100th meridian near the present-day cities of Uvalde and Carrizo Springs, approximates nature's arid fault zone. In the 1820s and 1830s, colonists in Stephen F. Austin's Colony who owned slaves established their cotton-based economy in the more humid, greener region of Texas to the east.[21]

West of the 100th meridian, dry-land agriculture often frustrated farmers in the nineteenth and twentieth centuries. Current research in Texas reinforces Powell's report on western aridity. Studies show that south of Odessa and west of Big Lake and Ozona, all crops require irrigation. North and east of this line, in the Panhandle and the rest of West Texas, some dry-land farming is possible during years of moderate or ample rainfall. In prolonged droughts, however, even dry-land agriculture in this region will fail. During dry years, farmers in this part of West Texas are also forced to rely upon irrigation.[22]

In the Trans-Pecos, large-scale agricultural endeavors tried to conquer the natural limits of this arid region and lost. Irrigated farming, which peaked during the 1960s, is now in decline. Currently, irrigation consumes 75 percent of the water in West Texas, and in the coming decades, urban and industrial water demands will marginalize those of waning agricultural interests. Federal Farm Service agents throughout the area confirm that large-scale irrigation in the Trans-Pecos is unsustainable in the future.[23]

While widespread irrigated farming in the South Plains and Texas Panhandle continues, they soon will share the same fate. Geoff Cunfer's research shows that in "coming decades" farmers in this part of West Texas will largely deplete the Ogallala Aquifer, from which they pump water for their crops. The region's reserves of underground water and natural gas (used to pump water) are not renewable, and when they are exhausted, "that's it." Cunfer says, "Farmers will eventually use up their underground water supply and will then be pulled back within natural limits imposed by climate." He predicts that these natural limits will force people to change their lifestyles. Some may return to livestock grazing on rangeland, supplemented with dry-land farming. During future droughts, however, dry-land farmers will have nothing to fall back on, leaving them vulnerable once again to widespread crop failures and Dust Bowl conditions.[24]

Beyond the 100th meridian in Texas, man's attempt to conquer aridity with irrigation has largely failed. Within this century, farmers living west of the 100th meridian will once again confront the constraints of Webb's institutional fault zone. Future scholars taking the long view of West Texas history will likely interpret large-scale irrigated farming in the region as a temporary phenomenon lasting from 1940 to 2040. From the times of John Wesley Powell, to Walter Prescott Webb, to today, aridity has always been and will remain a defining characteristic of the West. A more detailed environmental history of West Texas's agricultural and pastoral economies can be found in Chapter Four.

If West Texas's climate, terrain, and border with Mexico are decidedly atypical of states located in the American South, what can one say about its people? Native American tribes living in West Texas differed distinctively from those found in the eastern half of the state. The Backbone and Western Cross Timbers region discussed above not only marked a change from eastern to western ecosystems near the 98th meridian but also served as an east-west demarcation line for Native Americans. Todd M. Kerstetter describes this zone as "a tribal frontier." Anthropologists have determined that, from 1848 to 1861, the Caddos and Wichitas were the dominant tribes on the eastern side of Texas's shatterbelt region. On the western side, tribes more representative of the American West and Great Plains held sway, specifically the Kiowa, Comanche, and Apache (KCA) tribes.[25]

Along the antebellum frontier, the territory claimed by Comanches and their allies, the Kiowas, extended west from the Western Cross Timbers to beyond the Pecos River and south across the Edwards Plateau to just above San Antonio and Austin. The Pecos River served as another tribal frontier, in this case a buffer zone between Comanches and Apaches. West of the Pecos River to El Paso on the Rio Grande was primarily Mescalero Apache country although Comanches often traveled through the region. In the mid-nineteenth century, horses, buffalo hunting, trading, and raiding characterized KCA life in West Texas. By 1881 the U.S. Army had forced the KCA tribes onto reservations outside of Texas. The Kiowas and Comanches are now in Oklahoma while the Mescalero Apaches are in New Mexico. The Tiguas, a much smaller Native American tribe, still live at Ysleta, Texas, and in contrast to KCA Plains Indians, they are "classic Pueblo peoples."[26]

After Texas joined the Union in 1846, the first three counties created in the western half of the state were El Paso, Presidio, and Pecos (carved out of Presidio in 1871). For almost twenty-five years, these counties lying west of the Pecos River formed the nucleus of historic West Texas. Federal census records for these counties from 1860 to 1890 show that most of their population was Mexican American. Historically, blacks have always had a smaller presence in the American West than in the South, typically comprising no more than 4–7 percent of the total population. The same disparity held true between black populations in West and East Texas. In 1860 in Harrison County, for example, blacks accounted for more than 50 percent of the population,[27] whereas the total population of African Americans in West Texas comprised only .006 percent, proving that the institution of slavery never gained a toehold west of the 100th meridian.

An analysis of the 1860 federal census reveals that, as shown in the following table, the counties of El Paso, neighboring Presidio, and Maverick (with its county seat of Eagle Pass) had very few slaves.[28]

1860 POPULATION

County	Residents	Slaves	White Southerners
El Paso	4,000	15	83
Presidio	600	5	28
Maverick	725	1	25

In these three counties most inhabitants were Tejanos. Out of Maverick County's residents, less than 4 percent were white southerners. In El Paso County, Anglos of southern origin comprised only 2 percent of the population, Northerners and Europeans 5 percent, U.S. soldiers 3 percent, and Tejanos accounted for the remaining 90 percent. In Presidio County, southern Anglos represented just 5 percent of the population, while 16 percent were from the North and Europe, 24 percent belonged to the military, and 55 percent were Mexican American. In sum, the census figures show that in 1860 the vast majority of West Texas residents were not southern.[29]

Regarding southern identity among those living on Texas's antebellum frontier, two ethnic groups most suspect in the eyes of Lone Star secessionists were Tejanos and Germans. West of the 100th meridian, no Tejanos owned slaves. Slaveholding Anglos constantly worried that Mexican Americans in Texas would help runaway slaves escape across the Rio Grande to freedom in Mexico. In addition many white Americans in the antebellum period viewed Hispanics as racially and culturally inferior. The 1849 diaries of Gold Rush emigrants traveling across the Texas frontier on their way to California provide an excellent cross-section of Anglo perceptions toward Mexicans. In July 1849 John Murchison described the Tejanos near El Paso as both "miserable lazy [sic]" and "perished out [sic]." Murchison continued, "I am so disgusted at the country and people that I will forbear saying anything [further]." Camping downstream near San Elizario, Texas, in June 1849, L. N. Weed observed that the Mexicans "appear to realize that the Americans are a superior race." William P. Huff spent the summer of 1849 in the

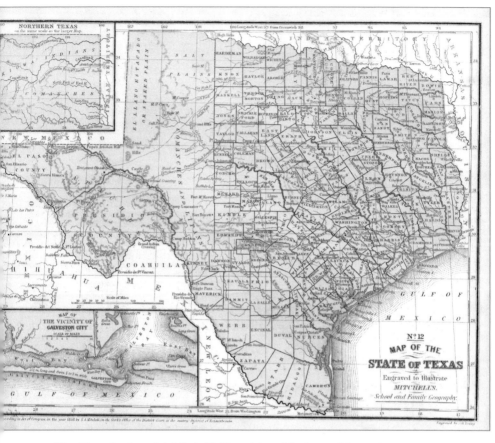

West Texas in 1859. *S.A. Mitchell's No. 12 Map of the State of Texas, 1859.* Courtesy of the Virginia Garrett Cartographic History Library, Special Collections, University of Texas at Arlington Library, Arlington, Texas.

neighboring town of Socorro and found most of its residents "mentally and physically in . . . [the] chains of ignorance." Huff concluded, "It is not a matter of wonder or surprise to see the Mexican but little removed from the days of Montezuma."[30]

Murchison, Weed, and Huff may have felt superior, but in antebellum Texas west of the 100th meridian, Tejanos vastly outnumbered Anglo Americans. For Anglos living in the region, circumstances forced them to adapt to regional realities. As a result, from 1848–1890, whites and Mexican Americans in El Paso, Presidio, and Pecos counties shared elected offices and conducted business transactions. Additionally, many of the white men moving to the Trans-Pecos during this period were single, and since there were few available white women in the area, a number of Anglo American men married Tejano women.[31]

Besides marriage, other frontier realities forced whites to make additional accommodations with Mexican Americans. Anglos needed Tejano assistance in settling and protecting the region. Whites also needed Mexican labor. Until Anglos could dominate Mexican Americans economically and politically, they were forced to bide their time and operate within what Richard White calls "The Middle Ground." While White uses the term to describe relations between Anglo Europeans and Native Americans in colonial North America, his concept also aptly characterizes race relations between Anglos and Tejanos on the antebellum frontier. White says, "The middle ground is the place in between: in between cultures, [and] peoples . . . On the middle ground diverse peoples adjust their differences." White observes that "this accommodation took place because . . . whites could neither dictate to Indians [in this case, Tejanos] nor ignore them. Whites needed Indians [in this instance, Tejanos] as allies, as partners in exchange, as sexual partners, as friendly neighbors."[32]

Although some whites moving to the western frontier during this formative period were from the South, one would be hardpressed to characterize Texas west of the 100th meridian as "southern." Certainly some whites brought southern attitudes with them, but Tejanos, not southern Anglos, were the majority population. Mexican Americans succeeded in keeping their culture and identity intact. Tejano historian Arnoldo De

León says that during the nineteenth century, the Tejano community was "forceful, robust, and resilient." Jesús F. de la Teja, who specializes in Texas colonial history, explains, "Although Tejanos had alliances with the Anglo American, they did not just think, 'Oh, we're going to become mint julip-drinking southerners.'" Jerry D. Thompson, whose work focuses on Civil War Texas and South Texas, agrees. Thompson notes that except for a few Mexican American elite, "Tejanos don't buy into Old South culture; they retain their own culture."[33]

While Tejanos managed to keep their customs and traditions intact, by 1890 whites west of the 100th meridian had accrued sufficient population gains and economic capital to seize control of the region. Just as Anglos after 1836 turned on their Tejano allies who had helped them win Texas's independence from Mexico, so, too, did Anglos in West Texas betray their Tejano allies after 1890. Whites in the Trans-Pecos deserted Mexican Americans they had previously shared power with, marginalizing those who had helped protect the frontier and settle the region. For the next six decades until after World War II, Anglos in West Texas dominated almost every aspect of economic and political life, creating a segregated society and treating Mexican Americans as second-class citizens.

West of the 100th meridian, Anglos segregated public pools, theaters, and schools. Restaurants posted signs that read "No Mexicans." Many towns and cities had residential segregation with whites living in their neighborhoods and Tejanos restricted to their barrios. The small numbers of African Americans living in the region also encountered discrimination. A 1909 article in the *Pecos Times* newspaper urged its readers "to keep the niggers out of Pecos and the West." Some southern historians might be tempted to view this segregation in West Texas as an extension of the Old South.[34]

On closer examination, however, one sees that segregation patterns in the region were more akin to those of the West than the South. Research shows that African Americans and Mexican Americans in California and Arizona also endured segregated pools, theaters, schools, restaurants, stores, neighborhoods, and churches. In their history of the American West, Robert Hine and John Mack Faragher note that "overt [racial] hostility was widespread" throughout the region. The authors point out that in Southern California, "segregation was an everyday fact of life." Los Angeles was "probably the most segregated city in the U.S.," where minorities were "subjugated and excluded . . . even more rigorously." *The Oxford History of the American West* observes that "racial and ethnic prejudice was pervasive" throughout the region. Gordon Morris Bakken writes that "California was at its birth an equal-opportunity racist state." Susan Lee Johnson says that even during the Gold Rush era, the laws and customs of California's Anglo-dominated society "barred Latin Americans, native peoples, and also African Americans from even the prospect of free participation in civic and economic life there."[35]

Testifying before the President's Committee on Civil Rights in 1947, Reverend John J. Birch lamented the "wide-spread discrimination" that "is practiced against the Spanish Speaking in the Southwest." The reverend pointed out that in almost "every city and town of California, Texas and Arizona, there are residential districts where persons of Mexican extraction . . . are not permitted to reside." In his landmark work on race relations, *Are We Good Neighbors*, Alonso Perales observed that in Texas, whites treated Mexicans as "inferior" and kept them "at arm's length." Perales found that the "same situation" existed in Arizona and California.[36]

Troubled race relations in America are nothing new. Anglo Americans have a national legacy of racism reaching back to the seventeenth century when whites first encountered Native Americans. The key to understanding race relations in West Texas is to examine the types of violence and the exact nature of segregation that whites were employing. Studies of racism in the western half of Texas found that from 1890 to World War II, the region was noticeably different from East Texas and the South. A detailed discussion of race relations in West Texas can be found in Chapter Three.

In the 1950s Anglo domination of Tejanos in the region began to crumble, concurrent with the national civil rights movement. Mexican Americans returned home from World War II with a new sense of empowerment and entitlement. During the 1950s West Texas Tejanos broke the exclusionary pattern established by Anglos during the Progressive Era and began serving on school boards, city councils, and county commissioners courts. By the 1980s Tejanos and Anglos were once again sharing power. Today, the region's dynamics are different. Mixed marriages have returned, and now Anglo women are marrying Tejano men. Jesús F. de la Teja observes that in the Texas Trans-Pecos, racism cannot "work in the long run. The oil is going to run out soon, . . . it is a poor area and the people who are left out in that area are the people who are native, the real natives, the ones who identify completely with the area. And they're going to be mixed races."[37]

From 1890 to 1980, Anglos, many of them with southern backgrounds, constituted a substantial part of West Texas's population. Today, the region's composition is rapidly changing. Whites in the Trans-Pecos are now the minority population, and by mid-century, this demographic trend will shift eastwards to include Anglos living in the South Plains, the Panhandle, and Edwards Plateau regions west of the 100th meridian. Many Tejanos, African Americans, and whites in West Texas now realize that the races must work together if they are to solve the region's serious economic problems. These pressing issues include depopulation, declining oil and water reserves, and for much of the region, a dwindling economic base.

Based on current demographic trends, Tejanos will outnumber whites west of the 102nd meridian, or a line from Lubbock to Midland, by 2020. By 2040, Mexican Americans in West Texas will constitute a solid majority west of the 100th meridian. State research shows (see the following table) that from 2000 to 2040, as whites become an ever-smaller minority, more of them will leave West Texas. Federal census records reveal that West Texas's population forecasts mirror the rest of the Southwest, specifically New Mexico, Arizona, and California.[38]

Cultural geographer Terry Jordan observes that "West Texas was settled largely by East Texans," but the record shows he is mistaken. From 1850–1890, most people living in historic West Texas (the Trans-Pecos) were Tejanos, not southern whites. It was not until after 1890 that a significant number of people from East Texas and the South moved west

WEST TEXAS POPULATION'S PROJECTED TRENDS
FROM 2000 TO 2040

Area	Decreasing % of Anglos	Increasing % of Hispanics
Concho Valley (San Angelo)	37%	107%
Permian Basin (Midland-Odessa)	54%	104%
South Plains (Lubbock)	43%	83%
Panhandle (Amarillo)	23%	237%
W. Rio Grande (El Paso)	71%	115%

of the 100th meridian. Prior to 1890 the primary population movement in the region was not east to west but south to north, from the northern Mexican frontier to West Texas. In the mid-1870s, the U.S. Army forcibly removed the Plains Indians from the High Plains, opening up West Texas's other major region to non-Indian settlement. In 1880 the Texas Panhandle had 1,607 residents. Of this number, Hispanics comprised 22 percent. Those from the North, Midwest, West, and overseas made up 36 percent of the region's population. Residents from the Upper South, Lower South, and Texas accounted for 25 percent. Ernest Archambeau says that in 1880, the Panhandle "was neither Northern nor Southern nor foreign. It was the culture of the Southwest, a culture as distinctive as the curl of the cowman's hat."[39]

As previously mentioned, prior to the Civil War, Germans constituted the other major ethnic group living along Texas's western frontier. Just as Tejano culture raised suspicions among Anglo Texans prior to the Civil War, so, too, did the worldviews of German Texans. Although some Germans living in Central Texas owned slaves, the vast majority

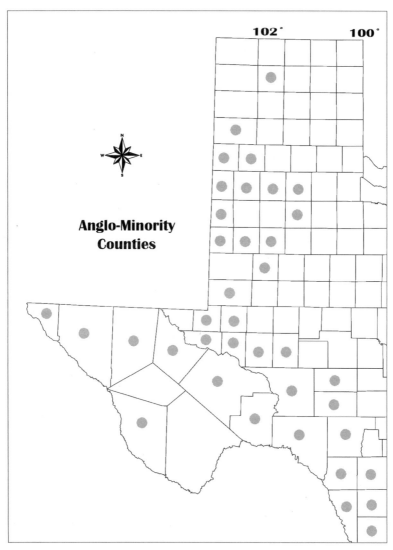

Anglo-minority counties west of the 100th meridian. Texas Counties Map courtesy of Texas Parks and Wildlife Department. Details added by author, incorporating 2008 U.S. Census data.

in the western Hill Country did not. Because Germans were white, they did not face the same prejudices regarding skin color encountered by African Americans and Mexican Americans. To some xenophobic Texans, however, the Germans seemed different and some of their customs a bit "strange." This response was typical of many in nineteenth and early twentieth-century America.

More recently, a newspaper noted, "The same debates that take place today over Latino immigrants and the Spanish language once centered around the German communities, which had their own newspapers, schools and theaters." During the antebellum period, some Texans of southern origin looked upon the farming traditions that emigrants brought with them to Texas from Germany as "foreign." These Germans employed unique agricultural practices unfamiliar to southerners accustomed to a slave-based cotton economy. In the western Hill Country, Germans were in large part non-slaveholding yeoman farmers. In his study of the subject, Terry Jordan found that "there is some fairly substantial evidence that German farms were producing more value per acre than the farms of Anglo Americans, and their farms reported a corresponding higher cash value per acre." German agricultural endeavors near New Braunfels using free labor "produced more cotton to the acre" and commanded "one to two cents more per pound than slave cotton at the Galveston market, on account of its greater cleanliness." Needless to say, some slaveholding Texans perceived the more efficient, free labor system of German emigrants as a threat.[40]

As the Civil War approached, Germans in the western Hill Country worried that an important and valuable part of their livelihood, specifically the federal frontier economy, would disappear if Texas seceded. If the U.S. Army pulled out of the Lone Star State, Germans would lose lucrative government contracts and markets for their agricultural products. They would also lose military protection for their western settlements against raiding Comanches. One major reason why Germans living on the Texas frontier were so resistant to serving in the Confederate Army is because they did not want to leave their families unprotected against Indian raids.

Finally, as Terry Jordan asserts, it is important to remember that "the average Texas German farmer in the western settlements" was not an "active abolitionist." Dale Baum writes, "Nevertheless, Germans throughout Texas showed very little sympathy for slavery." Discussing the nature of the strong opposition in the German Hill Country toward Texas joining the Confederacy, Rudolph Leopold Biesele says, "The vote against secession does not indicate opposition to slavery but a desire to preserve the Union." A number of Texas firebrands who clamored for secession, however, did not take the time to discern the finer points of German culture and perspective. As a result, in their rush to judgment, these hotheads formed some erroneous conclusions. Moritz Tiling notes that Texan planter-slaveholders "looked with disdain, mingled with contempt, on the German farmer." Such clashing conceptions subsequently sparked violent confrontations in the region during the Civil War.[41]

Numerous yeoman farmers of diverse backgrounds living in the western Hill Country shared the Germans' desire to keep both the Union and the federal frontier economy intact. Many among the first wave of settlers moving to the western frontier after 1848 sensed a golden opportunity to capitalize on the federal government's increased presence in the region. It is important to note that significant Anglo European settlement in western Texas did not occur until the federal government directly or indirectly provided the incentive.

The U.S. Army's outposts and the postmaster general's establishment of a transcontinental mail and passenger stage service between St. Louis and San Francisco offered the real prospect of making money from the federal government and related agencies on the Texas frontier. Howard Lamar says that it was not so much the pioneer but more the "government, both federal and local, [that] was a highly important factor in making . . . settlement . . . possible; therefore, to understand the nature and history of this last . . . frontier, the settler's concept and use of government must be closely examined." Lamar notes that "federal patronage and federal expenditures" subsidized the frontier economy through construction and maintenance of military outposts, road systems, and mail routes throughout the region. As in the case of antebellum West Texas, "government affairs became so financially important that they became the biggest business there."[42]

A major hallmark of the American West and West Texas is the region's dependence upon the federal government, specifically the U.S. Army and Postmaster General. A number of counties along Texas's northwestern and western frontier voted against disunion in 1861, namely, Maverick, Uvalde, Medina, Mason, Gillespie, Jack, Wise, and Cooke. In the Trans-Pecos, those casting ballots in Presidio County (which included Pecos County at the time) were unanimously against secession, 364–0.[43]

Some of these anti-secession counties on the western frontier shared a federal military presence, and their local economies depended upon military protection, local supply contracts, and army payrolls. Forts Davis, Stockton, Duncan, Inge, Mason, and Martin Scott were all located within counties voting against secession. In addition West Texas residents were much more isolated and removed from the South. The region's economy was far more influenced by the federal government and its agencies than by cotton slave culture.

So why did El Paso County not follow suit with these other frontier counties and oppose secession? Like the above counties, El Paso also had several federal forts, namely Forts Bliss and Quitman. The region's economy was based on transportation-related industries, primarily those in the service and supply sectors. Historian W. H. Timmons aptly describes the area as a "continental crossroads." Here the east to west San Antonio-San Diego and St. Louis-San Francisco roads intersected with the north to south Santa Fe-Chihuahua Trail. Wagon trains, freighters, stagecoaches, overland travelers, and the U.S. Army all relied upon El Paso as a major transportation and supply center. Merchants and businessmen comprised much of the local economy. In 1857 the U.S. Postmaster General selected the Southern Route through El Paso for the nation's first transcontinental mail line, the Butterfield Overland Mail. Local boosters from the "Pass of the North" lobbied heavily for a similar routing of the country's first transcontinental railroad.[44]

Situated in the Chihuahuan Desert, with less than ten inches a year in rainfall and little available irrigation water, antebellum El Paso County was clearly unsuitable for the South's cotton economy. With only fifteen slaves in the county, "the issue of slavery locally was hardly the burning issue it had become nationally." Timmons says Jefferson Davis' desire to bring a southern transcontinental railroad to the region was of far greater importance to local merchants than slavery.[45]

Like counties in Texas beyond the 100th meridian, New Mexico Territory, El Paso County's neighbor to the west, possessed a diminutive southern presence. In New Mexico, Hispanics comprised 50 percent of the population, Native Americans 45 percent, the military 3 percent, and Eastern immigrants 1 percent. Mark J. Stegmaier notes that out of 90,000 people, there were "probably less than twenty black slaves" in New Mexico. Before and during the Civil War, "most New Mexicans supported the Union," Stegmaier writes, "and the first major action taken by the territorial legislature after the war began was to repeal the territory's slave code." When rebel Texans invaded New Mexico in 1862, they found their presence unwelcome. "It had been erroneously supposed . . . that the citizens of New Mexico would greet us as benefactors and flock to our standard upon our approach." Lone Star troops instead discovered "that there was not a friend to our cause in the [New Mexico] territory, with a very few honorable exceptions."[46]

Regarding local demographics in El Paso County, Texas, in 1860, only 2 percent of the population was from the South. Tejanos, Northerners, and Europeans vastly outnumbered white Southerners. The area's two wealthiest Anglos and leading secessionists, James Wiley Magoffin and Simeon Hart, however, exerted much sway on local affairs. Largely because of the pair's significant economic and political influence, the county's pro-secession movement succeeded. A number of primary accounts reveal that members of El Paso County's secession ring utilized intimidation and voting fraud in order to influence the vote. El Paso has a long tradition of fraudulent elections dating back to the 1850s, typified by transporting Mexicans across the Rio Grande to illegally cast their ballots in exchange for liquor and money. While El Paso County voted for disunion, the remaining three Texas counties along or west of the 100th meridian did not, specifically, Uvalde, Maverick, and Presidio.

As previously mentioned, New Mexico Territory was also Unionist in its outlook. In short, El Paso County's tainted secession referendum was atypical of the region and is best viewed as a regional anomaly.[47]

As with secession voting trends, the history of western Texas during the Civil War was markedly different from the rest of the state. Unlike East and South Texas, the Trans-Pecos region was part of the Southern Confederacy for only sixteen months. In July 1862 after Confederate General H. H. Sibley's failed invasion of New Mexico, Texan and Confederate units abandoned Texas west of the Pecos River to Union forces. Union Troops from the Department of New Mexico under the command of Brigadier General James H. Carleton quickly moved in and administered the area under martial law for the remainder of the conflict.

East of the 100th meridian, in Texas's shatterbelt section, regional identity was mixed, with some frontier counties voting for, and others against, secession. In those shatterbelt counties voting against disunion, lawlessness, disloyalty, and desertion were rampant from late 1863 to 1865. West Texas historian William Curry Holden observed that "the number of disloyal citizens, to the Confederacy, at least along the entire frontier, was astonishingly high." Many residents in these shatterbelt counties were Unionist "Tories" who did not own slaves. These Unionists did not necessarily like abolitionists but desired to stay in the Union. As previously discussed, two of the region's major population groups were Tejanos and western Hill Country Germans, both typically non-slaveholders. Clearly, many Tejanos, Germans, and other frontier citizens did not warmly embrace Civil War-era Southern identity and all that it encompassed. No wonder then that Southern whites were often suspicious of these groups' loyalties, even those who fought for the Confederacy. A more in-depth examination of West Texas's identity during the conflict follows in Chapter Two.[48]

Regarding other aspects of West Texas's regional character, Holle Humphries' study of public monuments and architecture in West Texas reveals an overwhelming preponderance of western themes and icons illustrative of the region's western identity. Terry Jordan, in his geographical and cultural research on Texas, noticed several other notable distinctions between East and West Texas. Southwestern Hispanic architecture is present in much of West Texas, while the dog-trot, double log cabin of the South and East Texas is noticeably absent. Land surveys are also markedly different in West Texas. Since much of this area developed after the Mexican War and Texas's admission to the Union, "rigid rectangular surveys" in the region are typical of federal surveys elsewhere. In contrast, East Texas features long-lot surveys along major streams and rivers. Jordan puts the dividing line between these two survey systems at approximately the 98th meridian.[49]

Additional research on West Texas's identity reveals that residents west of the 100th meridian, when asked where they live, typically answer "The Southwest" or "The West." Cultural geographer D. W. Meinig places El Paso and the Trans-Pecos firmly in the Southwest. West Texans also perceive themselves as uniquely distinct from the rest of the state. William Curry Holden notes that "West Texans have the feeling that their section constitutes all but a state in itself. This intense feeling of sectionalism belongs distinctly to the people of the western part of the state."[50]

Part of what underlies this distinctive and separate West Texas identity is a rugged, self-reliant regional pride. In addition West Texans share a longstanding perception that they are often isolated from the rest of the state. There is a local sentiment that Austin does not always have the region's best interests at heart when setting policy. Area residents sometimes feel exploited, for in some instances, profits from sizeable state landholdings, minerals, and resources in the region flow out of the area, providing little economic benefit to the local economy. In the late nineteenth and early twentieth centuries, West Texans complained of being treated like a second-class colony of East Texas. Even today, citizens in West Texas will grouse that they feel ignored, or even worse, forgotten by the rest of the state. In the Lone Star pecking order, the local consensus is that West Texas often gets the "short end of the stick." These feelings are not just imagined slights but have some basis in historical fact.

During the early decades of statehood, significant debt, poor credit, and lack of capital hampered Texas's ability to expand its infrastructure and economy. As had been the case throughout the Texas Republic, the state looked to public land sales to solve its economic woes. In 1866 a motion in the state legislature proposed selling all of the Trans-Pecos to the federal government in order to finance a permanent school fund. Nothing came of this resolution, but in 1868 a new measure was introduced during the Texas Reconstruction Convention. This bill recommended selling much of Texas west of the 100th meridian to the federal government to help finance internal improvements, education, and immigration. Governor E. M. Pease believed that the land would be worth far more to the U.S. "than it can ever be to this state." Like its predecessor, this proposal failed to win passage.[51]

A 1912 *El Paso Times* article complained that there was a selfish tendency "to regard the western portion of the state as something to be exploited for the direct benefit of the remainder of the state." The newspaper noted that Austin "gave away" millions of acres of West Texas lands to get the railroads it desired, "and now when West Texas advances a plea for anything—no matter what—the west is ignored." During this period, residents frequently groused that Austin did not provide the western half of Texas its fair allotment of state services and institutions. Education proved the foremost grievance.[52]

West Texans demanded that the state establish an agricultural and mechanical college in the region, similar to Texas A&M, to help residents improve and expand their agricultural operations. Residents pointed out that "west of the 99th meridian," the soils and climate in the western half of Texas "were very different than that of other sections of the state." The nearest agricultural and mechanical institution was located at College Station, a considerable distance from West Texas. Locals argued that in order for "agriculture west of the 99th meridian in Texas to be successful [it] has to be handled as it has to be taught, on entirely different lines and by entirely different methods than in that part of the state east of said Meridian."[53]

If West Texans were going to improve their farming and ranching operations, they needed an agricultural and mechanical college close to where they lived, a college specifically designed to help residents address the land's unique natural conditions. If citizens could better adapt their agricultural operations to regional environmental realities, this would "greatly aid in the settlement and development of the country." Eventually, area cities joined forces to create the West Texas A&M Campaign Association, an early incarnation of the West Texas Chamber of Commerce. "Representatives of the various business, agricultural and commercial interests . . . from practically every part of West Texas, west of the 99th Meridian" held their first meeting in Sweetwater on April 5, 1916.[54]

Despite approval by the state legislature, Texas Governor Pat Neff in 1921 vetoed a bill creating West Texas A&M College on the grounds that the state possessed insufficient funds to support such an institution. Neff's veto created an angry backlash in West Texas and sparked calls for a regional secession movement. This was not the first time that Texans had discussed division. After the Civil War, legislators considered carving several additional states out of Texas, as allowed by law. All of these efforts eventually fizzled out as Texas identity and unity, forged early on during the Revolution and Republic periods (1832–1846), proved stronger than potentially divisive local concerns. The West Texas A&M College veto, however, breathed new fire into regional resentments. West Texans demanded "fair play," a "square deal," and the same rights enjoyed by other Lone Star citizens. Residents of the western half of the state, "many of them . . . native Texans, . . . would be sad to see the day when Texas should have to be divided" but refused to surrender their innate rights over "a question of sentiment."[55]

Finally, after further revisions by the state legislature, Governor Neff in February 1923 signed the measure creating a regional agricultural and mechanical institution, to be called Texas Technological College. Six months later, the State Board of Control selected Lubbock, Texas, as the site for Texas Tech. The law creating Texas Tech quickly silenced any talk of West Texas seceding. The seven-year push to secure a local college reveals, however, that by the early 1900s, West Texans had already formed a self-defined and clearly delineated regional identity, bounded on the east by the 99th meridian, by "Amarillo on the north," and "El Paso on the West."[56]

The Texas Tech case raises a larger question. It is evident that a strong West Texas personality had formed by the early 1900s. Was this regional identity first created during the college flap, or had it coalesced earlier? In January 1869 Judge Evans of Titus County in East Texas observed noticeable local distinctions within Texas, commenting that "the average man of the east and the average man of west Texas are as dissimilar as the average citizen of any two states in the American Union." William Curry Holden dates the origins of West Texas's unique character to before the Mexican War. Holden argues that West Texas's formative frontier period, which commenced with statehood in 1846, "was the beginning of a distinctive West Texas spirit," a spirit forged by a "common danger" and a "feeling of common interest and unity among the people."[57]

This distinctive West Texas spirit became markedly more pronounced immediately prior to and during the Civil War. As discussed earlier, up until 1861 the lands in arid West Texas beyond the 100th meridian loomed as a formidable environmental impediment to widespread Southern cotton agriculture. The following chapter examines how, from 1861 to 1865, the western half of Texas also emerged as a daunting cultural barrier to the expansion of Old South ideology, with many in the region rejecting southern identity and values as out of sync with West Texas and the Confederacy not worth defending or dying for.

GONE FROM TEXAS AND TRADING WITH THE ENEMY
NEW PERSPECTIVES ON CIVIL WAR WEST TEXAS

Governor Francis R. Lubbock understood Texas. Writing eighteen months into the Civil War, he demonstrated a keen awareness of the state's clashing identities, cultures, and divergent geographic regions. "Texas is . . . situated in many respects very differently from other of her Sisters [other Confederate states]," he observed, with "an immense frontier line" stretching from New Mexico and Indian Territory on the west and north, southwards to the Rio Grande. Unlike other rebel states, Texas shared a lengthy border with Mexico. During the war, effectively defending such an expansive frontier against raiding Indians, Mexican bandits, white renegades, and Union troops from New Mexico ultimately proved impossible.[1]

Lubbock also knew that he governed a very diverse and fragmented population, a number of whom were indifferent or opposed to slavery, secession, and serving in the rebel army. Lubbock lamented, "It is useless to disguise the fact of there being many disloyal people in various localities of the state . . . [with] vile tongues and [who set a] bad example." Some of these dissenters, hardworking and conscientious Germans, Anglos, and Tejanos living on the western frontier and along the border, might have taken offense to the governor's remarks. They cared deeply for Texas but not for the Confederacy or southern ideology. They identified with a different part of Texas and, in many cases, with the United States.[2]

In an effort to squelch all dissent and assert greater control over wartime Texas, Confederate and state officials adopted a number of forceful measures. They declared martial law and in 1862 violently suppressed suspected "insurrectionists" and "Unionists" across the state. In Cooke County a "kangaroo court" hung forty men, and in Wise County, a second ad hoc committee strung up five men. Five more died in Grayson County, another in Denton County, and in Gillespie County, vigilante mobs hung fifty. These harsh measures, however, only temporarily quelled dissent.[3]

Authorities also passed conscription laws compelling military service. In July 1862 at Ringgold Barracks in South Texas, a Confederate colonel reported that the conscript law "produced considerable alarm" among "many" Tejanos, who subsequently "left for the other side of the Rio Grande." In October 1862 Confederate Brigadier General H. P. Bee, commanding South Texas, observed that Mexican Americans "are at most neutral" to the rebel cause. Bee said the problem stemmed from the fact that "few" of the Tejanos "are of sufficient intelligence to understand" the issues involved.[4]

Bee also discussed ongoing conscription problems with "dis-affected [sic] and disloyal" Germans in the western Hill Country, part of Texas's shatterbelt region. "We need not disguise from ourselves," he wrote, "that it [disloyalty] is pretty general, although confined to the foreign element, living in the mountains . . . north and west of San Antonio." Fresh in Bee's mind, no doubt, was a recent firefight on the Nueces River in Kinney County in which Confederate troops killed thirty-five German Unionists attempting to leave the state to avoid military service. Additionally, State Conscription Officer Lieutenant W. H. Holland remarked that along the Pedernales River in the Hill Country, there were "very few Southern men . . . and those few are in constant fear of destruction." Holland reported that one area resident was waylaid because of "his Southern principles," and said that "others too have been threatened and live in constant dread."[5]

In addition to compulsory military service, rebel authorities required Texas citizens and merchants to accept Confederate currency. Those who refused were subject to having their property seized by the government. By October 1864 this currency had depreciated to "two cents on the dollar," causing a "lukewarm" feeling and "distressing apathy" in many Texans toward the Confederacy. Confederate Major General John G. Walker, commanding Texas, complained, "In more than half of the state," residents and merchants refused to accept Confederate money. "But for the conscription and the impressments law," Walker lamented, "not a man, nor a pound of subsistence could be procured in the length and breadth of this state, and a majority of them would not turn on their heels to save the Confederacy, unless paid for it 'in specie' [gold or silver]."[6]

During the latter half of the war, some West Texas ranchers, reluctant to accept a worthless currency for their cattle and unwilling to have their herds impressed by government agents, began driving their beeves westward to more lucrative markets. One destination was Mexico. Another was New Mexico, where the enemy needed considerable supplies of beef to feed its troops at Fort Sumner and Native Americans at the adjacent Bosque Redondo Indian Reservation. In both Mexico and New Mexico, cattle agents paid in hard currency. Just as Texas and Confederate authorities proved unable to protect the frontiers and contain dissent, so, too, did they fail in their efforts to stop citizens trading with the enemy and Mexico. Throughout the Civil War, Lone Star identity, attitudes, and events in the western half of the state differed significantly from those in East Texas and the rest of the Confederacy.

For example, in the spring of 1864, Texas Adjutant General Colonel D. B. Culberson sent his subordinate, Captain W. W. Reynolds, to assess conditions at Texas Ranger camps along the state's western defensive perimeter. Reynolds found widespread disobedience and desertion up and down the line. Arriving at Camp Colorado in Coleman County, Reynolds learned of the disappearance of two lieutenants and thirteen men from Captain Loyd's company and Captain Whiteside's entire company, excluding Whiteside and one man. Ranger patrols from Camp Colorado also discovered that several hundred families, including deserters from Loyd and Whiteside's units, were forming a wagon train on the Middle

Concho River, ninety miles to the west. This wagon train was part of a swelling exodus of Texans disillusioned by the Civil War who left the Lone Star State for a fresh start in New Mexico, Arizona, and California. While this mass migration troubled state and Confederate authorities, they proved powerless to interdict it. Summing up conditions on Texas's western frontier, Captain Reynolds said, "The most perfect anarchy prevails."[7]

In September 1864 thirty-five miles to the southwest of Camp Colorado at the junction of the Concho and Colorado rivers, cowboys working for Confederate beef contractor John Chisum assembled a herd for sale to the enemy at Fort Sumner, New Mexico. The fall of Vicksburg in July 1863, the loss of southern cattle markets east of the Mississippi, and a rapidly depreciating rebel currency forced Chisum and other Texas ranchers to look westward for new sales. In the fall of 1863, these cattlemen began moving their herds out to the western frontier and beyond the reach of inquisitive impressment agents.[8]

These are but several striking examples that dispel a number of erroneous popular perceptions regarding Civil War West Texas. The first misconception is that Lone Star troops adequately protected the western frontier. To the contrary, they failed in this endeavor. During the war, the frontier line collapsed not just once but twice, forcing authorities to relinquish control over much of West Texas.

A second accepted fallacy is that Texas's legendary cattle drives to Fort Sumner, New Mexico, and beyond did not commence until after the war, with Charles Goodnight and Oliver Loving's first trip in June 1866. Goodnight often claimed that he and Loving laid out the Fort Sumner route, but Texas, Confederate, and Union records reveal that Lone Star ranchers driving their beeves to the Union Army in New Mexico blazed this trail during 1864 and 1865. Confederate beef contractor John Chisum's Concho County ranch often served as the starting point for these westward drives. These new perspectives of a collapsing frontier, Texas's abandonment of half its territory, widespread desertion and disloyalty, and trading with the enemy all make for a fascinating examination of Lone Star identity and events in West Texas during the last years of the war.[9]

There has been much debate over the last eighty years concerning the Texas Rangers' Civil War service. Some scholars maintain that the Rangers failed to discharge their duties, and as a result, the Lone Star frontier fell back to its position in 1849. Other writers, however, claim that the state militia successfully defended the western perimeter. One historian carries this argument even further, holding that wartime Rangers outperformed federal troops stationed in Texas before the war. Admittedly, the U.S. Army failed to deter raids by Indians and white renegades, but the fact remains that prior to the sectional conflict, Texas's westward line of settlement kept advancing, not retreating. The army's frontier forts and their adjacent civilian communities stayed put. In addition, antebellum soldiers found their task much easier because they escaped the additional burden of dealing with Tories, large segments of a hostile, anti-Confederate frontier population.[10]

By charting the position of frontier defense lines throughout the war, one can accurately assess the performance of Texas troops. In May 1861 Colonel Earl Van Dorn, Confederate military commander of the Lone Star State, clearly defined Texas's two "western frontiers" when he issued orders for defending these perimeters. His first line, from the Red River to near present-day San Angelo, Texas, replicated the federal government's cordon of frontier forts in 1852. Texas troops garrisoned outposts at Camp Cooper, Fort Chadbourne, Camp Colorado, and the Concho River. Van Dorn's second frontier line mirrored the U.S. Army's 1860 defensive perimeter along the San Antonio-El Paso Road. The colonel positioned soldiers at Fort Inge, Fort Clark, Camp Hudson, Fort Lancaster, Fort Stockton, Fort Davis, Fort Quitman, and Fort Bliss.[11]

As it had done previously with the federal government, Texas now looked to Confederate authorities to safeguard its frontier. In 1861 Texans listed inadequate frontier security as one of their primary reasons for secession, after the protection of slavery. In April 1861 Confederate Secretary of War L. P. Walker assured Texas officials that the War Department would "exert all its energies and exhaust all the means at its command" to protect the frontier. In July 1862 following Confederate General H. H. Sibley's failed invasion of New Mexico, the Confederacy reneged on its promise and abandoned Van Dorn's second defensive line between El

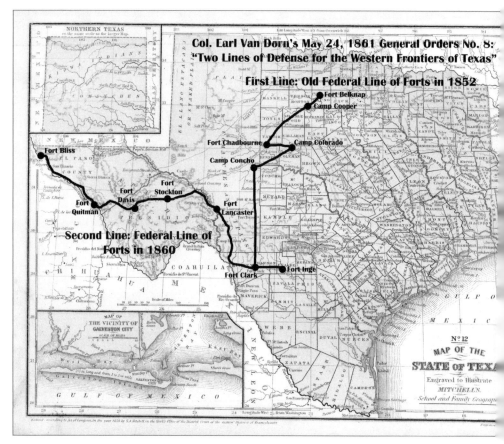

Colonel Van Dorn's two defensive perimeters for the western frontiers of Texas, May 1861. *S. A. Mitchell's No. 12 Map of the State of Texas, 1859.* Courtesy of the Virginia Garrett Cartographic History Library, Special Collections, University of Texas at Arlington Library, Arlington, Texas. Locations and frontier lines added by author.

Paso and Fort Clark. Union forces from the Department of New Mexico followed close behind Sibley's retreating troops and quickly occupied outposts in Texas's Trans-Pecos region for the duration of the war.[12]

After the Confederates pulled out of West Texas, defense of the remaining Lone Star frontier devolved upon the state. Texas found itself unable to defend even its first defensive line, based upon the 1852 cordon of frontier forts. By war's end the Texas frontier fell back once again, in some cases an additional 150 miles. In April 1865 the state's western defensive boundary in many places approximated its position in 1849, running from Gainesville, to Decatur, Weatherford, Gatesville, Fredericksburg, and Uvalde.

The withdrawal of the U.S. Army in 1861 clearly demonstrated that the Lone Star State did not have sufficient resources to protect West Texas residents. Texas military historian Colonel Thomas "Ty" Smith notes that "Texas, either as a republic or a state, lacked the economic clout to expend the funds necessary to secure its borders or to conduct large-scale operations on its frontier." Despite enduring popular legends concerning the prowess of frontier Rangers, it was the federal government, not Texas, that finally secured the state's boundaries.[13]

During the Civil War, Texas Rangers frequently scouted parts of the western frontier, but they, unlike the antebellum federal troops, could not hold the territory. Many Lone Star militiamen served courageously and with honor; however, the Rangers consistently lacked adequate manpower, supplies, and ammunition, significantly limiting their effectiveness. Desertion rates for these regiments also run counter to the common perception that Texas Rangers never shirked their duties. By the end of the war, official records showed that 25–50 percent of the men deserted their units. In a number of wartime engagements, Rangers found themselves outnumbered and outgunned by both Indians and renegades.[14]

Failing in its responsibility to secure the frontier, the Confederacy made matters worse by occasionally drafting portions of the state Ranger units to supplement rebel forces, much to the consternation of West Texas residents, who demanded protection for their frontier homesteads. Many of those living in the state's shatterbelt region, while disliking abolitionists, had strongly opposed secession. A number of shatterbelt

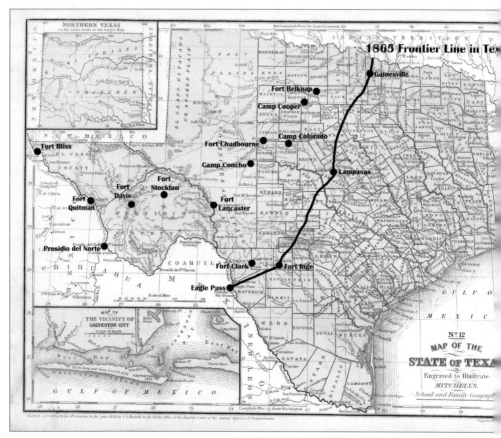

Texas's western frontier line in May 1865. *S. A. Mitchell's No. 12 Map of the State of Texas, 1859.* Courtesy of the Virginia Garrett Cartographic History Library, Special Collections, University of Texas at Arlington Library, Arlington, Texas. Locations and frontier line added by author.

counties had voted against disunion. When the Confederacy drafted militia regiments to bolster its army, such actions further disaffected citizens in these counties, creating serious conflicts of loyalty within wartime West Texas. As previously noted, one historian observed that "the number of disloyal citizens, to the Confederacy, at least, along the entire frontier was astonishingly high." Some of these disaffected frontier residents provided aid to and harbored deserters. In contrast, the antebellum federal army encountered no similar civilian resistance while discharging its duties.[15]

Interestingly, most Lone Star history books, in their discussion of the Civil War, neglect to mention that the Union Army occupied Texas west of the Pecos River from August 1862 until June 1865. Instead, the standard account presented in these works maintains that Texas, unlike other Confederate states such as Louisiana or Virginia, successfully repelled all Union attempts to invade and occupy her territory. Several recent scholarly studies claim that the only Union occupation to occur in Texas was along the Gulf Coast and in the Lower Rio Grande region, and that by mid-1864, Texas had driven all federal troops from its soil. The actual history that unfolded in the Trans-Pecos, however, runs directly counter to this traditional Civil War narrative of Lone Star exceptionalism.[16]

Another conventional story line acknowledges that the Confederacy relinquished control of the Trans-Pecos to Union forces but minimizes the consequences of this action. According to this explanation, the abandonment of Colonel Van Dorn's defensive line along the El Paso Road had little impact upon regional depopulation. This is incorrect. With no military presence to protect and sustain them, dependent civilian communities at or adjacent to abandoned frontier forts quickly became depopulated.[17]

For example, in early April 1861, rebel troops assumed control of Fort Quitman in El Paso County. A skeleton force of eight men manned the post, three of whom soon deserted. By late summer the fort stood empty. In September 1861 former El Paso County Judge, District Attorney, and State Senator Archibald C. Hyde (also one of Quitman's co-owners) implored the Confederate commander of Texas, Brigadier General Paul O. Hebert, to re-garrison the post as soon as possible. Hyde noted that because the rebels had left the area unprotected, "many farms and ranchos have been abandoned by the settlers, and families have sought refuge" elsewhere "from fear of the ruthless savages who are devastating that country."[18]

To accurately assess the extent of this regional depopulation, the 1860 census proves illustrative. In El Paso County, 132 civilians lived at Fort Quitman, another 127 in the adjacent community of Bosque Carmelo, and an additional eighty-two in the neighboring Camp Rice, Birchville, and Hawkins settlements. In adjacent Presidio County, thirty civilians lived at Fort Stockton and the hamlet of Comanche, located next to the post. At the county's other military installation, Fort Davis, there were sixty-one civilians. Next door at Las Lympias, there were 101 residents, and at nearby Wild Rose Pass, another forty.[19]

Regarding the remaining outposts on the El Paso Road abandoned by the Confederates, there are no period census returns for Fort Lancaster in Crockett County. Lacking hard numbers, a conservative estimate based on other similar-sized installations might place twenty-five civilians at Lancaster. Likewise, at Camp Hudson on the Devils River, there were probably twenty-five non-military inhabitants. Many of these West Texas settlers were making their living from the frontier economy as army contractors, farmers, ranchers, blacksmiths, clerks, freighters, and laborers.[20]

In sum, on the eve of the war, there were approximately 625 civilians living and working in these military dependent communities. After rebel troops marched away in the summer of 1862, these settlements (and much of Presidio County) became frontier ghost towns. When Union Lieutenant Albert H. French visited Fort Quitman, Fort Davis, Fort Stockton, Fort Lancaster, and Camp Hudson in September 1862, he found them all deserted. The captain noted that the first settlement he encountered east of the Pecos River was at Pedro Pinto, seven miles from Fort Clark. Major General Zenas R. Bliss, who served on the West Texas frontier from 1854–1861 and 1870–1886, says that during the Civil War, "all [the] settlers fell back to Uvalde, on the El Paso Road, and to Fredericksburg, north of San Antonio." Such accounts graphically illustrate the extent of the wartime depopulation occurring in this western section of the Lone Star State.[21]

Prior to the rebels' evacuation of West Texas, a number of citizens were making money from the Confederate frontier economy. Sam Smith collected rent from rebel authorities for use of his Fort Lancaster property; James Duff freighted supplies to many of the frontier outposts; A. Duclos supplied corn to Forts Clark, Hudson, Lancaster, and Stockton; F. M. Joiner worked as a butcher at Fort Davis; Lewis Lee was the farrier at Fort Stockton; and John Burgess delivered corn to Forts Clark and Davis. E. P. Gallagher furnished flour to Forts Stockton and Davis; Archibald Hyde served as an army guide from San Antonio to El Paso; Jesus de la Garza hauled military stores from Fort Stockton to Forts Davis and Bliss; and at Fort Davis, Moke & Brother, Daniel Murphy, and Patrick Murphy provisioned the troops. At Fort Stockton, C. G. James served as post sutler until replaced by John D. Holliday in March 1862.[22]

The Confederate forces occupying these West Texas outposts from 1861 to 1862 were "woefully small." At Camp Hudson on the Devil's River, troop strength fluctuated between twenty-five and forty. A similar-sized command was at Fort Lancaster, and at Fort Stockton, the garrison ranged from nineteen to thirty-one. At Fort Davis, Captain Adams oversaw a command of fifty-one, with only twenty-five rounds of ammunition per man. The limitations of such an anemic force quickly became evident. In August 1861 post sutler Patrick Murphy lost fifty animals in a raid by Apache Indians. Lieutenant Reuben Mays, accompanied by thirteen soldiers and civilians from Fort Davis, set out in pursuit, but Apaches ambushed the party, killing all save one. Over the next few months, the situation worsened as Fort Davis' military effectiveness continued to atrophy. By May 1862 troop numbers had declined to twenty-nine, which "precluded any significant military activity." By comparison, in June 1860 the U.S. Army had eighty-three men at Fort Stockton, fifty-four at Camp Hudson, seventy-nine at Fort Lancaster, and 138 at Fort Davis.[23]

The Confederates' dwindling defenses evaporated altogether after General Sibley abandoned New Mexico and the Trans-Pecos and retreated to San Antonio in the summer of 1862. In another example illustrative of the region's divergent identities, a number of Mexican Americans confronted Sibley's retreating soldiers in several violent engagements from Mesilla, New Mexico, southward to Socorro, Texas. Hispanic residents "became incensed by the acts of the Texans" when passing through their communities. When Lone Star troops demanded that area citizens provide them with transportation supplies, the locals refused. Rebel soldiers then attempted to seize the items, and a desperate hand-to-hand fight with more than 150 Mexican Americans commenced, claiming almost fifty lives and leaving many wounded. As the Texans continued to fall back toward San Antonio, Hispanic residents followed in pursuit, harassing them and attempting to run off their livestock.[24]

At Franklin, Texas (present-day El Paso), Confederates crossed over into Mexico and took fourteen cattle. That same night, a party of Mexicans crossed the Rio Grande and reclaimed them. Another severe fight erupted when the still-retreating Texans commandeered supplies and livestock at Socorro, Texas. Two hundred to three hundred Tejanos and Pueblo Indians from Socorro and nearby Ysleta attacked the rebel force in a bloody encounter that destroyed the town's church, left another twenty to fifty dead, and more wounded. A Houston newspaper lamented, "Instead of fighting the Yankees . . . we have to fight the Mexicans." The intense clashes demonstrated that a number of Mexican Americans in the region held no warm regard for Confederate Texans or the Southern cause.[25]

Regarding the rebels' abandonment of the territory west of the Pecos River, another popular narrative argues that the region was actually unimportant and its loss of little concern to the Lone Star State or the Confederacy. In truth, from the fall of 1862 until the spring of 1865, Confederate military authorities and die-hard secessionists in Texas actively worked on a number of plans to recapture the Trans-Pecos and the Southwest.

In January 1863 the Confederate commander of Texas, Major General John Bankhead Magruder, personally endorsed a two-pronged invasion of the Trans-Pecos and New Mexico Territory under the command of Colonel Spruce Baird. One force would travel along the Canadian River through the Texas Panhandle and sever the Union supply lines to Fort Union, New Mexico. The second group would move through the Trans-Pecos, capturing Fort Bliss and Franklin (El Paso), Texas. Other notable Confederates in Texas supporting invasion plans included Colonel John

Baylor, Colonel Dan Showalter, Major Sherod Hunter, Captain Bethel Coopwood, Captain Henry Kennedy, Jarvis Hubbell, James Magoffin, and John Burgess.[26]

In order to aid these military efforts and to prevent further territorial losses, Confederate General H. P. Bee in October 1862 established a spy network in western Texas. For the next several years, rebel agents monitored Union operations in the Trans-Pecos under the command of Brigadier General James H. Carleton and the Department of New Mexico. The leader of this spy company was Henry Skillman, noted Texas mail contractor and Butterfield stagecoach driver. Captain Skillman (originally from New Jersey) and his team collected military intelligence and served as couriers.[27]

Union offensives in the eastern half of Texas during 1863 and 1864 heightened Confederate concerns that General Carleton and the Department of New Mexico might also launch an attack east of the Pecos River, threatening the state's western flank. In fact, such a prospect did arise in November 1863 when Union General Nathanial P. Banks captured Brownsville, Texas. Banks wrote to Carleton, suggesting a coordinated movement into the interior of Texas.[28]

In January 1864 Confederate Colonel John "Rip" Ford in San Antonio learned of the proposed Banks-Carlton operation and immediately informed his superior, Major General Magruder. The Confederate commander's instinct told him that Carleton's forces would not be ready to move in the near future, "but I have no doubt that they will come sooner or later, and some time probably this spring [1864]." When Department of New Mexico troops did move east of the Pecos, Magruder wanted advance warning. The logical person to provide such notice was rebel spymaster Henry Skillman.[29]

In late January 1864 Magruder met with Skillman in Houston and ordered him westward with several new assignments. The first task was to proceed to El Paso and keep the enemy under surveillance. Skillman's second mission was to compile an accurate map of West Texas showing the best routes for the movement of rebel troops. Should the Confederates raise a sufficient force to reinvade the Trans-Pecos and the Southwest, Magruder wanted the logistics already planned. The Confederate commander designated Colonel Ford as Skillman's regional handler in San Antonio. After Ford outfitted Skillman's group during the month of February, the spy company finally set out on March 6, 1864. Ford wrote Magruder "that much may be expected from Capt. Skillman, who will give reliable information of the intentions and movement of the enemy." By the end of the month, the rebel spy party had reconnoitered the San Antonio-El Paso Road as far west as Fort Davis.[30]

With Skillman embarked on his new mission, Magruder turned next to implementing defensive measures against a Union advance from El Paso. The Confederate commander directed Colonel Ford to draft a plan to "occupy the Devils River with a considerable force to stop the further progress [of approaching federal soldiers] and defeat them." After carefully reviewing the topography of the Devils River (in Val Verde County), Ford ultimately selected Pecan Springs, located above Camp Hudson and a second site upstream at Beaver Lake (near Juno, Texas) as the best places to defend against General Carleton's troops. In late January 1864 Ford ordered his subordinates to keep a close watch on the El Paso Road for Department of New Mexico forces. Major Alexander and seventy-five men scouted westward from Fort Inge in Uvalde County to the Devils and Pecos rivers. Alexander's expedition and subsequent scouts during February detected no signs of the enemy.[31]

Despite repeated requests from his superiors to make a coordinated movement with Union General Nathanial Banks, as of late March 1864, Carleton's forces were still in the Trans-Pecos, unable to move east of the Pecos River. The lack of adequate manpower, supplies, and transportation for such an expedition was "sorely felt." Ultimately, the Department of New Mexico units stayed put. Causing additional headaches for Carleton were the activities of Henry Skillman's spy company, which proved a chronic irritant to Union operations in the region. For eighteen months the crafty and elusive rebel spymaster defied all federal attempts to capture him.[32]

Finally, Union Captain Albert H. French and the First California Volunteer Cavalry found Skillman in camp at Spencer's Ranch (now Presidio, Texas) and on April 15, 1864, gunned him down in a pre-dawn ambush. Skillman's death dealt a severe blow to rebel dreams of a

Confederate empire in the Southwest. Despite this setback, Lone Star rebels persisted in their efforts to recapture the Trans-Pecos. As late as April 1865, leading military authorities and diehard secessionists in Texas were still working on various invasion plans. None of these plans came to fruition.[33]

To summarize, after General Sibley's failed New Mexico campaign, the Confederacy abandoned Colonel Van Dorn's defensive perimeter along the El Paso Road. By August 1862 regional outposts and settlements between San Elizario, Texas, and Fort Clark had become depopulated. By 1864 this frontier line had receded even further to Uvalde, Texas. In comparison, the antebellum U.S. Army not only maintained this same perimeter but also provided protection for adjacent civilian communities and helped sustain the frontier economy. In addition, when federal troops returned to West Texas in 1867, the region's economic engine roared back to life, and civilian settlements adjacent to military installations quickly took root in Fort Stockton, Fort Davis, Brackettville, and San Angelo.

Turning now to that part of Civil War Texas lying east of the Pecos River, frontier defense in this section depended upon the state militia (Texas Rangers). At the beginning of the war, Texas had garrisoned outposts along Van Dorn's first frontier line, from the Red River to the Concho River. By 1863, however, the state had abandoned several of these outposts, and the line of defense had shifted eastward. In 1864 Texas further refined this defensive perimeter, dividing it into three districts.

Major William Quayle, succeeded by Brigadier General J. W. Throckmorton, supervised the First Frontier District from its headquarters in Decatur. This district covered the region from the Red River south to Shackelford County. Major George Erath, stationed at Gatesville, oversaw the Second Frontier District, which stretched southward to present-day Junction in Kimble County. Major James Hunter and his successor, Brigadier General John McAdoo, oversaw operations in the Third Frontier District from their headquarters in Fredericksburg south to the Rio Grande. The western defensive boundary for all the three districts was a north-south line running from just east of present-day Childress, to Abilene, Rocksprings, and Fort Clark at Brackettville.[34]

The disintegration of Van Dorn's first frontier line had started in early 1863 when Ranger Captain James Diamond in Gainesville reported Indians and outlaws raiding the region and residents on the verge of flee-ing eastward. Diamond warned that without immediate increased pro-tection, the settlements in the First Frontier District would dissolve, "and the whole frontier for miles and counties will give way." In February 1863 Brigadier General William Hudson echoed Diamond's grim forecast on a visit to Montague County, thirty miles west of Gainesville. Hudson found locals greatly excited after numerous Indian depredations. Those settlers who had not already fled the county had "forted up" at the county seat of Montague. Within a few weeks, continuing raids caused a whole-sale panic among settlers. Residents abandoned many sections of Mon-tague County and all of Clay County to the west.[35]

At Gainesville, Ranger Colonel James Bourland observed this flight firsthand as settlers flooded into town, filling all available housing. Simi-lar reports from across the First Frontier District reached Texas Gover-nor Francis Lubbock (1861–1863) during the summer of 1863. In Weath-erford, the county seat of Parker County, locals expressed dismay and bewilderment as the line of settlement along the frontier kept receding. In nearby Decatur, the county seat of Wise County, a citizen observed the region "in a state of the most wild excitement" and warned that if prompt relief was not forthcoming, the resultant chaos would force all loyal southerners to move into the state's more-populated interior.[36]

In mid-October 1864 one hundred miles west of Decatur, 600 to 1,000 Indians launched a massive attack along Elm Creek in western Young County. Ranger Lt. Colonel Buck Barry later recalled that the immense raid "caused a general desertion" among residents of counties along the northwest frontier, including Stephens, Palo Pinto, Jack, Wise, and Montague counties. Wise County historian Cliff Cates chronicled the "almost complete abandonment" of the frontier because of Indian attacks. Indian depredations "swept clean" western Wise and Parker counties, and Palo Pinto County suffered the same fate. Merchants in the county seat shuttered their stores and relocated eastward.[37]

On April 10, 1865, two months before Texas surrendered to Union forces, Young County Commissioners abandoned the county seat of

Belknap after declaring the courthouse and county offices "unsafe." Commissioners disbanded the county government and attached it to neighboring Jack County for judicial purposes. Excluding the town of Jacksboro, Indian raids also forced the evacuation of much of Jack County. Near the end of the war, repeated Native American attacks compelled Jack County Ranger Captain J. B. Earhart to leave his homestead and former Butterfield stage station on Hog Eye Prairie and move his family closer to Decatur in Wise County. Ranger Captain E. M. Orrick, who lived near Jacksboro, also relocated his family eastward and abandoned his homestead, saying that "it has become too dangerous for me to remain." The captain described the section of Jack County where he lived as "nearly depopulated." Taken together, all of these accounts chronicle a disintegrating western frontier and widespread anarchy across much of Texas's First Frontier District.[38]

Despite the above facts, some legends persist. According to one story line, significant depopulation in this part of West Texas did not occur until after the end of the war when the Texas Rangers dissolved, leaving residents defenseless. Proponents of this narrative argue that during the Civil War, many settlers did not leave the frontier but instead "forted up" in local settlements. Discussing this forting up of citizens, West Texas historian Joseph Carroll McConnell says that some of these area settlements included Fort Davis (in Stephens County), Davidsonville, Old Picketville, Old Owl Head, Mugginsville, Flattop, and Fort Murray.[39]

It seems clear, however, that the forting up of residents was the exception to the rule. One can deduce that West Texas's frontier line and population numbers were not holding firm when seats of government and counties were dissolving and when captains in the Texas Rangers were abandoning their homes and moving eastward because it was too dangerous for them to remain. McConnell says that the numerous Indian raids during the war "had a dynamic effect in decreasing" the frontier population, and "many of the early frontiersmen bagged their few belongings, and started toward the east."[40]

Two of the most knowledgeable persons regarding this depopulation issue were those in command of the frontier during this period, namely Buck Barry and Rip Ford. Writing in the 1880s, Lt. Col. Buck

Barry, the number two ranking officer in the Texas Rangers, recalled that the northwestern frontier counties "were *almost entirely abandoned* by the settlers" after the Elm Creek Raid of October 1864, with "*only a few* cowboys remaining at the large ranches—or as they were then called, 'forts' (emphasis added)." Confederate Colonel John "Rip" Ford, who commanded troops guarding the Rio Grande, Eagle Pass, the western Hill Country, and the El Paso Road recalled, "the Texas frontier suffered greatly from Indian depredations during the war. A tier of counties, at least three deep, was *quite depopulated* (emphasis added)."[41]

As the state's frontier line receded, dissent within Texas's military forces increased markedly. During the summer of 1863, Smith Bankhead, Confederate commander of North Texas, expressed concern that the unrelenting depredations pulled strongly on the loyalties of his troops. A number of them wanted to return home to protect their families in exposed frontier settlements. Many men seemed agitated and on the verge of deserting, compelling Bankhead to disarm an entire company. In addition, numerous deserters and disloyal civilians were congregating to the west in frontier counties. The military commander characterized Texas Rangers in the district as "utterly inefficient," providing no protection to local citizens.[42]

In the fall of 1863, Ranger Colonel James Bourland inspected a Texas Ranger camp at Red River Station in the First Frontier District and suggested that a number of the men posted there were disloyal. He remarked that many of them had joined the Rangers to avoid service in the Confederate army. A few months later, the colonel learned that two-thirds of the state troops at Buffalo Station and Fort Belknap deserted. In another troubling event, Ranger Adjutant Abner See reported that a lieutenant failed to prevent deserters from escaping because the officer lacked the men necessary to safely make an arrest. The deserters rode away and no one tried to stop them. See questioned whether there were any "good and true men" willing to make an arrest. Brigadier General J. W. Throckmorton, commanding the First Frontier District at Decatur, described the Texas Rangers as a "wretchedly inadequate force." Throckmorton despaired of his district's rapid depopulation, noting that many had left the region, and hundreds more appeared ready to follow.[43]

Smith Bankhead's successor, Confederate Brigadier General Henry E. McCulloch, inherited a quickly deteriorating situation in North Texas. In late 1863 significant desertions among four regiments led McCulloch to observe that many Rangers would only defend their local communities, having no interest in the Confederate cause. By early 1864 the district commander felt so frustrated that he considered leaving the frontier himself. He expressed astonishment at the type of people living in the district, calling them "perfectly worthless" cowards. Describing the region as a "sinking ship," McCulloch complained that he lacked a force sufficient to control Indians and deserters. Within the frontier counties, a paralysis existed among the civil governments, and local law enforcement was a "farce." It was next to impossible to apprehend deserters because of their many friends throughout the region. Thoroughly disgusted, the district commander recommended arresting one-fourth of the population, including civil officers, for aiding and abetting disloyal persons. The Texas Rangers were "perfectly unreliable." McCulloch remarked that many of them might feel more at ease with their Yankee friends than with rebel troops.[44]

By February 1864 as Texas's control of the frontier continued to slip away, McCulloch grew exasperated over widespread disloyalty among Confederate General Samuel Bell Maxey's men, who deserted "by the score." The remaining troops refused to obey orders. In addition, because so many men were hiding in the brush throughout North Texas, official Confederate travel in the region required a "strong guard." Numerous residents sympathized with the "brush men" and acted as informants for these deserters, reporting on local troop movements. These Tory lookouts prevented daytime scouting expeditions throughout the frontier country and limited operations to mostly nighttime maneuvers.[45]

McCulloch's superior, Confederate Major General John Bankhead Magruder, was also pessimistic regarding frontier conditions in the Lone Star State. He felt surrounded "by traitors, harassed by deserters and mutineers." One hundred rebel soldiers had recently deserted, and an entire regiment of 700 men, against orders, had discussed marching west, back to the frontier to protect their families. Magruder held an even lower opinion of Texas Rangers. Writing to Texas Governor

Pendleton Murrah (1864–1865), the commanding general remarked, "If the defense of the state rests to any great extent upon the organization of State troops, we shall be overwhelmed."[46]

During the last two years of the war, Texas Rangers on the frontier often felt overwhelmed. In the Second Frontier District, located in the middle part of the state, deserters, outlaws, and skulkers easily evaded and frequently outnumbered state forces. In early 1864 District Commander Major George Erath at his headquarters at Gatesville remarked that renegades and men with forged papers were a common sight in his section. Large numbers of deserters ranged through Erath and Johnson counties. The major, however, could not flush them from their hiding places. Unionist spies, in the community and within Erath's own Ranger unit, quickly communicated news of any state or Confederate troop movements to those in hiding. During the latter part of the war, hundreds of men deserting state and Confederate forces flocked westward to the Concho River region, which lay beyond the Rangers' defensive perimeter. Here fugitives rendezvoused, often forming wagon trains that included family members, before heading onto El Paso and points westward via the old Butterfield Overland Mail Road.[47]

One of the main rendezvous points was near the Rangers' Camp Concho, west of present-day San Angelo. While Camp Concho enjoyed a strategic location for deterring Indian raids or apprehending deserters, only twenty-five Rangers manned this remote outpost. Major Erath understood that such a small garrison offered little prospect of controlling the region, as "the various parties passing through the country [are] armed and often too large to engage." In June 1864 Erath reported that 200 disloyal men passed through his district and, after threatening his diminutive force at Camp Concho, departed for El Paso with the helpless Rangers looking on. Outnumbered and outgunned, the major acknowledged that he lacked the necessary men, supplies, and ammunition to adequately defend the Second Frontier District. In early 1865 Coleman County Chief Justice and Ranger Captain J. J. Callan wrote the governor that he knew of "but one" Ranger officer "worth one dime" in the entire district.[48]

Ranger reports from the Third Frontier District conveyed a similar, dismal tone. Major J. M. Brown of Burnet complained that state authorities were mistaken if they believed "the frontier regiment is . . . a <u>Chinese</u> wall by which Indians can never pass." Chaotic conditions in the region resembled the Runaway Scrape of 1836 when hundreds of Texans fled east before Santa Anna's advancing Mexican Army. Now, recurring Indian raids in the Third Frontier District had panicked local residents, creating a similar "stampede."[49]

In early 1864 Ranger Captain Charles Hurman reported large numbers of bushwhackers and deserters roaming the Texas Hill Country at will. Hurman observed that horse thefts and killings "by these villains are the order of the day." Ranger forces were too weak to attack the bandits. Conditions had disintegrated to where it was now too dangerous for a man to travel alone. Ranger Lieutenant Martin Casner lamented that Indians and renegades were close to overrunning the district. Writing from Fredericksburg, Ranger Major Albert Walthersdorff reported fifteen men killed, with Indians, deserters, and jayhawkers infesting the country and stealing livestock. Walthersdorff forecast that "this is only the beginning." The major complained that the outlaws had plenty of guns and ammunition, while his troops had "scarcely any."[50]

Early in 1865 New Braunfels resident Otto Wupperman relayed grim news about deteriorating frontier conditions in that section. Incessant Indian attacks were forcing residents to flee, and "many farms are given up already." Wupperman warned that New Braunfels would soon become the frontier line, with Blanco and the upper part of Comal County surrendered to the Indians. The same month, another district resident Niell Robison pleaded for immediate relief from marauding Indians and lawless men. Robison alerted state authorities that without immediate help the frontier line would quickly fall back to Austin, New Braunfels, and San Antonio.[51]

Mob violence also proved a problem in the Third Frontier District. During the summer of 1864, deadly clashes between Tories and Rebels broke out in Gillespie County. Ranger Brigadier General John McAdoo reported from Fredericksburg that violence within a three-month period claimed the lives of twenty men. McAdoo stated, "Some had been way-laid and shot; others taken from their homes at the dead hour of mid-night and hung, and their homes robbed; and some had been mobbed and murdered in jail and in irons." Throughout the region, no man felt safe, not even in his own home.[52]

Ranger Lieutenant William Holland informed Governor Murrah that he considered many people living in the district's Hill Country un-reliable and in collusion with deserters. Referring to the recent frenzy of hangings, he stated that the traitorous Germans lynched were "not entitled to protection." Holland asked Murrah to understand the difficult circumstances facing "true southern men" in the region. Third Frontier District Commander Major James Hunter told the Governor that a reign of terror existed in the area and characterized the civil government as powerless to intercede. The major noted that some local authorities, rela-tives of the murdered men, were too intimidated to arrest a "southern man for hanging a tory [German]."[53]

Several citizens of the county subsequently complained to the gover-nor about Hunter, saying that the major had married a German and was overly sympathetic to Germans, most of whom they considered disloyal. In July 1864 state authorities relieved Hunter of command "until further orders." While some of the "good and honest southern men" in the re-gion thoroughly approved of the vigilante hangings, saying the Germans "deserved their fate," they abhorred the subsequent robberies of lynched Tories' homes. Similar violence broke out in Uvalde and Dawson coun-ties during the spring of 1865. Ranger Major John Henry Brown report-ed that local officials asked him to investigate a vigilante slaying in which a mob murdered the sheriff.[54]

While other Confederate states experienced similar internal dissent, none shared West Texas's chronic Indian depredations or a border with Mexico. Only on the Lone Star frontier did chaos besiege residents from all sides. In early 1864 Confederate Colonel Rip Ford ordered Major Thomas Riordan, commanding state forces at Fort Inge near Uvalde, to move his defensive line westward to Fort Clark near present-day Brack-ettville. Upon arriving at Fort Clark, the major reported he had "no pro-tection whatever" and only twelve effective men scattered over a fifteen-mile range. Indians and Mexican marauders were driving off all the stock in the region, and Riordan lacked sufficient forces to pursue them. Riordan's picket remained at the outpost for only a short time. By the fall of 1864, regional lawlessness and disorder forced Confederate postal authorities to curtail local mail service because "'there are no troops at Fort Clark, and it is considered hazardous to go there with any kind of conveyance whatever.'" For the remainder of the war, the mail went no further west than Uvalde.[55]

In May 1864 Uvalde County Chief Justice C.C. McKinney reported that large numbers of renegades stole 2,000 cattle from Pedro Pinto in Kinney County and crossed them over the Rio Grande into Mexico. Across the border at Piedras Negras, Mexico, there were hundreds of outlaws threatening to take all available livestock. The following month, McKinney observed large groups of deserters and renegades freely roaming the region. In addition, "thieves and robbers" had stolen 4,000–5,000 head of cattle, driving them across the river into Mexico. The Chief Justice characterized the local Ranger force as "totally inadequate."[56]

In May 1864 Bandera resident W. A. Lockhart predicted the desertion of the entire country west of San Antonio within sixty days without adequate frontier protection. Lockhart noted, "Already robberies and murders are of frequent occurrence." Ranger Captain H. T. Edgar reported that the region between Camp Verde and the Rio Grande was "daily run over by bands of Indians and lawless men with impunity." The lack of a strong military presence in the jayhawker and robber-infested Third District was pressuring frontier residents to move farther east for protection.[57]

Summarizing developments across all three Frontier Districts in the spring of 1864, the head of the Texas Rangers, Colonel J. E. McCord, expressed great concern about the region's "destitute condition." In a revealing remark about state forces under his command, the colonel reported that without an immediate infusion of regular Confederate troops, not Texas Rangers, "the country will be devastated, and the good citizens reluctantly forced to retreat to the interior. The frontier will be broken up and the outer line thrown back to San Antonio and Austin, from 80 to 100 miles inside of the present line." Here McCord notes that the "present" frontier line in May 1864 was already back to its 1849 position, eighty to one hundred miles west of Austin and San Antonio, roughly from Fredericksburg to Uvalde. McCord's assessment, along with those cited earlier by Buck Barry, Rip Ford, and others clearly demonstrate that Texas failed to maintain its western defensive perimiters.[58]

Such chaos, lawlessness, and dissent throughout the entire frontier region, coupled with depressing news from the Confederate battlefront, prompted large groups of Texans, both civilian and military, to abandon the state. This westward exodus out of Texas had become an increasingly familiar phenomenon as the war progressed. As early as May 1861, a newspaper had reported twenty-five West Texas families in ten wagons leaving the state. The following month, the same newspaper mentioned sixty wagons full of Texans traveling between Fort Stockton and El Paso, heading for California, "and more are reported beyond."[59]

In late December 1862 W. W. Mills, customs collector in El Paso County, noted the arrival of five Hill Country Germans who survived the Battle of the Nueces, some four months earlier. In September 1863 ten refugees from North Texas arrived in El Paso via the overland mail route. By the early months of 1864, the number of Texans abandoning the state skyrocketed. In Wise County a rumor circulated that troops were coming "to hang or shoot" anyone who voted against secession. A widespread panic ensued, and on April 15, a "stampede" commenced, in which many citizens of the county abandoned their homes and fled westward, beyond the Rangers' defenses.[60]

Concerning this growing flight, Texas Ranger Colonel Buck Barry recalled that in the spring of 1864, his officers dispatched patrols to flush out deserters and their families congregating west of the state's frontier line, many of whom intended to move to California with their livestock and household goods. Barry lamented, "To see men apparently planning to remove to the country of the enemy or remain outside the settlements among the Indians and threaten to become criminals, was a queer sight when the times and conditions should have called up more than the best in them."[61]

In late May 1864 Captain Henry Fossett from Camp Colorado went on patrol along the Middle Concho River. He discovered five hundred deserters and some families, with many cattle and forty loaded wagons, recently departed from the old Butterfield Head of Concho mail station near present-day Barnhart. The group included a number of men from Ranger Captains Loyd and Whiteside's companies. A well-used wagon road blazed by deserters paralleled the Concho.[62]

A large exodus of Texans reached Union-occupied El Paso during the summer of 1864. Brigadier General James H. Carleton ordered rations for 152 of these since they were hungry and without funds. Carleton's troops carefully interrogated all refugees. The general required new arrivals to state their reasons for leaving the Lone Star State and any over the age of eighteen to take an oath of allegiance to the Union. Intelligence previously received indicated that the Confederates might plant spies among the group to reconnoiter Union troop strength and deployment in West Texas and New Mexico. Carleton's military intelligence proved correct. In March 1864 Henry McCulloch, Confederate commander of North Texas, recommended that Ranger Colonel McCord send spies among refugees heading west.[63]

A study of records kept by the Department of New Mexico provides a fascinating profile of the motivations and types of people leaving Texas. One group interrogated included close to thirty Texan deserters and refugees found at Fort Quitman in May 1864 by California Volunteers Captain Timmins and his men. Timmins' brother subsequently shot one of the party and relieved the dead man of $76 and two horses. The captain reported that another group of deserters and refugees was due to arrive shortly via the Upper Overland Road through Hueco Tanks. In questioning the Fort Quitman party, Timmins learned that state troops stationed on Texas's western frontier "have disbanded generally and left the country."[64]

A September 1864 descriptive roll of Texas deserters included Isaac Knight, a former Butterfield Overland Mail stage driver who boarded with Jack County Ranger Captain J. B. Earhart in 1860. All of the men on this particular list, which included Ranger Lieutenant Samuel Morrow, came from Jack and Parker counties. Carleton ordered this group carefully examined and in October convened a board of inquiry at Santa Fe. During their interrogations members of the group stated they deserted their Confederate and state regiments because they "did not wish to fight for the rebel government" and "disliked both [the] laws and [their] treatment" in Texas.[65]

In the summer of 1864, Union Colonel George Bowie reported the arrival at San Elizario of twenty families (including eighty-four children) and eighteen single men. The refugees appeared in El Paso County after a four-month journey with a large wagon train carrying supplies and livestock. Bowie ordered the party to camp at the Cottonwoods, Henry Skillman's old stage station on the Texas-New Mexico line, pending orders from General Carleton. Another roster of Texas refugees, this one from 1865, reveals that two-thirds deserted from state frontier regiments and the rest from the Confederate Army.[66]

One of the deserters, part of an 1864 wagon train, kept a diary of his journey from Texas to California. Thirty-year-old John Taylor of Comanche County, an Ohio native, wrote that in April 1864 he received permission from Ranger Major George Erath to transfer to a Concho County regiment. Not having any intention of serving in the Texas State Troops, Taylor used the transfer pass to travel to the Middle Concho River and join a wagon train forming there. The group left on May 11, following the old Butterfield Overland Road through Texas. "There were twenty-six men in this company" in addition to "fifteen or twenty Texas Rangers" who provided escort "as far as the Pecos River."[67]

The deserters' overland trip proved arduous and sometimes tragic. On May 22, 1864, eighteen-month-old Alice Foseman died, and the wagon train paused at Llano Estacado, the old Butterfield station in Upton County, Texas, where her parents laid her to rest a short distance southeast of the stage stop. Continuing westward, the refugees finally reached California in October 1864. Taylor and his wife, Margaret, stayed on the west coast after the war, settling in San Diego County. The Whitlows from Denton County and the Ward family from Mount Vernon in Titus County, Texas, accompanied Taylor's wagon train. During Reconstruction, Green Ward, John Ward, and their families returned to Titus County.[68]

In 1864 all across Texas, desertions by state and Confederate troops were rapidly increasing. In his memoirs Ranger Captain R. H. Williams recalled that soldiers "were going off in bands of from a dozen up to two hundred at a time." Many of those deserting were heading west to El Paso and beyond. Often these men and their families had to wait until rains replenished the grass and waterholes along the route in arid western Texas; therefore spring and fall proved the best times to travel. In early 1865 the now-annual westward exodus got underway once again. Ranger Major George Erath learned that 300 men were assembling on the Concho River to go to California and that a much larger group would soon follow. At the Rangers' Camp Colorado, Colonel Buck Barry heard similar reports. In a letter to his superiors, Barry stated that citizens from both the interior and the frontier were gathering supplies and forming wagon trains to leave Texas in the spring. The 1865 rendezvous on the Concho would be similar to that of the previous year.[69]

Departing wagon trains were but a small part of the spiraling frontier chaos that Colonel Barry and the Texas Rangers found themselves increasingly unable to control. In a postscript to his report concerning deteriorating conditions on the Concho, Barry warned his superiors of another serious problem, that of frontier residents trading with the enemy. The colonel remarked, "It might be well to inform you that we have five men here under arrest that say they were hired by one Patterson in New Mexico to drive beef from our frontier." Patterson and his party carried plenty of cash with them to buy all the beef that local ranchers would sell. In early January 1865 after visiting cattlemen in Coleman and Concho counties, Patterson's group traveled south to Fort Mason and the San Saba River in search of additional livestock. The Patterson that Barry referred to in his postscript was James Patterson, beef contractor for the Union Army at Fort Sumner, New Mexico. From 1864 to 1868, the U.S. Army purchased all the cattle that Texas ranchers were willing to supply for its Bosque Redondo Indian Reservation at Fort Sumner.[70]

During the previous year, James Patterson of Springfield, Illinois, and William Franks of Marion County, Alabama, had formed a partnership to drive cattle from Confederate Texas to the Union outpost at Fort Sumner on the Pecos River. Franks had left Texas in the spring of 1864 and met Patterson in New Mexico in July. The two men soon added a third partner, Captain Thomas L. Roberts, who retired from the First

Infantry California Volunteers in September 1864. The three men had an open-ended contract with the Union Army to supply beef on the hoof to Fort Sumner.[71]

Writing in July 1865, Union General James H. Carleton noted that Roberts "has some cattle en route up the Pecos River from Texas." The general ordered that a party of eight to ten men, with a wagon full of food, supplies, and ammunition go downriver to help Roberts trail his herd upstream. Roberts' herd was undoubtedly the fruits of Patterson and Franks' continuing efforts to acquire Texas frontier cattle. In a subsequent letter from September 1865, Carleton noted that Patterson, on two previous occasions, drove cattle from Texas to Fort Sumner. Alabama-born Bill Franks, well known and trusted by many West Texas ranchers, including John Chisum, handled details for the Texas end of the trade. Yankees Patterson and Roberts managed the New Mexico side of the arrangement.[72]

Across the entire frontier, Texas officials noted increased movements of cattle. In April 1864 Ranger Colonel James Bourland, commander of the frontier regiment at Gainesville, warned that 1,500 men were on the Concho and that these "jayhawkers . . . must have driven all the cattle from the border counties." In October 1864 Ranger General McAdoo in Fredericksburg reported that thirty to sixty men with 1,000 to 1,500 head of cattle had passed through his Third Frontier District, driving their herds toward the San Saba and Concho rivers. McAdoo suspected that the group was heading west for an eventual rendezvous on the Pecos River.[73]

The capture of Vicksburg in July 1863 gave the Union control of the Mississippi River, effectively preventing Texas cattle from reaching Confederate markets east of the river. During the last two years of the war, the Concho River country in West Texas became a major staging area for frontier cattleman trading with the enemy. Here they pooled their herds and cowboys before driving their beeves over the old Butterfield Mail Road to the Middle Concho, then west to Horsehead Crossing on the Pecos River. From Horsehead, the cowboys pushed their herds upstream to eager Union buyers at Fort Sumner, New Mexico. In 1864 and 1865, cattle prices ranged between eight cents and twenty-two cents per

pound, depending upon availability, competition, and market speculation. The Union Army paid in gold.[74]

This Texas-New Mexico beef road, used by former Union soldiers
and Texas cowboys to drive their beeves to market, became widely known
by the end of the century as the Goodnight-Loving Cattle Trail. James
Cox used the name in 1895, as did J. Evetts Haley in 1936. Both writers
claimed that renowned ranchers Charles Goodnight and Oliver Loving
blazed this cattle route. In one account Goodnight stated, "I laid off the
Goodnight Trail in 1866." In another he noted, "In my drive of 1866, I
had to lay out my own trail, as no trail had been made since 1859, and that
one not in my direction. . . . My course led through a trackless wilder-
ness." Goodnight told Haley that he sold his first herd to James Patterson
at Fort Sumner in July 1866.[75]

The hooves of countless Lone Star steers, however, had blazed this
path to New Mexico long before 1866. Patterson and Franks were already ranging throughout Texas in the fall of 1864, purchasing cattle for
the Union. On a trip through the Trans-Pecos in January 1865, Confederate Captain Henry Kennedy found evidence of Texas ranchers' lucrative
trade with the Union Army. Kennedy reported, "I discovered the trail of
about seventy or eighty Yankees who crossed the Pecos River at Horse-
ead Crossing, and went in the direction of the Conchas [sic] and Fort
Belknap, no doubt in search of beef cattle, as droves have already gone
out by that route."[76]

Throughout the Civil War a number of Texans went to great lengths
to avoid detection of their trade with the enemy. Despite their efforts to
keep this business hidden, records reveal that Lone Star cattlemen sold
their beeves to the Union Army at Fort Sumner and at El Paso. Some of
these ranchers also drove their cattle to buyers in Mexico, despite explicit
Confederate orders to the contrary.[77]

One notable Texas rancher who conducted business with the
Patterson-Franks outfit was John Chisum. In October 1863 Chisum, a
Confederate beef contractor, shifted 1,500 head of cattle from Denton
County to a new ranch in the northeast corner of Concho County at the
confluence of the Colorado and Concho rivers. In the spring of 1864, a
friend of Chisum's wrote Texas Governor Pendleton Murrah requesting

John Chisum, noted Texas-New Mexico cattleman and Confederate beef contractor, started selling beeves to the Union Army at Fort Sumner, New Mexico, in 1864. Photo from James Cox, *Historical and Biographical Record of the Cattle Industry and the Cattlemen of Texas and Adjacent Territory* (St. Louis: Woodman & Tierman Printing Co., 1895).

permission for the cattleman to finish moving all of his livestock operations to the Concho, noting that such permission "would be gratefully received by him and appreciated by his numerous friends in the community." The writer noted that Chisum had long been a friend to the Confederate States, supplying 4,000 cattle to the rebel Army.[78]

By March 1864, however, Texas authorities had become suspicious of the increased movements of Lone Star livestock. Two days after the above letter to Murrah, Confederate Brigadier General Henry McCulloch advised the governor that many Texans were heading west with their families out beyond the Rangers' frontier perimeter, driving large numbers of beeves. Several prominent stock raisers were among the group, including John Chisum. McCulloch believed that the group would rendezvous with deserters in the region "with whom these people doubtless have an understanding and from whom they expect aid."[79]

Unaware of the recent letter sent to the governor requesting permission for Chisum to move his cattle to the Concho, McCulloch warned Murrah that some Texas ranchers were seeking permits to move their livestock west, beyond the control of state authorities. The general wanted the governor to know about Chisum and the other cattlemen before issuing any permits; however, Chisum's friends persisted in their petitions to the governor. A month later, John Williams wrote to Murrah, requesting that he "please receive my friend John S. Chisum and if it is possible to give him any relief please do so. You can rely on any statement he may make." The author may be the same John Williams who worked for Patterson and Franks during the summer of 1865 driving Texas cattle to Fort Sumner.[80]

One cowboy knowledgeable about Chisum's business dealings with Union cattle agents was M. C. Smith. In September 1864 after working eleven months at the cattleman's Concho County ranch, Smith decided to strike out on his own. The cowhand left for Denton County to give Chisum the news and collect his back pay. Before Smith reached Denton, however, Ranger Colonel James Bourland collared him and on September 20, 1864, enrolled the hapless cowboy as a private in Captain Patton's regiment. In order to pick up his horse and blankets before reporting to

M. C. Smith worked for John Chisum during 1863 and 1864 and for Union beef contractor James Patterson during 1864 and 1865. Photo from Sidney W. Smith, *From the Cow Camp to the Pulpit: Being Twenty-Five Years Experience of a Texas Evangelist* (Cincinnati: The Christian Leader Corporation, 1927).

Captain Patton, Smith asked Bourland for a travel permit to Denton. The aging colonel granted him a three-day pass.[81]

The newly enlisted private had no intention of serving in the Rangers and quickly left North Texas. His name later appeared on a June 1865 deserter list from El Paso. Smith fled westward, stopping long enough at Chisum's Concho ranch to demand his $50 in back pay. Once again, Smith missed seeing his ex-employer, this time by a matter of minutes. He did manage to find the rest of the cowboys tending Chisum's herd. He recalled, "I was no better off in money matters, as I had failed to see Chisum, *so when they began making up the herd for Patterson, I proposed to put in enough of the Chisum brand* to bring $50.00" (emphasis added). In September 1864 then, M.C. Smith directly links Confederate beef contractor John Chisum to a Civil War business transaction with Union beef contractor James Patterson.[82]

Immediately after deserting the Texas Rangers, Smith went to work for the Patterson-Franks outfit. From late 1864 through April 1865, Smith and several other cowboys collected a new herd, trailing it west along the Middle Concho River, following the ruts of the antebellum Butterfield Overland route to Centralia Draw. Smith said the cowhands waited there for things to quiet down until after the Battle of Dove Creek (near modern San Angelo) on January 8, 1865, before moving the steers westward. During the Dove Creek fight, 500 Texas Rangers received a drubbing from a band of 400 to 600 Kickapoo Indians en route to Mexico. Ironically, after the battle some of these Rangers recuperated at Chisum's Concho ranch, unaware of the cattleman's trade with the enemy.[83]

After the Dove Creek excitement quieted down, M. C. Smith's first drive with Patterson was not to Fort Sumner but likely to El Paso. On May 1, 1865, the cowhands started the herd toward the Pecos, eighty miles distant, and then pushed onto El Paso. This sale of Confederate beef to the Union Army at El Paso also took place during the war, as Texas did not surrender until June 2, 1865. On all subsequent drives, Smith delivered the Texas cattle to Fort Sumner on the Pecos.[84]

Other Lone Star cowboys moving Patterson-Franks cattle up the Pecos were Robert Kelsey Wylie and Thomas Murray. Murray noted

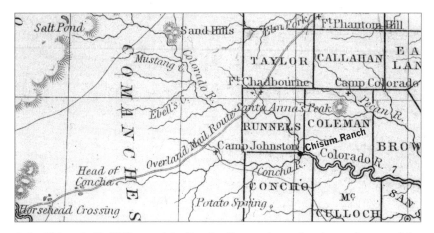

John Chisum's Civil War ranch in Concho County, located at the confluence of the
Concho and Colorado Rivers. Texas cowboys moved their herds westward from
Chisum's along the Middle Concho River to Head of Concho, a Butterfield
Overland Mail station, then onto Horsehead Crossing on the Pecos River.
From there, cowhands followed the Pecos upstream to Fort Sumner, New Mexico.
Map detail from *S. A. Mitchell's No. 12 Map of the State of Texas, 1859*. Courtesy
of the Virginia Garrett Cartographic History Library, Special Collections,
University of Texas at Arlington Library, Arlington, Texas. Chisum
Ranch location added by author.

that his employer's beeves came from Palo Pinto, Parker, and Concho
counties. He recalled that for these drives, "the old Chisum ranch was
the starting point—we left [from] the mouth of the Concho." In early
January 1865, Texas Rangers patrolling the Concho arrested five men
engaged in acquiring cattle for the enemy (Patterson), not far from
Chisum's Concho County ranch.[85]

Soon after moving to the Concho country in the fall of 1863, Chisum
met Bill Franks, owner of a store and saloon in the area located at present-
day Trickham, Texas. Chisum later took over the store but kept Franks
on the payroll to help run it with another man named Emory Peter. One
old-timer in the region recalled, "John Chisum would send Franks to
Austin after money to pay off his men, and Franks would return with his
saddlebags full of gold and silver." On other occasions after Chisum sold
a herd, he sent Franks to Austin to bank the proceeds. In the summer of

1865, Chisum's younger brother Pitser started working for Patterson and Franks, helping get their cattle to market and butchering their beeves at Fort Sumner. Chisum's niece remembered that James Patterson, Emory Peter, and Pitser Chisum oversaw the portion of the drives from "down about Horsehead [Crossing] . . . to Fort Sumner." Further evidence of Chisum's business relationship with Patterson and Franks is Chisum's later purchase of James Patterson's general store at Bosque Grande, near Fort Sumner.[86]

Besides freighting and running Texas cattle to New Mexico, in December 1863 James Patterson requested permission from the commander at Fort Stanton to rebuild the old Whitlock Sawmill located nearby at Tularosa, New Mexico. A Union report in 1864 noted that Patterson's sawmill was a frequent haunt for a number of unsavory types, including some dealing in stolen government weapons and supplies. The note mentions Bill Franks, "one of the Texan refugees," whose "movements are to say the least of a suspicious character." In an accompanying statement, a man named Apodoca claimed that in the fall of 1864 he sold a stolen army revolver to an American in the company of James Patterson, whom he believed to be William Franks. Dismissing these reports, the commander at Fort Stanton characterized the pair as loyal citizens in the community. Desirous of their Texas beeves, Department of New Mexico Commander James Carleton likely granted Franks and Patterson a certain degree of latitude.[87]

During 1864 and 1865, as the market for Texas cattle began to expand, Union, Confederate, and Ranger officers all tried to capitalize on the lucrative trade. In December 1864 Lieutenant James Conwell, recently retired from the Fifth Infantry, California Volunteers, announced his intention to enter into the Texas cattle business. Six months earlier, Conwell had provided escort for fifty-three Texan refugees from Franklin (El Paso) to Santa Fe. The refugees likely told the lieutenant about conditions in Texas. Conwell informed General Carleton that eleven men, six Texans and five discharged soldiers, were en route to the interior of Texas to round up beeves. Conwell's party may be the same men dressed in federal uniforms that Buck Barry's Ranger patrol apprehended on the Concho River.[88]

Authorities in Texas made additional arrests. In one case, however, the guilty parties were not Union agents but officers of the Texas Rangers. In 1864 Major George Erath of the Second Frontier District discovered that Ranger Captains M. W. Matthews of Johnson County, J. M. Luckey of Parker County, J. K. Carmack of Palo Pinto County, and Jack County Chief Justice J. W. Robbins were conspiring in a "traitorous" plot to defect to the Federals and deprive the Confederate Army of beef supplies. Carmack also allegedly polled residents of the frontier counties and found "that they were in favor of closing the war on any terms."[89]

In the fall of 1864, Confederate authorities charged Ranger Major James M. Hunter of the Third Frontier District with selling cattle to the enemy. The major denied the accusation. One should remember that some rebels wanted Hunter dismissed from the Rangers, believing him too familiar with Unionist Germans in the Texas Hill Country. In his defense Hunter claimed that Confederate agent John Burgess purchased Hunter's entire herd of 800 beeves at Presidio del Norte, Mexico. Union documents provide some support for this claim. Skeptical of Hunter's story, Confederate Major General John G. Walker and Captain Henry Kennedy endorsed Burgess's account of the transaction. Burgess stated that he acquired only 300 head from Hunter and that Union cattle agents in El Paso County, Texas, bought the remaining 500. On December 19, 1864, authorities granted Hunter a thirty-day leave of absence, and on January 19, 1865, Governor Pendleton Murrah accepted his resignation. The illicit cattle trade had brought down one of the Texas Rangers' highest-ranking officers.[90]

Officers of the Texas Rangers were not alone in attempting to deprive the rebel army of needed beef supplies. A number of Texans were participating in an illicit cattle trade with Mexico. Despite numerous orders over a three-year period prohibiting such transactions, state and Confederate authorities were unable to stem this border commerce. In November 1863 Confederate Major General John B. Magruder complained that "large numbers of beeves are being driven into Mexico and sold on speculation." Ranger General McAdoo in Fredericksburg called the traffic in Texas cattle "notorious." He observed that beeves were crossing unimpeded into Mexico every day after ranchers paid Confederate authorities bribes of one to two dollars per head. McAdoo also noted, "This is believed to be a regular <u>blackmail</u> arrangement."[91]

Confederate Major General John G. Walker asserted that the "avaricious" trade with Mexico had caused a fearful depreciation of rebel currency by introducing precious metals such as gold and silver into Texas. By the fall of 1864, paper money was essentially worthless. Many international merchants and brokers conducting business with Texas and the Confederacy now required payment in either hard currency or cotton.[92]

Lampasas rancher O.S. Nichols recalled that he and his father were part of an outfit driving 150 beeves to Mexico from the Hill Country in the fall of 1864. Nichols said the men paid Colonel Tobin, the Confederate commander at Eagle Pass, $150 for a signed pass. The cattleman wryly noted that "Colonel Tobin was just putting that money down in his pocket." To justify their actions, the group offered the same explanation used by other Lone Star ranchers selling their cattle in Mexico. "We put it up to Tobin that we were just a bunch of citizens driving over [to Mexico] to get supplies we could not get in Texas," Nichols said, "and with a little something for him [i.e., money] he was easy to convince."[93]

In early 1865 Ranger Brigadier General J. W. Throckmorton, commanding the First Frontier District, also received reports of persons illegally driving herds to Mexico. Throckmorton promised to fully investigate the claims and promptly punish any offenders. W. A. Peril of Harper, Texas, was one of those trailing cattle into Mexico. He recalled that the route he took in 1864 went from Fort McKavett, to the South Concho River, to Horsehead Crossing on the Pecos, to Fort Stockton, and finally crossed the Rio Grande at Presidio del Norte.[94]

Despite sporadic attempts at enforcement by Confederate and Texas authorities, the Lone Star beef trade grew rapidly during the last two years of the war. Many persons, whether rancher, Ranger, Union, or Confederate, all realized there was considerable money to be made selling Texas beeves. During the war Texas ranchers opened a new cattle trail to the Union Army at Fort Sumner, New Mexico. Charles Goodnight claimed that he pioneered this New Mexico route in the summer of 1866, but he did not.

Texans trading with the enemy, a collapsing defensive perimeter, and hundreds of families fleeing west were all clear indicators of the crisis facing frontier residents during the latter half of the Civil War. Over time, with rebel losses mounting and the economy failing, the political and social structure throughout the Confederacy and Texas unraveled. The farther west one traveled, the more pronounced the chaos. Frontier settlers learned early in the war that adequate protection from raiding Indians and renegades was not forthcoming.

In West Texas, people cared far less about slavery and the southern cause than about their own welfare. Events during the Civil War made clear that regional identity among Tejanos, Germans, and Anglo frontiersmen in West Texas was often not the same identity typical of East Texas and the Old South. Out on the western frontier, Confederate authorities had surrendered control long before the war's end.

By early 1865 a marked breakdown of law and order was evident across West Texas. Ranger General Throckmorton reported that 500 deserters passed through his First Frontier District in March, collecting cattle and "stragglers" before moving out beyond the Rangers' lines. The district was full of renegades and deserters, and local residents exhibited "a stolid indifference" toward aiding state forces in their efforts. A telling example of the widespread chaos and anarchy throughout the region involved eighty-eight men who deserted from a regiment near Crockett in East Texas. The deserters marched westward in formation "for four days through towns, villages on public highways and no effort [was] made to stop them . . . no information sent in by the citizens . . . to notify the authorities." Throughout the latter part of the war, state and Confederate authorities proved unable to control events and an often-hostile population in the western half of the state. During this same period, desertions among Texas Ranger companies sharply increased. Despite their efforts the Rangers failed to protect the frontier, which fell back in many places to its position in 1849.[95]

In the first half of the nineteenth century, the allure of Texas's frontier and its vast open lands attracted many new residents. During this period, thousands of settlers packed their belongings and moved to Texas, inspired by the prospect of a fresh start in a new land. Before leaving their old homes and farms, they sometimes paused long enough to scribble a note goodbye or carve the initials "G.T.T.," or "Gone to Texas." Once in Texas, those who settled on the state's antebellum frontier frequently complained about inadequate federal protection from Indian raids. This chronic complaint eventually became one of the reasons why Texas seceded.

After the Lone Star State joined the Confederacy, officials pledged much-improved protection for families living in western counties. The record shows that both Texas and the Confederacy reneged on their promises. By the end of the war, widespread raiding and lawlessness depopulated much of West Texas. As mentioned at the beginning of this chapter, state authorities had sent Ranger Captain W. W. Reynolds in May 1864 to investigate conditions on the Texas frontier. Reynolds' statement, "The most perfect anarchy prevails," proved all too accurate. During the last two years of the Civil War, hundreds of disillusioned and war-weary Texans left their homes and headed west to California, hoping for a fresh start in a new land largely untouched by the sectional conflict. Before leaving, perhaps a few of them paused long enough to scribble a note goodbye or carve the initials "G.F.T.," or "Gone from Texas."[96]

POSTSCRIPT

Near the south entrance to the Irion County Courthouse on a hill over-looking Mertzon, Texas, is a pink granite marker erected in 1963 by the Texas Historical Commission. The marker commemorates Confederate and Texas Ranger frontier service during the Civil War. Part of the text etched into the pink granite reads, "Texas and Confederate troops, despite poor arms and mounts, held defense lines until war's end."[97]

One-hundred-ten miles to the southwest, at the end of a remote dirt road in Pecos County, stands a 1936 gray granite state centennial marker. Located at Horsehead Crossing on the west bank of the Pecos River, the signpost memorializes not only this historic ford but also the Good-night-Loving Cattle Trail. Though often used for target practice over the years, the marker is still legible. One sentence carved in the gray stone states, "The Goodnight-Loving trail [sic], established in 1866 and trod by tens of thousands of Texas longhorns, came here and turned up the east bank of the Pecos for Fort Sumner [New Mexico]."[98]

Both of these historical markers raise an interesting point. Many Texans learn about their state's history by reading Texas Historical Commission road signs. The state's marker program, one of the finest in the nation, does much to promote and stimulate interest in local heritage. But what happens if a sign is inaccurate? If it is etched in stone (in the above examples, granite), it must be true, right? Not necessarily. Occasionally, the narrative presented in these signs is outdated or erroneous. Similarly, sometimes the way Texans remember their history is also inaccurate. While historical agencies can easily replace an imprecise marker, Texas identity, once engraved in the cultural consciousness, is often impervious to change. The Texas Historical Commission has a convenient link on its website to correct marker inaccuracies, but where does one find a corresponding link for Lone Star memory? It is likely that fifty years from now, many Texans will still believe the narratives on these granite markers, regardless of what historians uncover to the contrary. The state's myths and icons are that powerful.[99]

RACE RELATIONS AS A BAROMETER
OF WESTERN IDENTITY

The fact that Texas seceded from the Union might lead some to conclude that, like its sister states in the Confederacy, Texas was southern in outlook. Events in Texas's shatterbelt region during the Civil War amply demonstrated that not all residents of the state shared the same values. Many Lone Star citizens did embrace a collective Texan distinctiveness, forged during the Revolution and Republic periods of 1832–1846. When it came to slavery and secession, however, a number of people living on the western frontier firmly rejected a southern identity. The frontier, with its distinct environment, diverse cultures (Great Plains and Western Indians, Tejanos, Germans, and Anglos), and a traditional dependence upon the federal economy imprinted a distinctly more Western disposition upon some of its residents.

A key barometer in understanding these various strains of Lone Star identity is race. After the Civil War and Reconstruction, the eastern half of Texas marched in tandem with the South regarding race relations. Once again, Texas west of the 100th meridian proved itself different. Interactions between whites, blacks, and Tejanos in West Texas more often mirrored the American West than the Old South.

In the western half of Texas from the 1850s to today, race relations between Anglo Americans and Tejanos have moved from cooperation to segregation to cooperation once more. This circular and often painful journey contains a story both remarkable and compelling. Initially, Texans west of the 100th meridian enjoyed some measure of accommodation in their interactions. From 1850 to 1890, whites moving into the region demonstrated a spirit of cooperation with local Tejanos.

In a number of instances, the two groups worked together establishing the region's infrastructure, creating towns and counties, protecting the frontier, and sharing leadership positions in local government. Some historians argue that this spirit of accommodation was not necessarily the first choice of some Anglos. Given nineteenth-century racial attitudes in America, it is clear that a number of whites would have preferred dominating Mexican Americans rather than cooperating with them.[1]

When Anglos began migrating to Texas in the 1820s, "many found the presence of Tejanos . . . an unwanted sight." White Americans and Texans alike looked down upon brown-skinned people. Mexicans were often seen as dirty, lazy, and degenerate. Well into the twentieth century, state textbooks cast the Texas Revolution saga as a struggle of superior, divinely ordained Anglo Texans against inferior, treacherous Mexicans. Only within the past few decades have historians finally acknowledged the notable contributions of Tejanos to Texas and its independence. Tejanos signed the Texas Declaration of Independence, fought in the Texas Revolution, and served the Republic in official capacity, including as Vice President.[2]

Shortly after the victory at San Jacinto in 1836, however, white Texans developed amnesia and began vilifying their Tejano allies who helped defeat Santa Anna. Within a few months, fallout from the Battle of the Alamo and subsequent Goliad Massacre was negatively impacting many Tejanos. Anglos increasingly viewed all people of Mexican origin, even staunch supporters of independence, as "the enemy." For more than a century afterward, white Texans used the Alamo and Goliad myths to justify outrages against Mexican Americans. In some Texas counties throughout the 1840s, whites intimidated, harassed, and even forcibly removed Tejanos. Anglos also seized Tejanos' ranches and livestock. Relations between whites and Mexican Americans deteriorated further after the Mexican War when a "series of punitive expulsions" by Anglos ejected Tejano populations from Southeast and Central Texas.[3]

The Texas Revolution and Mexican War narratives shaped interactions between whites and Tejanos over the next century. Annual anniversaries commemorating the Alamo, Goliad, and San Jacinto served to "reinforce a collective memory of [Anglo] Texan superiority." Portions of this public consciousness evinced a selective forgetfulness, dropping Tejanos' contributions to Texas history from the narrative. Lone Star race relations eroded further during the Progressive Era, starting around 1890. Texans, like the rest of the nation, worried about the "disturbing" effects of industrialization upon society and the flood of "less-than-desirable" immigrants pouring into America from Eastern Europe and Mexico.[4]

From 1880 to 1930, more than one million Mexicans came to the United States and many of them settled in Texas. By the end of the nineteenth century, the immense expansion of America's industrial machine created a strong demand for labor. In the Southwest, including West Texas, Mexican immigrants filled that demand. "Lily-white" Texas Progressives, in their search for order amid these new and "unsettling changes" in the labor force, reaffirmed the state's old, post-1836 racial hierarchy. This ordering of Texas society by "reform-minded" racist progressives effectively kept Tejanos "in their place" until after World War II.[5]

Up into the 1890s, Anglos living west of the Pecos River were a minority population. From the 1850s to the 1880s, they were obliged to accommodate local Tejanos. Until whites could dominate Mexican Americans economically and politically, they were forced to bide their time and operate on a neutral ground. For their part, "even with concessions and accommodations," Mexican Americans in West Texas, New Mexico, Arizona, and California "still lost power [to the Anglos] when the numbers turned against them." Patricia Limerick dates this transformation to the 1880s when the railroad reached the region, bringing large numbers of whites to previously isolated sections of the American West. As a result Mexican American settlements "changed from pueblos to barrios, from towns in which Hispanics were the majority population to segregated enclaves in cities in which Hispanics had become a minority."[6]

Following the Mexican War, many of the white men moving to West Texas were single. As there were few available white women in the region, a number of early Anglo settlers married Tejano women. In many instances, these mixed couples gave their children Spanish first names. This intermarriage always manifested itself as a white man marrying a Mexican woman. Anglo women available for marriage rarely took Tejano husbands. West Texas Anglo society frowned upon white women marrying brown-skinned men and giving birth to mixed-race children. Local whites considered such practices taboo and shunned these women. Seventy-five year-old Fort Stockton native M. R. González recalls what happened when the daughter of a prominent and powerful Anglo family in Pecos County married a Tejano. González says, "They ran them out of town, they have never claimed them again."[7]

In the Texas Trans-Pecos up until the 1890s, a number of Anglo men married Hispanic women. From 1870 to the mid 1880s, 15–20 percent of all marriages in Fort Davis, Presidio County, were racially mixed. In El Paso County, many of the Anglo elite in 1860 had Mexican American wives. Prominent local merchants and businessmen such as James Magoffin, Simeon Hart, and Hugh Stephenson are but a few examples. By 1880, Anglo-Tejano nuptials accounted for 12 percent of all marriages in El Paso, and in the 1870s Texas Panhandle, several white cowboys also married Hispanic women. Beginning around 1890 and continuing throughout the Progressive Era, white Americans' attitudes toward persons of color hardened. Because of this harsher racial worldview and the influx of more white women, mixed marriages declined throughout West Texas.[8]

This hardening of feelings regarding mixing of the races was not unique to Texas, the West, or the South. It was a widespread American attitude. Peggy Pascoe's research shows that by 1865 most states, including those in the North and the West, had adopted miscegenation laws banning interracial sex and marriage. Pascoe notes that these laws "became the foundation for white supremacy across the nation, setting Whites apart" from other races. In October 1893 in El Paso, Texas, authorities arrested five Mexican women for marrying black men. In a telling example of the Trans-Pecos's more moderate racial climate, the city did not disperse a group of African Americans who assembled to protest the arrests a few days later. Throughout the American West, many states did not repeal these racial purity laws until the 1950s and 1960s. Once again, it bears repeating that racism has been an integral thread of the American fabric since the country's inception and is not just a southern problem.[9]

Before the onset of harsher Anglo attitudes during the Progressive Era, intermarriage was but one important facet of cooperation in the middle ground between early Anglo and Tejano settlers. Because the two races depended upon each other for survival in the vast expanses of the western frontier, they initially enjoyed a relatively peaceful co-existence. In all three counties comprising historic West Texas—El Paso, Presidio, and Pecos—Mexican Americans shared elected offices with Anglos. Pecos County records show that during the 1870s and early 1880s, Tejanos regularly served as constables, justices of the peace, election judges, and members of grand juries. In April 1875 in a representative example of racial cooperation, Tejanos supervised voting at two Anglo homes used as polling places. Two Mexican Americans, Hipolito Carasco and Cesario Torres, served as Pecos County commissioners in the 1870s. In 1872 Torres was one of four men selected to organize Pecos County. When he stepped down in July 1886 after fourteen years of public service, there were no Tejanos left in county elected offices.[10]

Throughout the 1880s there was a significant decline in the number of Mexican American officeholders in West Texas. Torres would be the last Tejano elected official to serve on the Pecos County Commissioners Court until the election of M. R. González in 1970. Minutes for the Fort Stockton City Council (the county seat) reveal that no Mexican Americans served as councilmen from the city's incorporation in December 1910 until 1955 when Pete Terrazas became Fort Stockton's first Tejano councilman. In neighboring Presidio County, starting in 1880, few Hispanics held county office until after World War II.[11]

In El Paso County, the Anglo-controlled political machine awarded token positions such as county clerk, district clerk, or county commissioner to Tejanos, but from 1882 to 1951, no Mexican Americans served as county judge, as mayor, or on city council. During the mid-1870s in Tom Green County (San Angelo), Tejanos served in a number of public offices, notably, election judge, constable, grand juror, and county commissioner. In the 1880s, however, "the political role played by . . . Mexican

Americans during Tom Green County's early years waned rapidly."[12]

By 1890 the spirit of racial cooperation in West Texas collapsed as Anglos seized control of local politics and the economy. Once again, as in the aftermath of the Texas Revolution, whites turned on their Tejano allies, seeking to dominate and control them rather than sharing power as in the old days. M. R. González remembers that in Pecos County this betrayal hurt Mexican Americans for many years afterward. He says the Anglos were "just using them for everything, you know." González recalls that his father warned him that whites were very good at manipulating. "My dad got burned twice on that. He always said, be careful dealing with Anglos, especially if they're over-friendly. Once they get the upper hand, they're dangerous."[13]

A number of Mexican Americans in the region were unfamiliar with Texas property laws and legal requirements for keeping title to their lands. Texas colonial historian Jesús F. de la Teja points out that while intimidation was a factor in some Mexican American land sales to whites, in many cases these transactions were perfectly legal. De la Teja says that Anglos had "cultural and economic information about the land that the Tejanos didn't have. If the Anglos buy out the Tejanos at a cheap price and clean up, have they cheated the Tejanos? No." In many instances, Mexican Americans sold their property, believing they had received a fair price. De la Teja notes that Tejanos "had no clue as to its real worth in the American [and Texan] system. By the same token, those who learn the ropes manage to not only survive but to thrive."[14]

M. R. González notes that "most of the people here came from Chihuahua, real poor people. Ninety percent of them were workers." Many of these immigrants had little education and were unable to read or write. "They were dominated by Anglos for a long time," González says. "There was no one to advise them. The Anglos knew about minerals, the Spanish people didn't know anything, nothing." During the period from 1890 to 1945, whites in the Trans-Pecos acquired numerous Tejano land holdings. One result of these land sales was that over time, some Mexican Americans in West Texas became "'a landless and economically dependent class.'"[15]

In another indication of decreasing influence, by 1918 fewer Mexican Americans participated in Pecos County politics. M. R. González says that historically low voter turnout among Mexican Americans in the county has always been a problem. In the early days, it was rare for the Mexican community to unify itself politically. González notes, "It wasn't until later [the 1950s and 1960s] that they organized into a bloc vote." Another factor complicating Tejano voting was the poll tax. For Tejano laborers earning twenty-five cents a day, putting food on the table was more important than paying the $1.75 poll tax. City and county officials allowed only "qualified voters" who paid their poll tax to cast ballots in local elections. Voting thus became a luxury that many Texans of Mexican descent could not afford.[16]

Anglo intimidation of those voters who could pay their poll taxes also proved effective in controlling Mexican American participation in West Texas elections. A number of Tejanos worked for farms, ranches, and businesses owned by the white elite and were afraid to take a political stance that might cost them their jobs. In another common electioneering practice, Anglo political bosses paid the poll tax for some Mexican Americans and instructed them how to vote. Political manipulation of Mexicans (transported across the Rio Grande to illegally cast votes) also occurred.

An 1889 newspaper report of an election in Eagle Pass, Texas, noted, "Mexicans gave their vote for a hack ride and some liquor. Reform is necessary to eliminate this practice." Reporting the same year, the El Paso paper observed, "The Republicans resorted to using illegal voters in the election. Steps ought to be taken to prevent this kind of abuse." In 1892 the same newspaper commented, "Many say that political bosses bring in the Mexicans to vote on an issue satisfactory to the bosses."[17]

On Election Day in Pecos County, some Tejanos faced intimidation from D. S. "Dud" Barker, County Sheriff from 1904 to 1926. Seventy-six-year-old Fort Stockton resident Joe Primera recalls his father telling him that Sheriff Barker typically stood behind the election judge and watched voters as they filled out their ballots. The sheriff would ask Primera's father, "How do you want to vote, Serapio?" Primera says that Mexican

Americans encountering such coercion at the polls "didn't have a chance of voting any other way."[18]

Barker also used his subordinates to harass minorities. Mexican Americans in Fort Stockton described one Hispanic deputy as a "co-coanut, brown on the outside and white on the inside," someone who betrayed his own community. Primera's uncle, S. L. González, told him that this deputy once planted a gun at a gathering of local Tejanos, and soon after, the sheriff came by and arrested them for having a weapon. Such intimidation effectively cowed area Mexican Americans.[19]

Pecos County Tejanos also recalled Dud Barker's slaying of eight "Mexicans" on November 8, 1912. Although the official inquest listed four "drunk Mexicans" killed, Fort Stockton historian Olan George says it was eight and recalls that the sheriff never fully explained what happened. George, whose father sold Barker some extra ammunition on the night in question, says the record is unclear as to how many of the slain men actually had guns. He observed that "it was like a small part of the War of 1836 [Texas Revolution] had erupted again . . . right here in Fort Stockton." After the killings, some Anglos, including George's father, began wondering if "Dud Barker was one of those men who thought that because Texas won political freedom from Mexico, the state should get rid of the cultural and language influence of Mexico too?"[20]

At the inquest, held "next to [a] Mexican restaurant" in Fort Stockton, Barker testified that he killed the men during a "shooting fight." Local Anglos and Tejanos both speculated that some of the slain were unarmed or that the sheriff must have been quite a marksman to overcome 8–1 odds. In death as in life, whites in West Texas classified Tejanos as "Mexicans." The Pecos County inquest book from 1912 to 1926 details a number of homicides, typically involving a white man killing a "Mexican." Several entries include an "unidentified Mexican . . . black," "a brown Mexican man," and "a dark Mexican."[21]

In 1926 Dud Barker, widely unpopular throughout the county by this time, lost his re-election bid to W. P. Rooney. Joe Primera recalls that the ex-sheriff "quickly left town." Olan George remembered that an oft-spoken local sentiment was that "'if Dud Barker had defeated W. P. Rooney in 1926 he would have been the second sheriff assassinated in Pecos

County's history.'" George's remark refers to a November 1894 murder when an unknown assassin gunned down A. J. Royal, another controversial and violent sheriff, at the Pecos County courthouse.[22]

Intimidation was but one practice that Anglos utilized against Mexican Americans in West Texas. Whites also limited the types of employment available to Tejanos. This trend started in the 1880s with the arrival of the railroad. Thousands of Anglos subsequently moved to the region, rapidly transforming local demographics. Many of the new arrivals were from East Texas and the South. Arnoldo De León and Kenneth Stewart note, "Anglos brought large amounts of investment capital with their institutions and culture to the newly conquered region and then reserved the better occupations for themselves." In Pecos County and Fort Stockton, county and city records reveal that the vast majority of contracts awarded went to Anglo businesses. In most cases the better-paying blue collar and white-collar jobs also went to Anglos or European immigrants.[23]

Typically, employment available to Mexican Americans in West Texas from 1890–1945 was of a menial nature. Seventy-five-year-old Pete Terrazas of Fort Stockton recalls that during this time "it was very difficult to find good jobs for the Mexican people, it was very difficult to obtain work in Fort Stockton that paid any amount of money, so most of the people worked as laborers, and they worked the farms and they worked the ranches." Tejanos hired by the county or city uniformly worked as street repairmen, street sweepers, truck drivers, and garbage collectors.[24]

In many cases local records show that when the city and county hired Tejano day laborers, they listed them only as "Mexicans," with no given names. Nowhere do the same records list Anglo day laborers simply as "whites." Because official minutes usually list Anglos by name, the inference is that Hispanics were not people worth noting by name; they were just "Mexicans." In one example, Pecos County Commissioners in January 1914 discussed payment for "the Mexican laborers employed in beautifying the courthouse." In another instance, the Fort Stockton City Council in July 1925 paid a "Mexican" $7.00 for street work.[25]

Such perceptions of Tejanos were common among whites in West Texas during this period. As Maria Eva Flores notes, local news coverage by the *Fort Stockton Pioneer* reveals much concerning Anglo views on race. In April 1908 the newspaper carried Sheriff Barker's report of a "Mexican" killed at Sheffield in the eastern part of the county. Two months later, the paper noted that a polecat bit a "Mexican" on the ear. In December 1908 local law enforcement officials arrested a "Mexican sheepherder" after he stabbed a white teenager. According to the article, the teen told "the Mexican . . . that he had better go home." Finally, another story mentioned a mad dog attacking a "Mexican child." When the same paper reported on Anglo children or adults, it was usually by name and with no mention of their race. Pecos County made racial distinctions only for "Mexicans" and "Negroes."[26]

Racial attitudes in the Trans-Pecos mirrored those of many Americans. Such attitudes were not unique to the South. Racism has been part of the national character from the Atlantic to the Pacific since the country's inception. David W. Blight says that in the Progressive Era, "most Americans . . . accepted segregation as a natural condition of the races." In West Texas the pattern of *de facto* segregation (where segregation occurs but is not officially sanctioned by a detailed code of legal statutes) that evolved differed from the *de jure* (an elaborate legal and officially sanctioned) system of Jim Crow laws that took root in the eastern part of Texas and the American South. While some references to segregation appear in county and city minutes, many exclusionary practices west of the 100th meridian were of a more informal nature and do not appear in official records.[27]

The *de facto* segregation occurring in West Texas during this period was typical of Arizona, California, and much of the American Southwest. Oscar Martínez observes that in California, "Public facilities such as hotels, restaurants, theaters, and barber shops routinely banned Mexicans and Mexican Americans." Margaret Montoya notes that during the 1920s in Southern California, "Two common examples of segregation were the movie theaters in the larger towns and the swimming pools in almost every community. . . . Many organizations, businesses, and homeowners associations had official policies to exclude Mexicans, but in many other instances it was more of a general social understanding among Anglos that Mexicans should be excluded."[28]

Another key characteristic in considering the nature of race relations in West Texas is violence. During this period, were Mexican Americans and African Americans in the western part of the state subjected to the same lynching culture typical of East Texas and the South? The record shows that racial violence beyond the 100th meridian was generally milder and of a different character than that of the eastern section of the state, where the lynching, burning (and occasional corpse dragging) of minorities was far more prevalent.

In 1929 Walter White noted that "Northern and Western states have almost completely abandoned lynching with the passing of frontier conditions." The last documented lynching in Texas west of the 100th meridian was in 1910 in Rocksprings. White observed that "only the Southern states, and especially those of the far South, more or less regularly resort to the practice." In West Texas, there was occasional racial violence, but Bruce Glasrud says that "only a handful" of lynchings occurred in the region. Of the 489 lynchings in Texas from 1882–1938, only seven took place west of the 100th meridian. Three of these involved Tejanos and the remaining four, African Americans. Glasrud and Paul Carlson found that in general, "black and white West Texans avoided much of the bitter black/white struggle that took place during Reconstruction."[29]

Historically, there have always been fewer blacks in West Texas (less than 6 percent). For African Americans living west of the 100th meridian, "the concept of western openness and freedom aided black American achievement." Winfred Steglich's examination of population trends in Lubbock, Texas, found that the "treatment of, and attitudes toward, . . . minorities are typical of the Southwest rather than the South." W. H. Timmons discovered much the same situation in his study of El Paso. "Because El Paso is more western than southern," Timmons says, "and because the number of Negroes did not pose a threat to the economic or political life . . . they could achieve a greater degree of political and economic freedom" than in the South.[30]

In the municipal election of 1923, El Paso citizens firmly rejected the political aspirations of the regional Ku Klux Klan chapter. Like many Americans, some El Pasoans were bigoted; nonetheless, area residents refused to condone the Klan and its practices. One local anti-Klan tract opined, "We all have a right to be here, and the right of the Klansman ends where the right of the Jew, the Catholic, the Negro or the Mexican begins. This is fundamental." Garna Christian found that in comparison with other parts of the country, "El Paso's racial news was mild." In May 1930 when a mob in Sherman, Texas, burned a black man alive and dragged his body through the city's streets, an *El Paso Times* editorial noted, "The 'roasting and toasting' of Negroes cannot be tolerated no matter what their crime." The newspaper insisted that African Americans "be accorded the right of trial by law."[31]

Pecos County residents Joe Primera and M. R. González, both in their mid-seventies, do not recall any lynchings, nor do they remember their parents mentioning such incidents. González says that unlike South Texas, Anglos did not lynch Mexican Americans in the Fort Stockton area. González recalls, "No we didn't have that, it wasn't that bad. There was discrimination, but not that bad, they still got along." In neighboring Reeves County, however, there were two lynchings at Toyah, one in November 1891 and the second in October 1906, when Anglos lynched an African American named "Slab" Pitts for marrying a white woman.[32]

Other parts of America also had active lynch mobs during this period. The Midwest witnessed 260 lynchings, including seventy-nine African Americans. In the West, mob violence claimed 485 lives, among them, thirty-eight blacks. William S. McFeely observes that "this method of death is part of a national past" and speaks directly to our nation's character. Over time, however, as lynching decreased in some parts of the country, it gradually became more emblematic of one particular region, the South. W. Fitzhugh Brundage notes that "by the late nineteenth century lynching had become primarily a southern and racial phenomena."[33]

Research shows that from 1882 to 1938, the Lone Star State ranked third in the nation in the number of people lynched. Only Mississippi and Georgia had more. Although African Americans were more likely to face violence in Texas, whites also targeted Tejanos. During this period in South Texas, vigilante mobs killed twenty-six Hispanics. William D. Carrigan notes that "lynching and anti-Mexican mob violence had been a consistent characteristic of south Texas since the mid-nineteenth century." Anglo attacks on Hispanics in South Texas "exploded in the second decade of the twentieth century," largely due to the Mexican Revolution and increased unrest along the border.[34]

Farther to the north, in Central Texas, violence against Tejanos occurred less frequently. On one occasion in 1911, however, a lawless group of one hundred whites in Thorndale, Texas (forty-five miles northeast of Austin), "beat, tortured, burned, and hanged a fourteen-year-old Mexican boy" and then dragged the body throughout the city. In Central Texas, Anglos employed the practice of lynching, burning, and dragging of minorities in a number of instances, although primarily against African Americans. Once again, the trends in racial violence that manifested across Texas during the Progressive Era prove a reliable indicator of regional identity. Despite such gruesome rituals taking place in other parts of the Lone Star State, race relations and racial violence west of the 100th meridian were different. In West Texas the lynching of minorities was rare, and the practice of burning and dragging almost unknown.[35]

Increasingly, a number of Texas historians now perceive racial interactions in West Texas as milder than in East Texas and the South. In his study of Fort Davis in Presidio County, Robert Wooster says whites understood that they could not be forceful in their relations with Mexican Americans. Anglos had to reach an accommodation with local Tejanos. "They had to use the labor of Mexican immigrants," Wooster observes. "They could not afford the luxury of overt Jim Crow type segregation and discrimination." Wooster believes that "segregation was milder in West Texas; it was a different kind of racism. I just don't see it as being as virulent as southern Jim Crow."[36]

Texas-Mexico border historian Jerry Thompson agrees with Wooster, believing the violence in West Texas to be far different from that in East Texas and even South Texas. Thompson says, "Certainly there was racism and segregation, but ethnicity was less-pronounced." Oscar Martínez, whose work focuses on the U.S.-Mexico border and El Paso Tejano history, also observes that "racism in West Texas . . . was milder than in East and South Texas." Arnoldo De León notes that because the

Trans-Pecos was far more isolated than the rest of Texas, it "was not as connected to the Old South . . . and Tejanos were not as numerous (nor threatening) as in other parts of Texas."[37]

Jesús F. de la Teja also believes that west of the 100th meridian, race relations do not fit the typical model for East Texas and the South. De la Teja says, "You can have racism without Jim Crow, and [in West Texas] you do." One case in point is cowboys of color. Notable black cowhands such as "Bones" Hooks (of Clarendon and Amarillo, Texas) and "80 John" Wallace (of Mitchell County, Texas) frequently encountered discrimination in post-Civil War West Texas but because of their considerable abilities, grit, and character, ultimately earned the respect of many whites in the region. Out in the "vast expanses of space" in West Texas, "the prejudices of the old order did not have the same power." Wallace's daughter recalls that among those working out on the range, "there were no racial or color considerations. Men were measured by other standards." The same held true for Tejano *vaqueros*, who comprised the vast majority of non-Anglo cowboys west of the 100th meridian. The cowboy is but one example of milder race relations in the American West.[38]

Attitudes regarding race hardened during the Progressive Era when whites in the American West began to segregate and control many aspects of daily life. In Fort Stockton, Texas, Anglos made it clear that Tejanos were not welcome on Main Street or in their establishments. As M. R. González recalls, Anglos "who opened restaurants, that's the first thing they put up, 'No Mexicans Allowed,' in their windows." Ninety-three-year-old Clara Duran says she "never went to restaurants, I knew I wouldn't get in, so what's the use to go to Main Street, to stand outside?" Pete Terrazas remembers that "the old pharmacy downtown wouldn't serve Mexicans either, in their fountain, drinks, cokes, etc. It was very difficult for us, very embarrassing and very humiliating." Occasionally, a few light-skinned Tejanos evaded the color barrier by passing for white. Mexican Americans located their own business district one block to the west on Nelson Street. The railroad tracks served as the northern boundary of "Mexican town."[39]

Numerous other period examples document the racial separation that permeated the daily lives of county residents. The Pecos Theater on Main

Street permitted Hispanics entry, charging them the same admission fee as Anglos but requiring them to sit upstairs in the balcony's "Mexican section." M. R. González says that when he was a boy in the 1930s, there was also a separate "colored" seating area behind the Mexican section, "even though we hardly had any colored people." In Pecos County, as in rest of the Southwest, Anglos utilized several levels and varying shades of discrimination. Local blacks found themselves at the bottom of the racial "pecking order." González notes, "In the first place, they didn't want any colored people at all, we don't have any colored people hardly in Fort Stockton." González says that at one time the city warned black travelers not to stop in town, erecting a sign on the old highway into Fort Stockton that said, "You Negroes Keep on Going."[40]

The city's main recreational attraction, the Comanche Springs Pool, was also off limits to Tejanos, lest they pollute the "whites-only" water. Clara Duran recalls that when Mexican Americans tried to use the pool, "They wouldn't let us, that's the truth and it's a shame." Trans-Pecos Tejanos also encountered difficulties regarding equal housing. In both Fort Stockton and El Paso, they typically lived in *de facto* segregated neighborhoods. Mexican American barrios soon developed in both communities, and sanitary conditions in these barrios remained substandard until after World War II.[41]

Mario Garcia observes that in El Paso, "while no legal restrictions prohibited Mexicans from living in the better homes . . . occupational and wage discrimination, in addition to racial and cultural prejudices kept them tied to the Mexican slums where the worst housing existed." In neighboring Presidio County, Tejanos also experienced many forms of discrimination, including separate neighborhoods, but there was no "strict pattern of racial segregation." In other West Texas communities, the stories were much the same.[42]

In Abilene, Texas, racial violence was rare, "probably more a result of the small numbers of both Hispanics and blacks than of Abilene's progressive actions in meeting minority needs." By 1900 there were 200–300 African Americans in Abilene out of a population of 3,400. Locals established the Abilene Colored School, which had one room, one teacher, and twenty-two students. School segregation ended in 1969.[43]

Blacks and Tejanos in Abilene faced segregation in housing, in restaurants, and at the movie theater. One city ordinance passed in 1921 and repealed in 1943 required that colored persons and whites use separate elevators. Minorities also encountered discrimination in the workplace. Despite such practices, local African Americans say that in comparison, "Abilene has not been tormented by racial tensions as much as some other cities have," and that in West Texas, "Abilene's always been considered a nice town for black people."[44]

A 1940s survey of racial practices in Texas west of the 100th meridian found the following. In the Big Bend city of Alpine, Tejanos "are segregated from Anglo Americans at the theater and are placed together with the Negroes." Even the local pool hall refused entry to Mexican Americans. In Big Spring, "Mexicans are denied service at the Cafes and are segregated from the Anglo Americans at the theatres." In Lubbock, numerous businesses refused to serve Hispanics, and "Mexicans are segregated . . . at the City Bus Station." In Midland, local movie theaters required that blacks and Tejanos sit together upstairs, the Ritz Café posted a "No Mexicans Allowed" sign in its window, and Tejano elementary school students attended a separate Mexican school. In Pecos, Texas, "Mexicans are denied service in . . . Hotels, Cafes, Beer Parlors and recreational Centers. In the theatres they are placed together with the Negroes." The situation was much the same in Ozona, Texas, and Tejano children in Ozona attended segregated schools. Finally, in San Angelo, Texas, a number of eating establishments throughout the city refused to serve Mexican Americans. Across West Texas, from Fort Stockton to Lubbock, Anglo attitudes regarding race proved similar.[45]

Writing about Amarillo's race relations during the 1930s, David L. Nail says that "the amorphous spirit of cooperation present in the city tended to transcend racial barriers, but it did not always surmount them." Nail notes that this cooperative spirit among the races "existed because apparently neither whites nor blacks felt threatened by the other group. The traditional racial roles were strong," and each group stayed within their respective spheres. In Amarillo, blacks lived on the north side of the city, while Hispanics lived on the east side.[46]

Although Amarillo saw little racial violence, eighty miles to the east in the Panhandle town of Shamrock, a mob in July 1930 threatened to "burn the niggers out." After local authorities charged a black man with raping and murdering a white woman, a crisis quickly developed. The governor of Texas sent five Rangers to protect the African American section of town, and law enforcement officials soon restored order. Several months after the event, a number of locals still advocated "running all the Negroes out of this 'white man's country.'"[47]

During the Progressive Era, "white man's country" was a common sentiment, not only in the Texas Panhandle, but also across America. Frank Van Nuys notes that in the American West, white pioneers crafted "their vision of the West as their land of opportunity and a 'white man's country.'" In 1927 the West Texas Chamber of Commerce boasted that the region's population was "96 per cent native born white," and that "the area remains a stronghold of the native-born white American." West Texas, the chamber proclaimed, was "the meeting ground of the old South and the new West and its population retains the characteristics of each section." From its headquarters in Stamford, Texas, the chamber described its constituency by observing, "Here is found the chivalry and unbounded hospitality of the South and the virility and progressiveness of the West." In characterizing itself as both southern and western, the chamber was exhibiting a mixed regional identity.[48]

Determined to compete with other area boosters, the Board of City Development of Amarillo in 1928 touted its local amenities, noting that the "ninety-six percent native born American white population" enjoyed "good homes, churches, schools and recreational facilities." The board claimed that "Amarillo presents a high class [of] labor, living under climatic conditions conducive to a high degree of efficient production." The Panhandle-Plains Chamber of Commerce, also of Amarillo, issued its own promotional tract in 1920, offering a "Home for Every Man." The chamber opined that "the thing that brings the real consolation to the hearts of those who dwell in this portion [of West Texas] . . . is the high grade, pure bred, pure American, white-faced boys and girls . . . the safeguards of our sacred institutions."[49]

During this period, whites in West Texas frequently described themselves as "pure Americans" and "native born Americans." Apparently, those terms excluded Mexican Americans and African Americans. West of the 100th meridian, Anglos viewed minorities not only as "less American" but also not entitled to the same standard of living and the same level of city services that whites enjoyed. For example, when Fort Stockton paved some of its dirt streets in September 1928, road crews worked only in white neighborhoods. Many streets in the Mexican barrio remained unpaved until the 1970s. M. R. González says, "My dad had a store here. In the evenings, God, you could see that dust. There was a dust cloud in that barrio all the time."[50]

Pecos County also had segregated Boy Scouts troops, and Fort Stockton had separate baseball teams. Hispanics took pride in their "Mexican" team, named *Los Lobos*. The county even segregated social functions at the courthouse. In February 1906 county commissioners voted that whites could use the courthouse for dances six times a year, while "the Mexican population" could use it four times a year, provided their dances did "not conflict with the dates given to the whites."[51]

Fort Stockton officials segregated East Hill Cemetery in 1939 after learning that "I. Scott (Negro) had been buried in the northeast corner" of the cemetery. Alderman Roberts suggested "that the grave be moved to a suitable location in the cemetery" and that this new location serve "for future negro burials." The city council immediately approved Alderman Roberts' motion. A year earlier, in June 1938, George Barton approached city council with "an idea of establishing a Negro settlement." Councilmen told Barton to pick a location and get back to the city with the information, at which time they would "discuss the suitability of the location selected." Barton got the message and never followed up on his "Negro settlement." In both instances regarding blacks in Fort Stockton, the word "suitable" kept cropping up. Municipal leaders clearly did not want large numbers of African Americans migrating into the region.[52]

Residents of San Angelo and Lubbock voiced similar sentiments. At a mass meeting in October 1909, white citizens in San Angelo protested Orient Railroad contractors importing black employees to work in the county. The contractors quickly agreed to house the 125 African

American laborers in Mertzon, twelve miles to the west, and to keep them out of San Angelo. One resident said that blacks coming to town was "ten thousand times worse" than a smallpox virus outbreak. Others spoke of keeping the city free of "black devils."[53]

At the meeting, District Attorney L. H. Brightman allowed that "he wasn't much of a 'nigger-lover.'" Brightman said "he believed in a white man's country," and "that there were plenty of white men to do the work without the negroes." Several hours after the gathering adjourned, a white man named J. D. Waddle assaulted and critically injured R. F. Carruthers, an African-American janitor at a San Angelo bank. The sixty-year-old Carruthers, whose face looked "as if a horse had kicked him," also suffered a broken rib and injured back.[54]

White residents of Lubbock were also wary of large numbers of blacks "slipping" into town. In 1910 the *Lubbock Avalanche* newspaper noted that "last week a 'she' coon was seen to come in and go prancing . . . with a white man." The paper continued, "This is white man's country and it should not be polluted by a bunch of worthless 'nigger' [*sic*]." The newspaper argued that the city could prevent trouble by banning Negroes within the city limits. "It is nice to theorize about the 'sweet-smelling' coon," the *Avalanche* observed, but "when Mr. Coon oversteps the bounds . . . he will get all that is coming to him." In January 1923 the city commission of Lubbock drafted an ordinance to limit black housing to the southeast section of town. There is no evidence that this ordinance ever became law; nonetheless, "the white population was successful in its effort to restrict the blacks to one particular section of Lubbock."[55]

For several years the *Fort Stockton Pioneer* newspaper featured a regular advertisement from the city's Commercial Club (early Chamber of Commerce) featuring a column entitled "Why You Should Come to Pecos County." Reason Number 4 on this list of local attributes read: "No negroes in the county." Another advertisement in the paper, this one for a blackface minstrel show in 1908, proclaimed, "There are no niggers in Pecos county, but just to relieve the monotony of things, an aggregation of thick-lipped, lantern-jawed, mirth-producing coons will appear at the school house on Friday night." These racist remarks may have been a deliberate slap at African American soldiers posted to the region from

1867 to 1886, when local Anglos depended upon black regulars at Fort Stockton to protect them. After 1886, however, ungrateful white residents quickly forgot the courageous and competent protection these African American troops provided for their families and businesses against raiding Apaches and Comanches.[56]

Deteriorating race relations also affected educational opportunities in West Texas. El Paso established its first segregated Mexican school in 1887. The first black school had opened four years earlier, in 1883. By the 1890s San Angelo had a Mexican school, and Lubbock opened its one-room Mexican school in 1922. Amarillo constructed a school for African Americans in 1914 and one for Tejanos in 1919. Odessa, founded in 1881, had five black families by 1927 and segregated its school system and its branch libraries. Presidio and Pecos counties segregated their schools by 1909 and 1912, respectively. In Fort Stockton the school board built one "Mexican school" in town and another at "Little Mexico," a few miles outside the city limits. In July 1918 "the Mexican population," dissatisfied with their children's quality of education, petitioned the school board for "a satisfactory teacher."[57]

Up until World War II, Hispanic students in Fort Stockton received only an eighth-grade education. Whites felt this was an adequate level of schooling, believing that Tejanos were best-suited for vocational jobs of a menial nature. In contrast, Anglos in Pecos County received a high school education. Due to an influx of blacks into the county after World War II, the Fort Stockton School Board segregated the district yet again, creating a separate "colored school" in May 1950, and the district hired Theresa Mason to teach at the "Negro School," where she remained until the building closed in 1961.[58]

Prior to 1956, Anglos in Fort Stockton prevented Tejanos from serving on the school board. Pete Terrazas remembers that "in the beginning the city had an at-large voting system and we couldn't get Hispanics elected to the school board or the city council." When Fort Stockton officials changed the elections from an at-large system to single districts in the mid-1950s, voters once again elected Hispanics to public office after a seventy-year hiatus. In April 1956 George Pina became the first Mexican-American school board member. During the 1960s, the board started integrating the Fort Stockton Independent School District, a process not completed until 1972.[59]

Two of the most important events challenging racial segregation in Pecos County, events representative for much of West Texas, occurred in the 1940s. During World War II, local Mexican Americans who had served in the armed forces returned home with new and more militant perspectives regarding segregation. These Tejanos felt that if they risked their lives for their country, they deserved equal rights at home. As a result, Fort Stockton Hispanics became more politically active and formed a local chapter of the League of Latin American Citizens (LULAC).[60]

M. R. González says that his father, Manuel González, and others in LULAC Council #62 decided to pressure local segregation policies using two test cases, one at the Comanche Springs Pool and the second at the Pecos Theater. In late 1935 the county discussed using a government grant to build a bathing facility "for Mexicans exclusively," but commissioners never built the Mexican "bath house." After four years of waiting, twenty-two Fort Stockton Tejanos in August 1939 protested to county commissioners about discriminatory policies at Comanche Springs Pool. In their letter they argued that, as local taxpayers, they enjoyed the right to use the pool. The all-Anglo commissioners court never responded.[61]

In her study of Fort Stockton Tejanos, Maria Eva Flores notes a Local Council #62 letter to the national LULAC headquarters involving another pool test case four years later. On July 6, 1943, Corporal Jesse Garcia attempted to swim at Comanche Springs but was forced to leave because he was "Mexican." Garcia subsequently got into an intense argument with several Anglos and law enforcement officials, protesting "that if he was good enough to fight alongside" white boys, then "he would also be good enough to swim with them." Within minutes an ugly confrontation developed between Tejanos and Anglos, almost leading to a "race riot." Leaders in both groups prevailed, managing to defuse tensions and avert violence.[62]

The following day, the lessee of Comanche Springs, Pecos County Water Improvement District No. 1 (whose president was former County Judge J. A. Casebier), defiantly issued a refusal to integrate the pool. In a July 7, 1943, resolution, Casebier and the water district members reasserted their restrictions concerning use of the pool. Only Anglo Americans could swim in the pool, and "no person or persons of the Latin-American race shall be permitted to use said property for swimming, bathing, drinking, or for any other purpose." The water board ignored the obvious fact that local Mexican Americans paid for the pool's maintenance with their tax dollars. Instead, the board reminded Tejanos that Commissioners Court "has made provision for said Latin-American race to use the waters of Comanche Creek at a point near or back of the Old Catholic Church."[63]

Even after the near race riot, the pool remained segregated. Pecos County commissioners refused to tackle the issue, so the local LULAC chapter, in conjunction with the national headquarters, devised an ingenious strategy. Throughout the first half of the twentieth century, Texas farmers became increasingly dependent on Mexican labor to work their fields. Under the *Bracero* Guest Worker Program, Pecos County farmers obtained all the field hands they needed from Mexico. M. R. González says his father discovered a Mexican statute that prohibited sending braceros to any county in the U.S. that practiced discrimination.[64]

Manuel González wrote the Mexican Consulate in El Paso, informing them of the segregation in Pecos County, specifically at the swimming pool and movie theater. After reviewing the situation, the Mexican government wrote Pecos County officials that they were not going to permit braceros to work in the county. M. R. González says the "farmers got really irritated, they needed the braceros; they had a lot of cotton." The strategy paid off, and the county finally capitulated, desegregating the pool around 1950 (González does not recall the exact date).[65]

While testing county statutes regarding use of the Comanche Springs Pool, the Fort Stockton LULAC chapter mounted a concurrent assault on the local movie theater's segregation policy. In March 1949 an usher at the Pecos Theater on Main Street denied Adam Terrazas and his wife admission to the "whites-only" section downstairs. When Terrazas asked why he could not sit downstairs, a theater employee told him that he was a Mexican and had to sit in the balcony. Angry and hurt, Terrazas responded by hitting the usher. The theater manager quickly phoned for the police. Shortly thereafter, in a response to a protest letter from

LULAC Council #62, the owners of the Pecos Theater denied using discriminatory policies toward patrons.[66]

Manuel González knew this claim to be false and sent his light-skinned son and brown-complexioned daughter into the movie theater to prove it. González instructed his children to purchase their tickets and attempt to sit in the "Anglo-only" seating area. Soon after, the usher took the boy's ticket and let him pass into the white section, but when the youth's sister attempted to join him, the usher refused her admittance and instructed her to sit upstairs.[67]

González thoroughly documented the incident and Council #62 sent it into the company that owned the Pecos Theater. After receiving this second protest from LULAC, the owners finally gave in and instructed theater manager Guy Moses to drop the discriminatory seating policy. Moses fully integrated the Pecos Theater by April 1949, and soon local Tejanos were enjoying a ground-floor view of the latest Hollywood movies.[68]

It has taken half a century, but today the past wounds of racism and segregation are gradually healing in West Texas. As in many parts of the American Southwest, Mexican Americans and Anglos are once again cooperating and sharing power. Today, however, local residents have established a new and different kind of middle ground, one that is more economically, politically, and socially acceptable to both groups.

In West Texas, as in the American West, the period of Anglo domination that began in the 1890s gradually faded after World War II. It is important to remember that the harsh race relations typical of this period were not unique to the West; they were occurring across much of the nation. What *was* different is how race manifested in various regions of the country. A key indicator of regional identity is how segregation and racial violence are exhibited locally. During this period, Jim Crow statutes, lynching, burning, and dragging typified the southern racial culture that dominated the eastern half of Texas. In West Texas, however, race relations were more typical of western states along the Mexican border than of East Texas and the South.

West of the 100th meridian today, Tejanos, whites, and blacks know that they need each other if they are to weather the tough economic times forecast for the region. M. R. González says, "Now we have a lot of intermarriage, I see a lot of people who used to be prejudiced, now their daughter or their son marrying a Spanish person. There's quite a few here right now. You still have a little of that [old] mentality, but eventually it will change." Pete Terrazas notes that "Now, we're sixty-three percent Hispanic, we've made a lot of headway, we're also working together with the Anglo community. I see a lot of improvement."[69]

Looking back on their many years in West Texas, M. R. González, Pete Terrazas, and Joe Primera, all now in their mid-seventies, proudly remember their individual contributions to the Tejanos' struggle for civil rights. Summing up those years, Joe Primera says, "For all my life they called me a Mexican, Mexican American, Latin American, or a Hispanic, when all I ever wanted to be was an American."[70]

THE "GARDEN OF EDEN" AND THE "COWMAN'S PARADISE"
NINETEENTH-CENTURY MYTHS CONFRONT TWENTY-FIRST-CENTURY ENVIRONMENTAL REALITIES IN WEST TEXAS

Driving across West Texas's Rolling Plains and South Plains regions, with acre after acre of cotton fields, one might form the impression of being in the American South. After all, cotton remains one of the South's most enduring icons. Because of the Lone Star State's diverse regional identities, however, such appearances can sometimes be illusory. In Texas west of the 100th meridian, the profusion of cotton, like racism and segregation, does not automatically indicate a southern identity. For example, Arizona is also a large producer of cotton, but few would claim that Arizona is part of the South. Ultimately, environment, like race, becomes an accurate indicator of regional identity.

The American West is a place distinguished by a number of unique geographic and economic characteristics. For example, it is only west of the 100th meridian, says Donald Worster, that one finds both a "pastoral" West (ranching) and a "hydraulic" West (irrigated farming). During the last 150 years, both the rancher and the farmer have become important Western icons, each for differing reasons. This chapter examines what happened in Texas beyond the 100th meridian when man's idealized symbols confronted the region's harsh environmental realities.[1]

In the nineteenth century, a number of national myths and symbols inspired settlers to move to the American West. The most famous myth was Manifest Destiny, which proclaimed that God had ordained Anglo

Americans to conquer and settle the continent from the Atlantic to the Pacific. For many Americans the West represented a fresh start, a place of "rebirth" and "regeneration." Period newspapers and books described the West as a "land of golden opportunity" with "limitless prosperity" and an "inexhaustible reservoir of natural wealth." Western boosters characterized the region as the "Garden of Eden" and the "Cowman's Paradise," ideally suited for both farming and ranching.[2]

The main character in this "Garden of Eden" story was the farmer. Thomas Jefferson and Progressive-Era historian Frederick Jackson Turner believed that the educated, hard-working independent farmer embodied the essential characteristics necessary for sustaining a healthy American democracy. To Turner, the yeoman farmer represented the cutting edge of the nation's "frontier democracy." Even today, some still see the small, independent farmer as the backbone of America. *Farm Aid*, in its website and annual concerts featuring Willie Nelson and Neil Young, promotes those who till the soil as "the most resourceful, heroic Americans," citizens who are "active in civic life," "pillars of their communities," and "stewards of the land."[3]

In another popular Western myth, the "Cowman's Paradise," the primary protagonists were the rancher and his cowboys. Theodore Roosevelt was convinced that the ranching life produced the ideal democratic role model for America, citizens whose experiences in the wild imbued them with "a capacity for [the] 'strenuous' life." Roosevelt believed that those who worked cattle in the West were "a vigorous and masterful people" possessed of "energy, resolution, manliness, self-reliance, and a capacity for self-help," characteristics "without which no race can do its life work well." In 1902 author Owen Wister immortalized the cowhand in his classic western novel *The Virginian*. During the same period, artists Frederick Remington and Charles Russell celebrated cowboys in many of their paintings and sculptures. Beginning in the 1880s Buffalo Bill Cody popularized trick-riding, fast-roping trail hands in his immensely popular Wild West Show. In the twentieth century, Hollywood firmly cemented the cowboy's place in the national mythology through hundreds of its western movies.[4]

While these narratives provided Americans with a sense of purpose and a national identity, they also did a great disservice to settlers moving westward. Because they were myths, these stories were not always grounded in reality, especially in western environmental realities. When settlers holding these popular notions encountered the often harsh and arid truths concerning life in the American West, the settler and the environment suffered. Today, both are still suffering.[5]

The State of Texas, where the legend of the rugged, free-spirited cowboy still rides tall in the saddle, proves an excellent case in point. For many, the cattleman remains an integral component of Lone Star identity. Those who work the range embody many admirable, defining traits, including self-reliance, bravery, loyalty, and a strong work ethic. Cowboys did not whine; they got the job done. Many of Texas's early histories revered the state's ranchers and their tough trail hands, whose legacy was "as strong as stout saddle leather" and who lived on "as genuine legends who had ridden through a golden moment in American history." Along with the Texas Ranger, the cowboy remains one of the state's most enduring symbols. Nowhere in the Lone Star State is this myth stronger than in West Texas, home to some of the state's most colorful Old West history. During the late nineteenth and early twentieth centuries, newspaper accounts described West Texas as ideally suited for ranching, variously calling it the "cowboy's paradise" or "the cowman's paradise."[6]

Another notable, albeit less-glamorous, Lone Star icon is the farmer. Although not as celebrated today as he was in the last two centuries, the farmer is still part of the basic fabric of Texas identity. In the early 1900s West Texas newspaper editorials celebrated tillers of irrigated lands as educated, upstanding citizens. Just as the rancher conquered the frontier's open range with his lariat and barbed wire, the western farmer subdued nature with his plow and irrigation ditches, proving that man could make the desert bloom like a rose. The irrigated empire that developed in West Texas after World War II, with its dependence upon federal funds for water projects and dams, mirrored similar efforts in other western states. To irrigation proponents in the Progressive Era, cultivators in the American West assumed heroic, mythical powers as they created their manmade "Garden of Eden." Trumpeting scientifically based irrigated farming as the future civilizing savior of wild West Texas, the *Fort Stockton Pioneer* noted, "The coyote is already packing up his grip preparatory to going farther west, and his shrill cry will soon be but a memory."[7]

For more than a century, avid boosters like the Fort Stockton newspaper promoted the benefits of farming and ranching in West Texas, carefully avoiding discussion of negative state and federal environmental research regarding these industries. As a result these boosters have often ignored the unpleasant regional realities of overgrazing, rangeland desertification, and the "salting up" of farmland. In truth, however, early farmers and ranchers in West Texas dramatically altered the land they worked. New arrivals to the region from the East and Europe possessed little understanding of their environment, employing traditional agricultural methods from more humid regions. After several generations many still relied upon their old practices, refusing to adapt to the arid environment's natural limitations. At this point their lack of knowledge became a stubborn determination.

In the process some West Texas farmers and ranchers put a price tag on nature, making the environment into a commodity. Conditioned by market forces of the American (and more recently global) economy, the farmers and ranchers viewed grass, water, and the land in terms of dollars instead of finite assets requiring wise stewardship. Romantic myths about the West, a desire for economic gain, and a number of environmental preconceptions guided these early settlers. Many of them gave little thought to the damage they inflicted upon the land, grabbing as much of the region's resources as they could before moving on. The scarred, boom-bust landscape today bears graphic testimony to these two industries' chronic abuse of West Texas's fragile, rain-starved environment.[8]

In much of the region, rainfall averages from below ten inches a year at El Paso to nineteen inches a year at Del Rio, Texas. An 1878 federal report on aridity by John Wesley Powell stated that successful agriculture in the West required rainfall of at least twenty inches a year. In the Lone Star State, this break point occurs west of the 100th meridian, and a number of early West Texas settlers who attempted dry-land farming beyond this line failed miserably. One popular, quasi-scientific theory in America during the nineteenth century stated that wherever one culti-vated, the rain followed the plow. According to this reasoning, plowing released moisture into the air, thus promoting more rainfall.[9]

Ultimately, however, the rain did not follow the plow, and periodic droughts ruined many West Texas farmers. The catastrophic farm fail-ures of the 1930s amply demonstrated the inherent pitfalls of dry-land farming. The Dust Bowl's disasters illustrated the national disconnect in America between agrarian myths and environmental realities. Current research in Texas still supports Powell's findings. Interviews with U.S. Farm Service agents show that the break line for dry-land farming in the Lone Star State is east of Ozona and north of Odessa. Dry-land agricul-ture in this region is possible during wet or moderate years but requires irrigation during droughts. Farmers raising crops south and west of this line are entirely dependent upon irrigation.[10]

Starting in the late 1860s, a number of early irrigation endeavors in West Texas utilized the waters of the Pecos River, one of the region's most important watersheds. Federal and state research over the last one hundred years, however, found that high salinity levels rendered the Pe-cos's water quality marginal, making it a real threat to area farming. An 1890 Texas A&M study concluded that high salt levels in both the soil and Pecos River would create over time a "fatal" combination for irri-gated agriculture. Scientists predicted that the salt accumulation would kill even alkali-tolerant crops. It is no surprise then that agricultural op-erations along the river met with little success.[11]

Recent studies revealed that near the Texas-New Mexico line, salt lev-els in the river were seven times higher than federal standards for safe drinking water. Downstream near Girvin, Texas, state research found that from 2000 to 2003, salinity levels were thirteen to seventeen times the federal standard for safe drinking water. Such water poses "consider-able risk" to livestock, including pregnant cows. Near Girvin the health hazard is so high that the Pecos is not recommended for human or live-stock use "under any conditions." Reports of the river's abysmal water quality are nothing new. One member of an 1850 California-bound

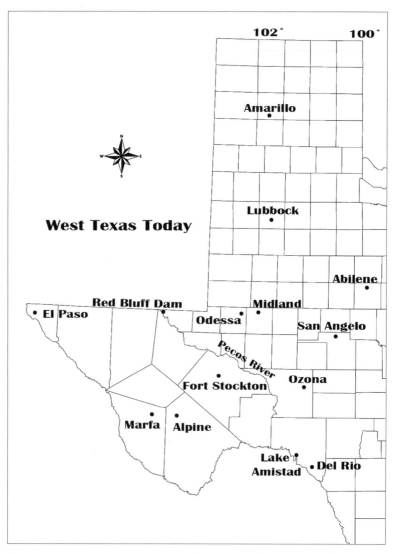

Pecos Basin Map. Pecos River watershed in Texas, from Red Bluff Reservoir on Texas-New Mexico line, southeast to Lake Amistad near Del Rio, Texas. Texas Counties Map courtesy of Texas Parks and Wildlife Department. Details added by author.

wagon train fording the Pecos near present day Sheffield, Texas, reported, "Our animals and men . . . suffered considerably from drinking the muddy water."[12]

Agricultural salinity studies show that river water, such as that sampled near Girvin, kills many crops and reduces yields on even salt-tolerant varieties by 50–75 percent. Farmers irrigating with water from the Pecos typically worked their fields for ten years. When the river finally salted up their acreage, they abandoned it and moved on to new lands, starting the same cycle in motion once again. Up and down both sides of the Pecos today are thousands of acres of abandoned farmland. Old, weed-choked irrigation canals and dilapidated homesteads illustrate the futility of trying to farm with the river's briny water. Discussing regional irrigation efforts over the last century, Fort Stockton Extension Range Specialist Charles Hart observes that much of the deserted farmland is ruined for generations to come. "A lot of that ground . . . is worthless right now. When the wind blows, all the topsoil and ground blows away."[13]

Ignoring adverse research about the Pecos River's effects on crops, the Fort Stockton newspaper continued extolling the watershed's virtues for farming. Challenging all naysayers, the *Pioneer* in 1909 predicted that irrigated farming would bring "an era of unprecedented prosperity for the entire west." The paper boasted that "irrigation is transforming a desert into a garden of productivity." Newspaper advertisements informed readers that there was plenty of superior farmland available. In one ad The Fort Stockton Irrigated Lands Company offered the "finest fruit and garden lands the sun shines on" for $80 an acre. The company only had 5,000 available acres of choice, "strictly high-class irrigated lands," and encouraged those interested to "act at once, as it will not last long at this price." In a 1911 article the *Pioneer* claimed that an industrious person tilling just ten acres of irrigated lands could, in a short time, be guaranteed a comfortable income with a good standard of living "assured."[14]

In an appeal to prospective large-scale farmers, business, and industry, the *Pioneer* proclaimed that there was no shortage of labor in Fort Stockton. The editor noted, "We have a quite a number of Mexican residents here. They are intelligent law abiding citizens, doing cheerfully a great deal of the manual labor . . . They have a separate school." During the Progressive Era, western irrigation boosters predicted that a new generation of white yeoman farmers who epitomized the American spirit would transform the bleak and barren desert into green fields and gardens. In reality, however, irrigated farming in the American West created a class system of those who controlled the lands and the water and those who did the manual labor. In Pecos County, the second-largest county in Texas, the typical field hand was not the romanticized white yeoman farmer but a segregated, brown-skinned Mexican.[15]

Despite boosters' attempts to whitewash regional realities such as segregation or the toxic salinity of the Pecos, by 1916 ten irrigation districts along the river found themselves in serious financial trouble. Nine miles above the city of Pecos, farmers reliant upon the Biggs-Cedervale Irrigation District discovered that the river water "was too salty to support most irrigated agriculture." At the Porterville District near present-day Mentone, there was never enough water to successfully irrigate with, and the river "was too saline to grow crops." Also, Porterville residents had to truck in their drinking water because the Pecos was "too salty for human consumption."[16]

In the American West private capital proved insufficient to manage large-scale water projects. Economic realities forced westerners intent on reclaiming their region through irrigation to rely upon the federal government. Only the federal government possessed the resources to build the West's hydraulic infrastructure. When agricultural interests in West Texas failed in their free enterprise efforts to bend the Pecos and Mother Nature to their will, they demanded that the U.S. Department of the Interior save them. Despite the Pecos River's proven toxicity upon agriculture, seven irrigation districts banded together in an effort to convince federal officials to build a dam on the Pecos. The two-million-dollar Public Works Administration project, funded with federal funds and irrigation district bonds, got underway in 1934. Two years later, workers completed Red Bluff Dam just below the New Mexico state line. Three-quarters of a century later, the Pecos's water remains lethal to many area crops.[17]

Other indicators of the river's condition are recurring golden algae blooms. In 1986 an algae bloom killed 99 percent of the fish in the lower half of the Pecos watershed. Two years later, another killed 1.5 million fish in the upper half of the river near Red Bluff Reservoir. From 1985 to 2007, Pecos algae blooms killed more than two million fish. Regional fishermen have long complained about the chronic fish kills and the river's briny nature. Many anglers now prefer the cleaner waters of Amistad National Recreation Area to the south near Del Rio, Texas.[18]

Even at Lake Amistad, however, recreational enthusiasts cannot escape the Pecos's problems. At Amistad National Recreation Area, the Pecos empties into the Rio Grande, and National Park Service officials now warn that salt deposits from the Pecos are rendering the lake unhealthy for aquatic wildlife. Twenty-six percent of all salt inflow into Amistad comes from the Pecos. Since the 1850s the variety and numbers of native fish at Amistad have been halved. During this same period "the number of non-native fish species that prefer saline waters has increased significantly." Federal and state scientists are currently studying strategies to halve excessive salt infusions into the river upstream in New Mexico at Malaga Bend and in Texas near Girvin and Grandfalls.[19]

Until the late 1930s, agricultural operations in the Pecos Basin had few options for water, forcing many to irrigate from the river. Prior to World War II, the Pecos's high salt and mineral content made farming problematic. Jim Ed Miller, former manager of Red Bluff Power and Control District, remembers that during periods of ample rainfall, there was plenty of water to flush out the salts and minerals. During periods of drought, which is often the case in the Trans-Pecos, farmers were left "with the dregs and then the water is horrible and it will kill crops." Studies show that there have been seventeen major droughts in the Pecos River Basin since the 1860s, including one that lasted for most of the 1950s. In addition the river's water supply was frequently insufficient for irrigation purposes. For example, from 1990 to 2007 water levels in Red Bluff Reservoir were typically less than 40 percent of capacity. The combination of poor water quality and an inadequate supply disillusioned many farmers along the river. Miller recalls that "the farms went to hell, people were just disheartened, and a lot of them moved away. Now there's hardly anything planted, less than ten percent of what it was." Miller believes that river farming was a doomed project. While agricultural endeavors along the Pecos did well at first, for the last fifty years they have not been an economically viable proposition.[20]

With the development of affordable well-drilling technology on the eve of World War II, regional farmers were no longer at the mercy of the Pecos River. As hundreds of new wells began tapping the region's subterranean aquifers, the amount of arable farmland quickly increased. Jim Ed Miller notes that in the 1940s and 1950s, conditions were ideal for pump farming. The land was cheap, the water table high, and financing "ridiculously easy." In addition labor costs were low, thanks largely to the U.S.-Mexico Guest Worker Program, where up to 30,000 braceros worked Trans-Pecos fields. In 1964 irrigated farming peaked, with almost 120,000 acres under cultivation. Pecos County produced 33 percent of all irrigated crops west of the Pecos River. It seemed that the *Pioneer* newspaper's predictions had indeed come true: irrigated agriculture had triumphed over Mother Nature, even in the desert.[21]

One inherent weakness in modern irrigated farming is its dependence on natural gas. Natural gas powers the pumps that draw the water out of underground aquifers. The higher the energy costs, the more expensive the water. When natural gas prices get too high and water levels are too low to economically pump, western farmers can no longer afford to stay in business. In the 1970s the water table dropped and natural gas prices quadrupled, making it much more expensive to pump water to the surface. Some local aquifers also had high salinity levels, which increasingly reduced crop yields. In addition, commodity prices failed to keep pace with rising labor and heavy machinery costs. Soon a number of area farmers were losing money while others had to quit altogether.[22]

Prices for farmland fell from $500 per acre in the 1960s to $100 per acre in 1979. Acreage under cultivation in Pecos County dropped from 120,000 acres in 1964 to 16,000 in 2006. Figures for neighboring Reeves County are similar, where irrigated agriculture declined from its high in 1964 of 118,200 acres to 10,759 acres in 2002. Ward County irrigated acreage plummeted from a high of 6,500 in 1969 to 284 in 1984. During the same period, Loving County went from 200 acres to zero. A 1979 state study found that many area farmers had "moved, gone bankrupt, or simply left their land idle." Today, tens of thousands of empty, barren acres bear witness to the futility of trying to farm in the region. Jim Ed Miller recalls that at the peak of irrigated farming, there were thirty-two cotton gins in a four-county area comprised of Loving, Ward, Reeves, and Pecos counties. Today, only two gins remain. Reflecting upon agricultural trends in the region, Extension Range Specialist Charles Hart says that irrigated farming in much of the Trans-Pecos today is "a recipe for disaster."[23]

Intensive use of regional underground aquifers created additional environmental problems. In Pecos County large irrigation wells adversely affected the flow of traditional water sources, including historic Comanche Springs. When agricultural concerns west of Fort Stockton began pumping the local aquifer after World War II, Comanche Springs and Comanche Creek dried up. Farmers along Comanche Creek, including the Moody family, watched their crops wither. Bill Moody says that when his family and his neighbors finally gave up and sold their lands along the stream, it was "heart-breaking." For decades Comanche Springs had filled Fort Stockton's municipal pool and the picturesque, tree-lined canals in the adjacent Rooney Park. Now the pool relies upon regular municipal water, and the park's canals are often dry. Whenever irrigation pumping slows west of Fort Stockton, however, both the springs and the creek bounce back to life. Research reveals that out of fifty healthy, flowing springs in the region in the 1850s, only ten remain today, thanks largely to irrigation pumping and drought.[24]

Once touted as the civilizing savior of the arid Trans-Pecos, irrigated farming now has, according to federal and state agricultural agents, a limited future. Increasingly, the global economy is affecting agricultural operations in the region. Alpine lawyer, rancher, and water conservationist Tom Beard says, "We're not meant to be doing large-scale farming in the Trans-Pecos. It's not the basis of our economy now." Robert Kinucan, agricultural and natural resource science specialist at Sul Ross

State University in Alpine, agrees with Beard's assessment. "As demographics shift, as emphases shift, local truck farming and agriculture just isn't as important for our community today as it was previously," Kinucan says; "we have supermarkets and long-haul trucking; we don't have to have it."[25]

Irrigated agriculture currently consumes 75 percent of West Texas's water. As battles over the region's water supply intensify in the coming decades, urban and industrial demands will increasingly trump those of irrigation. Jim Ed Miller believes that "they are not going to let cities starve for water so people can farm crops. They are not going to let El Paso perish so those farmers can grow onions and cotton for government subsidies." Large-scale farming is no longer economically viable west of the Pecos, and farm costs are considerably cheaper in more humid regions east of the 100th meridian. When asked if Mother Nature ever meant for man to farm in the Trans-Pecos, Loving County Judge Skeet Jones, a long-time rancher near Red Bluff opines, "not farm, not out in this desert, no." Jim Ed Miller agrees, saying, "What people should have done maybe was never farm to start with. It's not nice to fool Mother Nature."[26]

Farming is not the only industry in West Texas facing an uncertain future. Local ranching prospects have also dimmed. Over the last 130 years, the region's cattle and sheep business has experienced significant change. In the second half of the nineteenth century, when large-scale livestock operations moved into the Trans-Pecos, the area's abundant tobosa, grama, and bluestem grasses appeared an ideal rangeland. Visiting the area in 1884, a federal range specialist commented on the copious, nutritious grasses covering the broad valleys of the Pecos River. Eyeing the vast acreage, ranchers commenced stocking the semi-arid open range with as many cattle and sheep as they could acquire. In Pecos County, livestock numbers soared from 227 cattle and 150 sheep in 1890 to 109,000 cattle and 61,000 sheep in 1910. In 1908 the Fort Stockton newspaper boasted, "Pecos County is the Cowman's Paradise."[27]

As cattle and sheep men expanded operations in Texas west of the 100th meridian, they suffered environmental consequences stemming from poor land-use practices. Despite these consequences, some ranchers refused to adapt to the region's environmental realities and continued making the same errors in range management. From 1898 to 1950, six studies of western rangelands conducted by officials with the U.S. Department of Agriculture and the U.S. Forest Service documented a consistent pattern of chronic abuse and neglect by ranchmen, including those in West Texas. Following the Civil War, Texas's grasslands were in excellent condition. One federal range agent estimated that one square mile could support 300 head of cattle. A cattleman driving a herd from Tom Green County to Taylor County in the summer of 1867 recalled "that the grass was everywhere from one to three feet high, and that sometimes it was as high as a cow's back." In the late 1880s Charlie Walter of Odessa, Texas, recalled seeing grama grass that "grew one and a half feet high everywhere."[28]

The first ranchers to West Texas took advantage of the open, free range and its abundance of grass. As more settlers moved into the region after 1880, cattlemen realized that the days of the open range and free forage were rapidly closing. In an effort to make as much money as possible before the grasslands were fenced off, cowmen engaged in a frenzied range rush. This onslaught on free grass was similar to previous gold, silver, and timber rushes in the West, where man exploited the natural resources of the region and after using them up, moved on. In an effort to maximize profits, ranchers packed the range with as many cattle as possible.

In the 1880s, severe weather savaged the western cattle industry. A major drought hit West Texas, and lacking sufficient water and grass, livestock died by the thousands. During the decade's "Big Die Up," Lone Star ranchers lost tens of thousands of cattle. In May 1886 a Big Spring newspaper reported 20,000 dead animals rotting on the plains of West Texas and noted that the stench was unbearable. Cowmen rushed to sell their livestock before they lost their entire investment, flooding the cattle market. Beef prices crashed, and banks called in their loans, forcing many ranchers out of business. Ironically, even in midst of the decade's manmade and natural disasters, the San Angelo newspaper in 1886 still proudly promoted West Texas as "the cowboy's paradise."[29]

The Certain Result of Overgrazing.

"The Certain Result of Overgrazing." Photo from Will C. Barnes, *Western Grazing Grounds and Forest Ranges* (Chicago: The Breeder's Gazette, 1913).

Heavy stocking of cattle at Pope's Crossing on the Pecos River in the 1920s. Courtesy of the J. Evetts Haley Collection at the Haley Library, Midland, Texas.

Characterizing the overstocking frenzy of the 1880s as "madness," a federal range specialist in 1898 noted that less than two decades later, cowmen seemed to have learned little from their folly. Ranchers were rapidly returning to their old destructive practices and were seriously injuring if not ruining West Texas grasslands. One major problem was that few stockmen possessed any education regarding range management. The federal agent recalled a meeting of West Texas cattlemen who adopted the following resolution, stating, "none of us know, or care to know, anything about grasses, native, or otherwise . . . and we are after getting the most out of them while they last."[30]

Chronic overgrazing in West Texas from 1874 to 1936 diminished the range's carrying capacity by 50–70 percent. In the early 1880s pasturage could support one cow per five acres. By 1898 it was one cow per ten acres and by 1913 one cow per thirty-five acres. Western ranchers, including those in West Texas, were stocking private lands with more than 12 million animals on acreage that could support only 7.5 million. During the drought of 1934 that devastated western grasslands, the federal government allocated $100 million to purchase starving livestock. In the midst of this drought, federal agents along the Pecos River in West Texas shot cattle en masse to reduce grazing pressures on the parched and exhausted rangeland. Summing up rangeland practices in 1936, the USDA concluded that in the West, "the stockman has inevitably gone seriously wrong." The agency's report found that an attitude of wanton greed characterized much of the ruthless destruction of rangeland, with every rancher thinking only of himself.[31]

Recent research by soil conservation experts throughout the Trans-Pecos region confirms the USDA and Forest Service data. Thadis W. Box, a range management professor at Texas Tech, says that overgrazing reduced the carrying capacity of West Texas ranges by two-thirds. Statistics for Pecos County show that chronic and excessive overgrazing by all types of livestock since the 1880s has depleted native vegetation to the point that brush, cactus, and weeds have now invaded 80 percent of grasslands. Widespread erosion and desertification, or the denuding of rangeland, have also become serious problems. Prolonged droughts

1934 drought along the Pecos River and federal elimination of excessive livestock. Courtesy of the J. Evetts Haley Collection at the Haley Library, Midland, Texas.

Barren cattle country along the Pecos River near Mentone, Texas, in the 1930s. Courtesy of the J. Evetts Haley Collection at the Haley Library, Midland, Texas.

common to the region have greatly aggravated stressed conditions on overused, fragile pasturage.[32]

A 1980 soil survey of neighboring Reeves County found that original grasslands in much of the county were "greatly depleted by continued excessive use" by livestock. Most of the native range was now infested with brush and weeds, and the amount of grass produced had decreased by more than 75 percent. A similar 1971 study in El Paso County noted that heavy grazing had substantially changed the rangeland's original condition. By 1920 in Midland County, "the effects of overgrazing on the pastureland had become a matter of grave concern to ranchers." A 1975 federal environmental survey of Hudspeth and Culberson counties concluded that extensive overuse of grasslands by grazing livestock since 1895 had significantly altered the native range, leaving 50–75 percent only in fair condition and 30–50 percent in poor condition. Widespread overgrazing in both counties had also created a dramatic increase in the numbers of invasive plants and weeds.[33]

In tandem with the destruction of West Texas grasslands by livestock, area ranchers unknowingly worsened the condition of their acreage by eradicating coyotes and grey wolves. With no natural predators to keep their populations in check, prairie dogs and jackrabbits flourished, causing further erosion and diminishing the range's available forage and carrying capacity. The USDA estimated that five jackrabbits or twenty prairie dogs consumed as much grass as one sheep.[34]

Today, the issue of overgrazing remains a sore point with cattlemen. Ranchers blame the grasslands' poor condition on drought and early settlers' ignorance of environmental conditions. The historical record, however, shows that besides drought and settlers' misconceptions, primary range problems also included chronic overstocking, overgrazing, and fire suppression. Prior to the Civil War, wildfires occurred with regularity on the plains of West Texas, significantly retarding the spread of brush. It also bears noting that drought afflicted West Texas long before cattlemen moved there, yet the region still boasted grasses as tall as a cow's back. Naturalist David Schmidly blames Texas ranchers' high-impact relationship with the land. Schmidly's detailed research found that "semidesert grasslands in good condition in western Texas are rare today." Earle H. Clapp, Associate Chief of the U.S. Forest Service, notes, "Other peoples have destroyed their natural resources but none have shown greater efficiency in the process [than Americans]."[35]

Despite this gloomy assessment, some positive changes are now taking place. After 1945 both the federal government and the State of Texas began making significant headway in range management education, thanks to programs by the U.S. Department of Agriculture, Soil Conservation Service, Texas Department of Agriculture, and the Texas A&M Agricultural Extension Service. Important education outreach efforts that provide practical solutions toward improving the range are now taking hold in a number of West Texas communities. Following World War II, many ranchers started sending their children to leading Texas universities offering comprehensive, professional range management programs, notably, Texas A&M University, Texas Christian University, and Sul Ross State University.

Currently, range management specialists are focusing on brush encroachment, invasive plant management, and restoration of rangelands, three of the most pressing issues facing West Texas ranchers. Historically, healthy grasslands limited the spread of woody plants such as mesquite and juniper. These plants proliferated only after the 1880s, when widespread overgrazing depleted grasslands and ranchers implemented fire suppression practices. By 1963 mesquite occupied almost fifty-seven million acres and juniper, almost twenty-one million acres. Federal and state research focusing on combating brush encroachment and restoring rangelands found that the two best strategies were herbicide treatments and mechanical removal of woody plants. Ranchers say that these treatments, ranging from $35 to $150 an acre, often cost more than what the land is worth. The only landowners who can afford such improvements are often those who have other sources of outside income and do not depend upon ranching for their livelihood.[36]

Current range research also recommends that ranchers use regularly prescribed fires to help retard or eliminate brush encroachment. For many cattlemen in the region, however, controlled burning remains a controversial topic. Some have concerns that a fire might burn fence lines or buildings, while others feel that grass on the ground, even marginal grass, is still free livestock forage. A number of stockmen are unwilling to gamble existing feed for potentially higher yields in the future.[37]

In West Texas, range management continues to evolve, as does local land use. Over the last decade ranch management specialists at Texas universities have noticed a distinct shift from cattle ranching to wildlife management among those enrolling in their programs. Hunting currently provides more than 50 percent of the annual income for many Texas ranchers and is expected to increase. Students are capitalizing on this growing trend and the need for trained wildlife and habitat managers. Recreation and eco-tourism, which includes hunting, fishing, hiking, and wildlife viewing, are projected to become among the leading industries in the region. Robert Kinucan says, "I think you'll always have ranching, but I don't think it's going to be as pre-eminent as it had been through the 1960s." Kinucan observes that, "the range students are a lot smaller number than they used to be. In traditional ranching we don't have as many kids going back to the ranch doing livestock management that we had 20 to 30 years ago." Tom Beard notes that many of the economic pressures facing area stockmen are the same as those facing farmers. "Ranching is ultimately going to be a sideline," Beard observes. "Because of NAFTA and free trade, we can't compete with foreign beef and at that point cattle ranching becomes a sideline, in that you do it to generate some income, but something else has to pay the bills."[38]

Another rapidly growing trend in the Trans-Pecos is the percentage of absentee landowners. Range specialists note that out-of-town residents are rapidly becoming some of the region's largest landowners. Many area ranches are being snapped up by wealthy people wanting weekend homes in the area, or as Tom Beard puts it, "their own private national park." Some of the ranches being cobbled together by absentee landowners are immense in size. A number of these new property owners have no interest in raising livestock and are managing their acreage strictly as wildlife preserves. The decline in the number of West Texas ranches is already being felt at local feed and grain stores, where orders have sharply dropped. The West Texas economy is changing, forcing local residents to adapt. Despite these changes, ranching will continue. Properly managed and in balance with available resources, rangeland grazing of cattle, like the grazing of bison centuries before, is a historic and "natural" use of the region's ecosystem.[39]

After more than a century of confronting the harsh environmental realities of West Texas, the once-popular myths of the "Cowman's Paradise" and the "Garden of Eden" have lost some of their luster. Despite their best efforts to bend the environment to their romantic dreams and desires for economic gain, area residents have learned that in the arid West, Mother Nature dictates the terms. Taking a long view of West Texas history, the region, besides a brief one-hundred-year interval, has never been and never will be a manmade "Garden of Eden." State and federal agricultural agents report that from Odessa and Ozona westward to El Paso, large-scale irrigated agriculture is largely finished.[40]

In a recent study of the South Plains and Texas Panhandle north of Odessa, agricultural historian Geoff Cunfer found a similar trend developing in those regions. Cunfer's research shows that by mid-century, higher energy prices and the depletion of much of the Ogallala Aquifer will force agriculture endeavors in the area "back within natural limits imposed by climate." In this century those natural limits may compel a switch from irrigated farming back to the old days of livestock grazing and dry-land farming. Dry-land agriculture west of the 100th meridian, however, will become an increasingly risky venture. Cunfer notes that West Texas could see a return to the Dust Bowl days. "When the next multiyear drought strikes the plains," he says, and farmers find themselves "without irrigation water as a fallback, the farm economy may suffer severely."[41]

Competition for local water sources in West Texas over the last decade has increasingly diverted water away from irrigated agriculture to rapidly expanding urban centers such as El Paso. Currently, El Paso is aggressively seeking additional sources of water throughout West Texas, including Dell City's underground aquifer in neighboring Hudspeth County. With El Paso's population projected to double from 800,000 to 1.6 million in the next seventy-five years, this thirsty desert city will continue its relentless search for additional water in the region. Irrigated agriculture currently consumes three-quarters of West Texas's water supply. In future confrontations over water rights, however, urban needs will increasingly eclipse those of waning irrigation interests.[42]

In contrast to irrigated farming's marked decline in the region, ranching will remain an important, albeit also reduced, component in the local economy. It will be interesting to watch what impact the hard environmental lessons of the past have upon the faded myth of the "Cowman's Paradise." Assessing the influence of state and federal range management programs upon the region since World War II, Loving County Judge Skeet Jones estimates that only 40 percent of his neighbors rotate their pastures, follow carrying capacity guidelines, or work on brush eradication. The other 60 percent still do things the old way. A number of cattlemen continue to overstock the land, graze it until the grass is gone, and then move on. After 150 years of ranching in West Texas, man still has an abusive relationship with nature. Echoing federal and state reports over the last century, Jones laments that some area ranchers are "trying to get out of it all they can. They're not looking ahead and trying to take care of the land."[43]

In the nineteenth century, America's idealized myths and free enterprise mindset helped spur the nation's economic development and settlement. As ranchers in the arid American West soon discovered, however, Mother Nature has a way of working on people, forcing them to alter their old beliefs and practices. In West Texas, cattlemen cannot continue abusing the grasslands for another century if they expect to stay in business. The choices are clear. Those who do not align their livestock operations to regional environmental realities are destined to suffer the same painful lessons as other countless ranchers before them.

Ultimately, West Texas's environment, like its racial attitudes and Civil War mindset, proves a reliable indicator of regional identity. Our examination of environment, race, and Civil War identity in West Texas over the last four chapters brings us back to where we started, to "where the West begins." Applying these criteria to what we now know about Texas, we can form some accurate conclusions concerning Lone Star identity west of the 100th meridian. Our final chapter, then, looks at West Texas, its people, and their relation to the American West.

TEXAS IDENTITY WEST OF THE 100TH MERIDIAN

The motto on the side of the Fort Worth police cruiser reads, "Where the West Begins." Fort Worth, located near the 97th meridian, is not where the West begins. That distinction belongs to Del Rio, San Angelo, Sweetwater, Lubbock, and Amarillo—all beyond the 100th meridian. Fort Worth lies at the eastern edge of Texas's shatterbelt region, where environmental and cultural fragments of the West and the South collide and intermingle and where regional identity is mixed.

Geographically, Fort Worth lies well east of the 100th meridian and John Wesley Powell's twenty-inch rainfall line. In Texas the break point for aridity, the point at which successful agriculture requires irrigation, is west of the 100th meridian. In addition, beyond the 100th meridian, one discerns a distinct difference in the terrain and ecosystems. This is where the West really begins in Texas. Fort Worth, situated in an ecological shatterbelt region, lies in between the South and the West.

Culturally, while Fort Worth manifests distinct, authentic elements of western identity, it also retains deep southern roots. Both the city and Tarrant County voted for secession by an overwhelming majority. In 1860 residents fearful of abolitionists and slave insurrections lynched two men at Crawford's Limb on the west side of town. Clearly, a city that enthusiastically votes for secession and is worried about slave revolts and abolitionists is exhibiting southern sentiments. Ultimately, Fort Worth's core characteristics lie somewhere between West and South; part of Texas's identity jumble.

Fort Worth's adept image branding, notably, "Where the West Begins," "Cowtown," and "Cowboys and Culture," has yielded significant economic dividends. The Old West brand has proven popular with both tourists and business conventions. With its frontier fort, Sundance Square, Stockyards, cattle drives, and livestock shows, the city certainly exudes a western character. Some of the western characteristics that Fort Worth "naturally" claims, however, were created during marketing campaigns, part of the city's carefully cultivated image dating to the 1920s and Amon Carter.[1]

Marketing benefits aside, by focusing on Old West elements of its heritage, Fort Worth is simply doing what much of Texas did during 1930s—escaping C. Vann Woodward's "Burden of Southern History" by replacing it with a Western identity. Randolph Campbell says that by selectively viewing itself as more western than southern, the Lone Star State escaped the embarrassing legacies of slavery, the Civil War, and Reconstruction that confronted former Confederate states. Campbell notes that by hiding behind cowboys, cattle drives, and outlaws, Texans "do not have to face the great moral evil of slavery and the bitter heritage of black-white relations that followed the defeat of the Confederacy in 1865."[2]

The first scholar to explore this Texas escapism thread was John Stricklin Spratt. Writing in 1955, he pondered why Texans focused on the "romantic appeal" of their "Cattle Kingdom." Spratt observed that the "continuing deluge of fiction, folklore, and mythology about the cattle country tends to shroud factual material in a fog of obscurity." He speculated that Texans ignored certain parts of their history, most notably their "Cotton Kingdom," because "cotton may be associated with the servile condition of slavery or the poverty of sharecropping."[3]

Echoing Spratt's conclusions, Walter Buenger found that the interpretive exhibits at the Texas State History Museum in Austin promoted a selective public memory. At the museum, King Cotton once again takes a back seat to the Cattle Kingdom. Buenger notes that the story of a state "dependent on cotton and coerced black labor fall[s] beneath the hooves

of stampeding longhorns." In this instance, however, Texas's mixed identity proved helpful in creating a selective past. Other southern states had
no similar Old West identity with which to cloak discomforting elements
of their history.[4]

Texas's sister states in the Confederacy also lacked the Alamo, Goliad,
and San Jacinto. The Texas Revolution narrative conveniently provided
Lone Star residents a second escapist identity or passport with which to
avoid their southern burden. Richard Flores and James Crisp date this
second escapist thread in public memory to the Progressive Era. "It was
no accident . . . that the veneration of the Alamo as a shrine of patriotic
sacrifice crystallized" in the late 1800s and early 1900s "after more than
60 years of virtual neglect."[5]

During the Progressive Era, Texas's historical memory and identity
underwent a complete makeover. Gregg Cantrell says that beginning in
the 1890s the state's new image, rooted in the glorious triumph of the
Texas Revolution, reflected the "progressive values and aspirations of
modernizing society." By 1910 this shift in public memory was complete, and Texas had appropriated a new state identity. Governor Oscar
Colquitt "wanted his fellow Texans to forget about slavery, the Civil War,
and Reconstruction, but also he wanted them to remember a whites-only
version of the Texas Revolution." In this new Anglo version, Hispanics
"appear only as the enemy." In the adoption of this "highly sanitized collective memory," Texas ignored its Hispanic heritage and adopted a Progressive Era identity that utilized "western symbols: the self-sufficiency
of the pioneer, the valor of the Alamo, the rugged individualism of the
cowboy, and the entrepreneurial spirit of the oil wildcatter."[6]

While these multiple identities and selective memories have enabled
Texans to avoid unpleasant parts of their past, they have also confused
historians. These scholars are unsure where to place the Lone Star State
in their regional studies. Texas does not fit any facile categorizations.
Walter Buenger says that interpreting the state's heritage "offers such a
challenge that some historians of the South have simply ignored Texas,
leaving its history for the indiscriminate use of historians of the West."
Indiscriminate use aside, some western scholars ignore Texas for exactly
the same reasons as their southern colleagues.[7]

Western historians typically include Texas as part of the Old West. In their works Texas blends seamlessly into the standard, stereotypical Wild West history of cowboys, Indians, cattle drives, and gunslingers. A number of New West studies, however, largely ignore Texas. Perhaps these scholars conceptualize a "Western" Texas as existing only up to 1890 and the closing of the frontier. Perhaps the authors are unaware of the many collective narratives that link New West Texas and the New West. Complaining about the New West School's exclusionary treatment of the Lone Star State, Ty Cashion queried, "What's the matter with Texas?" Ironically, two Lone Star historians writing in 1935, Rupert N. Richardson and Carl Coke Rister, are among the first scholars to use the term "New West." Describing Texas's identity, the pair observed, "Texas belongs to the Old South as well as the New West."[8]

In her book *Something in the Soil*, New West historian Patricia Nelson Limerick provides a geographical definition of the West as bounded on the east by the 100th meridian, with less than twenty inches a year rainfall. Much of West Texas, then, fits her criteria. In addition, New West Texas shares many of the New West issues that she examines in her writings, including her chapter, "Burdens of Western American History."[9]

Among New West historians, standard topics include: Native Americans, Mexican Americans, the Mexican border, the federal government's imprint upon the West, the frontier, aridity, water resources, farming and irrigated agriculture, ranching and western rangeland management, extractive industries, nuclear waste disposal, gentrification of the West, and the romantic myth of the West as a place of escape and renewal.[10]

Examining the above list, New West Texas proves an excellent fit with the New American West. Native Americans have always been a defining component of the West. The prominent tribes in West Texas during the eighteenth and nineteenth centuries were the same ones that played major roles in the history of the West, specifically, the Apaches, Comanches, and Kiowas. In the 1850s the federal government operated two Indian reservations in Northwest Texas. During the 1870s and early 1880s, the U.S. Army forced Apaches, Comanches, and Kiowas who traditionally ranged throughout much of West Texas, onto reservations in New Mexico and Oklahoma.[11]

Besides Native Americans another traditionally important "Western" group is Mexican Americans. As previously discussed, Tejanos are currently West Texas's fastest-growing ethnic group and are rapidly becoming the majority population in county after county. Additionally, the border with neighboring Mexico remains a major influence and issue for residents of West Texas and other Southwestern states.

As in other western states, the federal government played a far greater role in shaping West Texas than did the state government. After the Lone Star State's admission to the Union in 1846, the U.S. Army and the Postmaster General quickly became West Texas's major benefactors. Soldiers built roads, forts, and sub-posts; guarded passenger, mail, and freight traffic; and gave an enormous boost to the local economy. Many of West Texas's earliest towns owe their existence and survival to the federal presence. The Butterfield Overland and San Antonio-San Diego Mail lines also spurred development of the Texas frontier, helping to establish much of the regional infrastructure that later became modern West Texas.[12]

Both the Republic and the State of Texas lacked sufficient resources to protect West Texas residents. Without a U.S. Army deterrent, raiding Comanches, Kiowas, and Apaches depopulated much of Texas's western frontier during the Civil War. Ultimately, it was the federal government's manpower and materiel, from 1848 to 1881, that permitted Anglo, African American, and Tejano settlement in the Lone Star State west of the 100th meridian. Robert Wooster aptly describes the region as "a child of federal subsidy."[13]

Like other parts of the West, federal water projects at Red Bluff on the Pecos River, Elephant Butte above El Paso, and Lake Amistad near Del Rio, Texas, helped ensure a dependable water supply for inhabitants of the arid region. In California, Arizona, and West Texas, irrigated farming promoters attempted to transform vast sections of southwestern desert and semi-arid plains into a manmade "Garden of Eden." Large-scale irrigated agriculture in West Texas has proved unsustainable. Urban centers such as Amarillo, Lubbock, El Paso, Midland-Odessa, San Angelo, and Abilene are demanding an ever-increasing share of West Texas's precious water supply.

In West Texas today, water futures are rapidly becoming more valuable than oil. The Texas General Land Office debated marketing water underneath its university lands, only to back off after their plan created a furor. Regional businessmen T. Boone Pickens and Clayton Williams, Jr., are working on plans to sell water from regional aquifers to the larger cities. Worried residents are scrambling to create local water boards or strengthen existing ones in hopes of restricting excessive and potentially ruinous water mining. In early 2010 Williams filed suit against a Pecos County groundwater district "for denying his application to pump water beneath his land" near Fort Stockton, Texas.[14]

Depopulation remains one of the most pressing problems facing West Texas. With oil reserves projected to run out by 2100, more small towns will undoubtedly be shuttering their windows. Elliott West notes that in the last century, a number of counties in the region experienced population declines ranging from 50–75 percent. If the lessening of water supplies become acute, even more people will abandon West Texas, returning the arid region back to a *despoblado*, or depopulated land, much as it was during the time under Spain and Mexico. Without water there is no sustainable future for those living in parched West Texas or the American West.[15]

Like other western states, West Texas also faces severe problems related to chronic livestock overgrazing and poor rangeland management since the Civil War. Western and environmental historian Todd M. Kerstetter likens this "range rush" by western cattleman to grab all available free grass to a gold rush, land rush, and other natural resource stampedes in the West. Federal, state, and county studies of overgrazing in the Trans-Pecos from 1898 to 1980 reveal that 80 percent of the acreage has serious brush and weed encroachment. The grasslands produce 60 percent less forage now than in the 1880s. Forty percent of the range shows severe depletion, erosion, and desertification. Besides livestock grazing of grasslands, pumping underground aquifers for irrigated farming, and tapping the region's oil reserves, West Texas has a long history of extractive industries, including sulphur, gypsum, silver, and quicksilver mining.[16]

As in other parts of the American West, some now envision West Texas's sparsely populated landscape as an ideal location for dumping radioactive waste. In May 2008 state regulators licensed a radioactive dump in Andrews County, Texas, for "waste from nuclear weapons processing and uranium mining." A year later, local voters gave their approval for the site. In marked contrast, during the 1990s residents of Sierra Blanca, Texas, repeatedly rebuffed state attempts to store nuclear waste near that town.[17]

If some parts of West Texas are attracting nuclear waste dumps, other locales are becoming gentrified. The Big Bend region now boasts its own Texas version of Santa Fe and Sedona. The Marfa-Fort Davis-Alpine triangle is rapidly becoming one of the new "hot spots" in the American West for people to visit, retire to, or purchase a second home in. With mile-high elevations, scenic mountains, desert, and gorgeous western sunsets, the area has seen real estate values skyrocket. Artisans, professionals, and the wealthy are flocking to this increasingly popular West Texas destination. Internet cafes, specialty coffee shops, wineries, upscale bookstores, restaurants, bed and breakfasts, galleries, boutiques, and the like are proliferating throughout the region.[18]

In the last decade a number of wealthy outsiders purchased ranches and large tracts of adjoining lands, creating what one local describes as "their own national parks." Many of the new landowners are absentee and only come to West Texas for weekends or holidays. As in Aspen, Vail, Santa Fe, Sedona, and other chic Western destinations, local residents are complaining about soaring property values and increased taxes. The number of cattle ranches in the region is also decreasing as more and more landowners switch to ecotourism, a rapidly growing industry. As wealthy hunters discover West Texas, wildlife management is gaining priority over livestock management, and landowners earn more on hunting leases than they do from raising livestock. Rafting, hiking, backpacking, and camping are also popular recreational activities in the region.[19]

All of the above issues are defining characteristics and issues that New West historians have examined in a number of recent studies. As the side-by-side comparison reveals, New West Texas shares many common issues and traits with the New American West. Just as West Texas was once part of the Old West, it is still part of the New West.

This brings the discussion back to where it started. Is Texas southern, western, or unique? The answer is all three. East Texas is primarily southern in its identity and history. While West Texas certainly exhibits southern influences, it is decidedly more western than southern. In many respects Texas's character west of the 100th meridian is more akin to other southwestern states that share a border with Mexico, namely New Mexico, Arizona, and California. In the long duré of history, future scholars will likely view the 1890 to 1980 period in West Texas with its southern Anglo majorities and irrigated cotton fields as almost a mirage, a temporary phenomenon, or an atypical blip.

It is important to note that several regional factors influence identity beyond the 100th meridian. The Trans-Pecos and the western portion of the Edwards Plateau are primarily western in nature, both environmentally and culturally. The High Plains that comprise the South Plains and Texas Panhandle, while western in many aspects, also exhibit environmental and cultural characteristics typical of the Great Plains and the Midwest.

Geographically, this region is part of the Great Plains. The High Plains ecosystem starts in northern Nebraska and ends at Midland-Odessa. Underlying much of this region is the immense Ogallala Aquifer, 177,000 square miles in size. In the High Plains the two largest cities are Amarillo and Lubbock.[20]

Amarillo exhibits a mixed identity and is both western and midwestern in nature. Its climate is often similar to that found in Nebraska, and many of its earliest Anglo residents were originally from the Midwest. Paul Carlson says that while "Amarillo remains a western town . . . it is the hub of a huge marketplace that looks more often . . . toward the Midwest." In regards to Lubbock, Roy Sylvan Dunn describes it as the "hub city—the market place—of the rich South Plains . . . the capital of 'West Texico,' embracing West Texas and part of New Mexico." The first census of Lubbock County in 1880 reveals that half of its residents were from the Midwest and Northeast.[21]

Two prominent local icons, the cowboy and the farmer, are also emblematic of the larger Great Plains region. James Shortridge says the yeoman farmer and the cowboy represent the Plains' self-image, that of "industrious, honest, humble, and self-reliant citizens who acquired and maintained these values by working for themselves and by being in close contact with the earth." Regional identity on the Great Plains, especially west of the 100th meridian, often parallels that found in West Texas.[22]

In closing, some final thoughts on Texans and how they use identity. Texans need to confront their past instead of avoiding it. Walter Buenger and Randolph Campbell have long lamented the fact that in Texas, myth and memory often obscure history. Instead of facing less-than-pleasant realities, some would rather swathe themselves in legends, myths, and symbols. For far too long, Texas has cloaked itself in a Western identity to escape its southern legacy of racism, segregation, and lynching.

For those seeking refuge in the Old West, the Lone Star's western history proves equally embarrassing. Those venturing out to West Texas will encounter a legacy of racism, intimidation, and segregation there, too. As in much of the American West, the region's mythic cowboys, county sheriffs, and gunslingers have their fair share of unsavory baggage. Ultimately, there is no safe place to hide in a Texan West since its past is just as problematic as that of the South.

Texans must also come to terms with a second escapist identity, one forged in the Texas Revolution's hallowed "Trinity" of 1836, namely, the Alamo, Goliad, and San Jacinto. In the ensuing 175 years since Texas won its independence from Mexico, whites have often forgotten or ignored the significant contributions of Tejanos to the Texas Revolution, to the Texas Republic, and to the settlement of the state. David J. Weber illustrates this point when discussing the writings of Texas historian Joe Frantz, who claims that "'a group of upstart Anglos'" won the Texas Revolution. Weber responds that "it was not just 'upstart Anglos' in Texas who defeated Mexican forces, but those Anglos had the help of Texas Mexicans too."[23]

Even now, some Anglos who celebrate the Texas Revolution's annual anniversaries fail to understand why Mexican Americans, discriminated

against, segregated, and often marginalized in the state's public memory, may not share their enthusiasm. In the second half of the nineteenth
century, Anglo Texans turned their backs on their former Tejano allies,
relegating them to second-class status. For many years standard Texas
Revolution and Mexican War narratives frequently disparaged Mexican
Americans. Whites became the "Good Texans," and Tejanos became
the "bad guys." Today, tourists who focus on a "whites-only" version of
Texas history during their visits to the Alamo, Goliad, and San Jacinto
may find themselves confronting this awkward Tejano betrayal baggage.
Just as one cannot forget the state's legacy of African-American slavery, one cannot ignore Anglo mistreatment and segregation of Mexican
Americans. In the end not even these Revolutionary shrines offer a safe
haven from the unpleasant realities of Texas's past.[24]

There is hope, however. If old wounds among Anglos and Tejanos in
the Trans-Pecos are now starting to heal, perhaps other Texans can take
courage and begin facing their past too, instead of avoiding it. The legacy
of slavery, racism, and segregation are too heavy a burden for the Lone
Star State to continue carrying in the twenty-first century. By coming
to terms with its mistreatment of minorities over the last two centuries,
whether in the aftermath of the Alamo, on a West Texas cattle ranch, or
an East Texas cotton plantation, Texas can start to shake free of its cum-
bersome past.

Simply put, much of the burden of Texas history is its heritage of
race relations, including a longstanding tradition of excluding minorities
from the historical narrative. There has been considerable progress. A
careful reading of Texas's current social studies standards reveals numerous references to both Hispanics and African Americans. Some Tejanos,
however, maintain that the curriculum still needs to say more about
Hispanics and their contributions to Texas. Native Americans have also
"complained that their history . . . [has] been given short shrift" in state
textbooks.[25]

During recent curriculum hearings at the Texas Board of Education,
revisions proposed by Mexican American board members "were consistently defeated." Mary Helen Berlanga of Corpus Christi stormed out of

one session in frustration, saying that the board "can just pretend this is a white America and Hispanics don't exist." An African American board member, Mavis Knight of Dallas, also expressed displeasure over the curriculum content. "Yes, we have come a long way," Knight observed, "but we have not arrived." Texas's culture war over history and identity continues. As the preceding chapters reveal, whenever the Lone Star State ignores portions of its past by appropriating unrepresentative or alternate identities, this only adds to the unwieldy burden that it already shoulders. Texans must fully embrace *all* of their history, including all of the participants in that narrative.[26]

Texas's multiple identities provide invaluable lessons and insights into how people remember history. In the Lone Star State there is an ongoing battle between mythology and history. Texas history often seems to be more about larger-than-life characters and myths than about what actually took place. In no other state in the union are legends and icons so deeply entrenched and so pervasive. In creating their public memory and identity over the last two centuries, Texans have often chosen mythology over history. Today, Texas is carrying a heavy load indeed. Like a lumbering Atlas staggering under the weight of the world, the Lone Star State is shouldering its own unique and exceptional "Burden of Texas History." Perhaps it is time that Atlas shrugs.

NOTE LEGEND

AGO: Adjutant General's Office
BB: J. B. "Buck" Barry Papers
C60: United States Eighth Census (1860)
C70: United States Ninth Census (1870)
C80: United States Tenth Census (1880)
DT: Department of Texas
LR: Letters Received
LS: Letters Sent
NA: National Archives
NM: Department of New Mexico
OR: *Official Records of the Union and Confederate Armies* series
PF: James Patterson and William Franks Claim
PM: Pendleton Murrah Papers
RF: John "Rip" Ford Papers
RG: Record Group
TAG: Texas Adjutant General's Department Records
TNMA: District of Texas, New Mexico, and Arizona
TST: Texas State Troop Records
Confederate Citizens File: Confederate Papers Relating to Citizens or
Business Firms, 1861–1865

NOTES

CHAPTER I

1. Fort Worth Police car photographed by author, April 2009 (quotation one); Cashion, *The New Frontier*, 6; Sparling, "Texas Frontier Centennial," *Handbook,* online, (quotation two); Kleiner, "Fort Worth Star-Telegram," *Handbook,* online. The author found an early masthead from Nov. 10, 1925, for the *Fort Worth Record-Telegram,* Amon G. Carter, President and Publisher, with the motto, "Where the West Begins."

2. Cashion, *The New Frontier*, 6 (quotations one and two).

3. Reynolds, *Editors Make War*, 97–117; Reynolds, *Texas Terror*, 83–8, 148–52, 153 (quotation), 154–67.

4 Texas Library and Historical Commission, *Journal of the Secession Convention of Texas, 1861*, ed. Winkler, 88–90.

5. The author adapted C. Vann Woodward's famous phrase to fit Texas History. See Woodward, *The Burden of Southern History*.

6. Woodward, *The Burden of Southern History*, 17, 18 (quotation), 19–22.

7. Ibid., 19 (quotations one and two), 20. Texas historians John Stricklin Spratt, Randolph Campell, Walter Buenger, and Gregg Cantrell all agree that since the Progressive Era, Texas has been trying to escape the legacy of its defeat in the Civil War and the subsequent humiliation of Reconstruction by appropriating alternative, escapist identities. For more on this, see Chapter Five.

8. "The Burdens of Western American History," in Patricia Nelson Limerick, *The Legacy of Conquest*, 322–9, 330 (quotations one through three), 331–49.

9. Walter L. Buenger talks about the dangers of Texas history and myth becoming cartoonish in his article, "'The Story of Texas'? The Texas State History

Museum and Forgetting and Remembering the Past," *Southwestern Historical Quarterly*, 486–9; *The Official Site of Texas Tourism*, "Texas: It's Like a Whole Other Country." A recent series of Texas braggadocio postcards entitled "Everything's Bigger in Texas!" features a gargantuan roadrunner, armadillo, and longhorn. These cards are distributed by: Smith-Southwestern, Inc. of Tempe, AZ.

10. Buenger, *The Path to a Modern South*, xvi (quotation one); Lack, "In the Long Shadow of Eugene C. Barker: The Revolution and Republic," *Texas through Time*, 134 (quotation two).

11. Lack, "In the Long Shadow," 135–6; Graham, *The Texas Literary Tradition*, 4, 15.

12. Weighing in on Texas identity, Randolph Campbell says that Texas "is far more southern than western and has been so for nearly two hundred years." Regarding public memory and Texas's western identity, he argues that despite enduring legends of Texas cowboys and gunfighters, the West "is not the essence of Texas." Harking back to C. Vann Woodward's "Burden of Southern History," Campbell says that for some people, "the cold history of being southern is not as pleasing as the warm memory of being western." Campbell, "Entangled Stories of the Lone Star State," in *Lone Star Pasts*, 279 (footnote quotations one through three). Campbell's views on Texas's southern identity are shared by James W. Lee, a professor emeritus of English specializing in southern literature. In an essay discussing the Old South literary tradition in Texas, Lee argues, "It seems evident to me that until well after World War II many Americans and most Texans saw the state as southern, not western." Lee, "The Old South in Texas Literature," *The Texas Literary Tradition*, 46 (footnote quotation four). Lee's opinion taps into the ongoing debate over text and context, and whether literary theory constitutes history. For more on this, see Clark, *History, Theory, Text*, and Sewell, *Logics of History*.

13. Jordan, *Texas*, 7–17.

14. Vernon Bailey's 1905 USDA Report, "Biological Survey of Texas," can be found in: Schmidly, *Texas Natural History*, 68 (quotation one), 73 (quotations two and three).

15. Byrkit, "Land, Sky, and People: The Southwest Defined," *Journal of the Southwest*. Byrkit's well-researched and documented definition of the Southwest provides a far more precise cultural and physiographical baseline as to what constitutes the region than does Vandiver's more general commentary, *The Southwest*.

16. Maptech Terrain Navigator Pro Version 8.0 U.S.G.S. Texas Series, topographic and aerial maps of Greenwood and Era, Texas. See also Francaviglia, *The Cast Iron Forest*, 38–40, 50.

NOTES

17. The author developed this shatterbelt concept over a seven-year period through dialogs with Ben Johnson, Robert Wooster, Frank de la Teja, Jerry Thompson, Todd Kerstetter, Sherry Smith, David Weber, and Bruce Dinges, all of whom offered helpful suggestions regarding regional identity in Texas.

18. Webb, *The Great Plains*, 8 (quotations one and two); Cunfer, *On the Great Plains*, 200 (quotation three).

19. Powell, *The Arid Lands*, 11–13; Plate LXVII, Map of "Arid Region of the United States, Showing Areas Irrigated" in Powell, *Eleventh Annual Report of the Director of the United States Geological Survey, Part II: Irrigation*, 21; Texas Parks and Wildlife Department, "Precipitation in Texas;" Buenger, *Secession and the Union in Texas*, 109 (quotation). According to www.citytowninfo.com/places/texas/ (accessed Nov. 12, 2009), Amarillo, Texas, receives 19.56 inches per year; Lubbock, Texas, 18.65; Colorado City, Texas, 19.00; and Del Rio, Texas, 19.00. Powell placed the 20-inch rainfall line in Texas at the 100th meridian, but it is actually slightly farther west. Fort Worth rainfall is 34.00 inches.

20. Cunfer, *On the Great Plains*, 174–5. Also see Green's earlier study, *Land of the Underground Rain*, which remains a classic.

21. Weber, *The Mexican Frontier, 1821-1846*, xix; Carey, *Map of Mexico, 1822 National Atlas*; Finley, *Mexico, 1831 World Atlas*; Tanner, *Map of the United States of Mexico*; Tanner, *Mexico and Guatemala, 1836 World Atlas*.

22. Cunfer, *On the Great Plains*, 198–200; author telephone interviews with Farm Service Agency agents in the following Texas counties: El Paso (June 11, 2007), Tom Green (June 12, 2007), Midland (June 12, 2007), Lubbock (June 12, 2007), Crockett (June 12, 2007), Bailey (June 12, 2007), Gaines (June 12, 2007), and Andrews (June 12, 2007).

23. Texas Water Development Board, *Far West Texas Regional Water Plan*, 5–39; Farm Service Agency representative interview, El Paso County, Texas, June 11, 2007 (author telephone interview); author interview with Tom Beard, Alpine, Texas, March 14, 2006.

24. Cunfer, *On the Great Plains*, 198 (quotation one), 199, 200 (quotation two), 237.

25. Wallace and Hoebel, *The Comanches*, 7, 12, 14; Kerstetter "Tribal frontier" comment to author in September 2008; La Vere, *Life Among the Texas Indians*, 15; Newcomb, *The Indians of Texas*, 157; Hämäläinen, *The Comanche Empire*, 176.

26. La Vere, *The Texas Indians*, 93 (quotation), 134. The U.S. Army subdued the Kiowa and Comanche tribes by 1875. Federal troops and the Texas Rangers did not force all Apaches out of the Trans-Pecos until six years later in January 1881 when Rangers defeated remnants of Victorio's Warm Springs Apaches in the Sierra Diablo Mountains. For more on the 1874–1875 Red River War, see Wallace, *Ranald S. Mackenzie on the Texas Frontier*, 128–68. For information on the 1880–1881 Victorio Campaign in the Trans-Pecos, see Sonnichsen, *The Mescalero Apaches*, 173–97; Baylor, *Into the Far, Wild Country*, 304–22.

27. Gournay, *Texas Boundaries*, 59–61, 89–90; East Texas census comparison data from Campbell, *A Southern Community in Crisis*, 20; U.S. Census Bureau, "Harrison County, TX 2000 QuickFacts," online (accessed July 22, 2008). West Texas Data from: U.S. Eighth Census, 1860 (C60), El Paso County, Texas, Microfilm Series (M) 653, Roll (R) 1293; ibid., Presidio County, Texas, (this also includes Fort Stockton, later in Pecos County); U.S. Ninth Census, 1870 (C70), El Paso County, Texas, M593, R1583; C70, Presidio County, Texas, (this also includes Fort Stockton, later in Pecos County), M593, R1601; United States Tenth Census, 1880 (C80), El Paso County, Texas, MT9, R1301; C80, Presidio County, Texas, MT9, R1323; Texas State Data Center and Office of the State Demographer, Thematic Maps, "1990 U.S. Population Density-Black Persons," (accessed July 22, 2008).

28. C60, Slave Schedules, El Paso & Presidio counties, Texas (both counties' slaves schedules appear on the same single page), Series M653, online, www.ancestry. com (accessed July 22, 2008); C60, Slave Schedules, Maverick County, Texas, and Uvalde County, Texas, M653, online, www.ancestry.com (accessed Nov. 10, 2009). Two of the three slaves listed for Maverick County in 1860 were actually in Frio County on the Frio River. Uvalde County (most of which is east of the 100th meridian) and its county seat of Uvalde had twenty-seven slaves.

29. According to the *Handbook of Texas*, "the term *Tejano*, derived from the Spanish adjective *tejano* or (feminine) *tejana* (and written in Spanish with a lower-case *t*), denotes a Texan of Mexican descent, thus a Mexican Texan or a Texas Mexican." The author uses the terms Tejano, Mexican American, and Hispanic (people of Spanish descent, Spanish-speaking people) interchangeably. See also, C60, Maverick County, Texas, M653, R1300; C60, El Paso County, Texas, M653, R1293; C60, Presidio County, Texas, M653, R1293 (this includes Fort Stockton, later in Pecos County). Uvalde County, situated on the western edge of Texas's shatterbelt, listed 479 residents in 1860, a fair number of which were from the Upper and Lower South. Uvalde County voted against secession by a 76 to 16 margin. See Texas Library and Historical Commission, *Journal of the Secession Convention of Texas, 1861*, ed. Winkler, 90; C60, Uvalde County, Texas, M653, R1307.

30. July 4, 1849 entry by John Murchison, diarist, for May 27–July 28, 1849 portion of "La Grange Company-John B. Cameron Journal," M0082, (quotations one through three); L. N. Weed, "Overland Journey to California in 1849," WA MSS 517, 38 (quotation four); "Journal of William P. Huff," online (accessed April 24, 2007), July 22, 1849 entry (quotation five and six).

31. Martínez, *The Chicanos of El Paso*, 6; C60, El Paso County, Texas, and Presidio County, Texas, (including Fort Stockton, later in Pecos County), M653, R1293; C70, El Paso County, Texas, M593, R1583; C70, Presidio County, Texas,

(including Fort Stockton, later in Pecos County), M593, R1601; C80, Pecos County, Texas, MT9, R1323; Twelfth Federal Census, 1900 (C1900), Pecos County, Texas, MT623, R1664. 1880–1900 Tejano and Black population figures in Fort Davis, Presidio County from Wooster, *Frontier Crossroads*, 125, 144. Wooster says that from the 1870s to the mid-1880s, Anglo-Hispanic nuptials accounted for fifteen to twenty percent of all local marriages.

32. White, *The Middle Ground*, x (quotations one and two).

33. De León, *The Tejano Community*, xviii (quotation one); author interview with Jesús F. de la Teja, San Marcos, Texas, Dec. 4, 2006 (quotation two); author interview with Jerry D. Thompson, Laredo, Texas, Dec. 5, 2006 (quotation three). Many of those moving to the High Plains and Trans-Pecos sections of West Texas after the 1880s were from East Texas and the South. Southern majorities accrued more rapidly in the Rolling Plains than in other areas lying west of the 100th meridian. This demographic shift in West Texas made southern life ways and worldviews a dominant culture in the region from the 1890s until the 1980s, when the population began changing once again. For more on this southern Anglo migration to West Texas, see Kerr, "Migration into Texas, 1860–1880," *Southwestern Historical Quarterly*, 184–216; Jordan, "A Century and a Half of Ethnic Change in Texas, 1836–1896," *Southwestern Historical Quarterly*, 385–422; Buenger, *The Path to a Modern South*, 148–50.

34. Racial discrimination and segregation in West Texas covered in author interview with Pete Terrazas and Clara Duran, Fort Stockton, Texas, May 6, 2002; Flores, "The Good Life the Hard Way," Ph.D. diss., 31, 84–6, 99, 150–1; García, *Desert Immigrants*, 5, 99, 110–1, 127, 132; Thompson, *History of Marfa and Presidio County, Texas*, Vol. 2, 61; Ramirez, "El Pasoans: Life and Society in Mexican El Paso, 1920–1945," Ph.D. diss., 102, 104, 108, 182–5; Perales, *Are We Good Neighbors*, 213, 215, 219, *Pecos Times* article quoted in *Fort Stockton Pioneer*, Sept. 30, 1909 (quotation).

35. The following provide a thorough discussion of segregation and racism in Arizona, California, and the American West: Hine and Faragher, *The American West*, 425 (quotation one), 427 (quotations two through four); Milner, A. O'Connor, and Sandweiss, eds., *The Oxford History of the American West*, 442 (quotation five); Bakken, "The Courts, The Legal Profession, and the Development of Law in Early California," in Burns and Orsi, eds., *Taming the Elephant*, 81 (quotation six); Johnson, *Roaring Camp*, 234 (quotation seven); Menchaca, *The Mexican Outsiders* xiv–xv, 8–9, 12–3, 24–5, 30, 58; Almaguer, *Racial Fault Lines*, 4–7, 18–9, 28–9, 58–9; Ruiz, "South by Southwest," *OAH Magazine of History*, online (accessed June 18, 2006); Salter, "In the Steps of Esteban," *University of Arizona*, online (accessed June 18, 2006); Knox, "Racial Integration in the Public Schools of Arizona, Kansas and New Mexico," *The Journal of Negro*

Education, 290–5; Montoya, "Chicana/o Desegregation Cases," *The University of Dayton School of Law*, online (accessed May 20, 2007); *Arizona State University Libraries*, "Chicanos in Arizona, 1864–1985" online (accessed July 2, 2007); *The Arizona Republic*, "A History of African-Americans in Arizona," online (accessed July 2, 2007); Bowman, "The New Face of School Segregation," *Duke Law Journal* 50 (2001), online (accessed July 2, 2007).

36. Perales, *Are We Good Neighbors*, 54 (quotations one and two), 55 (quotation three), 223 (quotations four through six).

37. For more on this, see Chapter Three. De la Teja interview (quotation). For more on mixed marriages in West Texas, the West, and America as a whole, see Pascoe, *What Comes Naturally*.

38. Current and future population figures and trends for West Texas based on study done by author using: *U.S. Census Bureau*, "Texas Quick Facts," online and "Texas County Selection Map," online (both accessed on July 1, 2007); Texas State Data Center, online (accessed July 12, 2007); Murdock, White, Hoque, Pecotte, You, and Balkan, "The Texas Challenge in the Twenty-First Century," 46–7.

39. Gournay, *Texas Boundaries*, 59–61, 89–93; El Paso's 1850–1890 Tejano population percentages in Martínez, *The Chicanos of El Paso*, 6; C60, El Paso County, Texas, and Presidio County, Texas, (this also includes Fort Stockton, later in Pecos County), M653, R1293; C70, El Paso County, Texas, M593, R1583; C70, Presidio County, Texas, (this also includes Fort Stockton, later in Pecos County), M593, R1601; C80, Pecos County, Texas, MT9, R1323; Twelfth U.S. Census, 1900 (C1900), Pecos County, Texas, MT623, R1664; Jordan, *Texas*, 28 (quotation one). Tejano and Black population figures in Fort Davis, Presidio County from Wooster, *Frontier Crossroads*, 125, 144. Also, Sherry Smith comments to author, 2006, (south to north migrations); Archambeau, "The First Federal Census in the Panhandle—1880," *Panhandle-Plains Historical Review*, 45 (quotation two).

40. Kulish, "As German as . . . America," *New York Times*, July 24, 2008 (quotation one). The article says that according to the 2000 federal census, there are more Americans of German ancestry (43 million) than of English or of Irish descent. See also Jordan, *German Seed in Texas Soil*, 106 (quotation two), 178 (quotation three), 179 (quotation four).

41. Jordan, *German Seed in Texas Soil*, 182 (quotations one and two); Biesele, *The History of German Settlements in Texas, 1831–1861*, 206 (quotation four); Baum, *The Shattering of Texas Unionism*, 53 (quotation three); Tiling, *History of the German Element in Texas*, 130 (quotation five).

42. Lamar, *Dakota Territory, 1861–1889*, xxv (quotation one); Lamar, *The Far Southwest, 1846–1912*, 6, 7, 13 (quotation three), 19 (quotation two).

43. Texas Library and Historical Commission, *Journal of the Secession Convention*, 89–90 (This journal omits the Presidio County and Maverick County returns). The Maverick County secession vote (3 votes for secession, 80 against) can be found in Sumpter, *Paso Del Águila*, 83. The Presidio County secession vote is reported in the *San Antonio Alamo Express*, March 25, 1861 (Presidio County unanimous against secession, 364-0), and in two letters from Fort Davis merchant Daniel Murphy to Elisha M. Pease. See: Murphy to Pease, Feb. 25, 1861, and Murphy to Pease, March 1, 1861, Elisha M. Pease Papers, Austin History Center. For more information on the organization of Presidio County, see Gournay, *Texas Boundaries*, 59–61.

44. Timmons, *El Paso*, 80–3, 103–17, 135 (quotation), 136–47.

45. C60, El Paso County, Texas, Slave Schedules (see footnote 28); Timmons, *El Paso*, 147 (quotation); Strickland, *The Turner Thesis and the Dry World*, 5–6.

46. Stegmaier, "'An Imaginary Negro in an Impossible Place'?," *New Mexico Historical Review*, 263–4, 265 (quotation one), 284 (quotations two and three); Wilson, *When the Texans Came*, 305 (quotations four and five). The Texan officers submitted their assessment in May 1862.

47. Ely, "Riding the Butterfield Frontier," Ph.D. diss., 274–81. Dale Baum says that the statistical evidence does not support the charge of voter fraud in El Paso County. The author has conducted a detailed study of El Paso County from the 1850s to the 1880s, utilizing numerous primary sources and documents, and has found that there is a strong circumstantial case for voter fraud in the secession referendum. The county has a long history of voting irregularities dating back to the 1850s. Next, Baum says that in Young County, there may or may not have been pro-secession voter padding. Unlike Jack County, its neighbor to the east, Young County voted for secession. The author's research reveals that on the eve of the Civil War, a reign of terror existed in Young County, with both county officials and residents afraid to act or speak out against it for fear of physical attack and/or murder. A local vigilante mob led by avid secessionist John Baylor created a violent and powerful deterrent to any Unionist, pro-Sam Houston sentiment in the county from 1859 onwards. The county may have indeed voted for secession, but one must also consider the influence of the Baylor mob on those casting ballots and on the final tally. For more on this, see Ely, "Bedlam at Belknap," *West Texas Historical Association Year Book*, 85. Finally, Baum suggests that Uvalde County's anti-secession vote may have been fraudulent. Although there is no evidence to date of Unionist improprieties in Texas's secession referendum, Baum advances several theoretical scenarios suggesting that in Uvalde, the anti-secession county judge influenced the outcome. See Baum, *The Shattering of Texas Unionism*, 63–9. Despite the above comments, Baum's excellent work along with Buenger's *Secession and the Union in Texas* remain the finest studies to date on the subject of Texas Unionism.

48. Holden, "Frontier Problems and Movements in West Texas, 1846–1900," Ph.D. diss., 99–100 (quotation); Buenger, *Secession and the Union in Texas*, 80; Marten, *Texas Divided*, 26, 29.

49. Humphries, "Public Monument Sculpture in West Texas," presentation to West Texas Historical Association Annual Meeting; Humphries, "Conceiving a Texan West," presentation to Texas State Historical Association Annual Meeting. Humphries' work is part of a chapter in a forthcoming book edited by Ty Cashion. Terry Jordan's studies on architecture and land surveys in Jordan, *Texas*, 185–205.

50. Author's interviews sampling regional identity from 2006 to 2009 with residents of the following West Texas counties: El Paso, Midland, Ector, Pecos, Reeves, Loving, Presidio, and Brewster. Most respondents said they lived in the Southwest, and the remainder said they lived in the West. In Jordan's identity survey, residents of West Texas said they lived in the West. See Jordan, *Texas*, 279-80; Meinig, *Imperial Texas*, 93, 102; Holden, *Alkali Trails*, 98 (quotation); McConnell, *Social Cleavages in Texas*, 15–6.

51. McConnell, *Social Cleavages in Texas*, 45–7, 51, 52 (quotation), 53.

52. *El Paso Times* article reprinted in the *Fort Stockton Pioneer*, Sept. 6, 1912 (quotations one and two); Hamilton, "University of Texas at El Paso," *Handbook*, online (accessed Nov. 12, 2007); Graves, "Texas Tech University," *Handbook*, online (accessed Nov. 12, 2007). See also earlier *El Paso Times* article reprinted in the *Pioneer* on Dec. 29, 1911, concerning Austin's exploitation of West Texas's resources and the region's meager allotment of state services and institutions.

53. Crane, "The West Texas Agricultural and Mechanical College Movement and the Founding of Texas Technological College," *West Texas Historical Association Year Book*, 4 (quotation two), 9 (quotations one and three); McConnell, *Social Cleavages in Texas*, 23–4; Ernest Wallace, *The Howling of the Coyotes*, 143–5; Holden, *Alkali Trails*, 124–6.

54. Crane, "The West Texas Agricultural and Mechanical College Movement," 4 (quotation one), 6, 8 (quotation two); Wallace, *The Howling of the Coyotes*, 143–5; Holden, *Alkali Trails*, 124–6.

55. McConnell, *Social Cleavages in Texas*, 45; Holden, *Alkali Trails*, 98, 100; Wallace, *The Howling of the Coyotes*, 4, 8, 15, 18, 23, 135, 141; Crane, "The West Texas Agricultural and Mechanical College Movement," 28 (quotations one through four).

56. Crane, "The West Texas Agricultural and Mechanical College Movement," 6 (quotations one and two), 29, 33.

57. McConnell, *Social Cleavages in Texas*, 83 (quotation one); Holden, *Alkali Trails*, vi (quotations two through four).

CHAPTER 2

1. Lubbock to Hebert, Sept. 26, 1862, National Archives (NA), Record Group (RG) 109, Dept. of Texas (DT), Letters Received (LR), Entry 106, Box 2, Folder 36, (quotations one and two). Additional note: An earlier version of this chapter first appeared in Vol. CX, No. 4 (April, 2007) of the *Southwestern Historical Quarterly* (pages 439–63) and is reprinted here with kind permission of the Texas State Historical Association. This updated and expanded version includes corrections, along with additional primary and secondary sources. This chapter has its origins in a continuing conversation between the author and Harwood Hinton, dating back to 1996 when Hinton first introduced the author to this topic. Over the years Hinton has graciously provided much invaluable insight and criticism.

2. Lubbock to Hebert, Sept. 26, 1862, NA, RG109, DT, LR, Entry 106, Box 2, Folder 36 (quotation). During the Civil War, Confederate Texans sometimes referred to their fellow citizens who opposed secession and rebel military service as Tories. The term, used to denote citizens favoring British rule, originated in the American Revolution. Six decades later, in the Texas Revolution, those fighting for independence also applied the label to Texans who remained loyal to Mexico. Regarding dissent in shatterbelt counties along Texas's western frontier, Walter Buenger notes that this opposition never coalesced into a unified or cohesive group. "Different interests and values," along with "culture, environment, and local self-interest" created "dissimilar attitudes." See Buenger, *Secession and the Union in Texas*, 8 (footnote quotations one through three). Some of the shatterbelt counties voting against secession included Uvalde, Medina, Mason, Gillespie, Blanco, Burnet, Jack, Montague, and Cooke.

3. McCaslin, "Great Hanging at Gainesville," Texas State Historical Association, *Handbook*, online (accessed May 23, 2009); Ralph A. Wooster, "Civil War," *Handbook*, online (accessed May 23, 2009).

4. Luckett to Bee, July 25, 1862, NA, RG109, DT, LR, Entry 106, Box 2, Folder 31 (quotations one through three); Bee to Davis, Oct. 15, 1862, NA, RG109, DT, LR, Entry 106, Box 2, Folder 40 (quotations four through six).

5. Bee to Davis, Oct. 15, 1862, NA, RG109, DT, LR, Entry 106, Box 2, Folder 40 (quotations one through three); "Battle of the Nueces," *Handbook*, online (accessed May 23, 2009); Holland to Walsh, Jan. 20, 1864, Rip Ford Papers, UDC Collection, Haley Library, Midland, Texas (RF), TCM94.1.0122a (quotations four through six). Although many Tejanos and Germans were ambivalent or opposed to the Confederacy, it should be noted that a number of them did serve in Confederate regiments during the war.

6. Walker to Boggs, Oct. 10, 1864, NA, RG109, District of Texas, New Mexico, and Arizona (TNMA), Letters Sent (LS), Ch. II, Vol. 123 (quotations one through six).

7. Reynolds to Culberson, May 5, 1864, Box (B) 401–386, Texas Adjutant General, Departmental Correspondence, Part 1, Texas State Library & Archives Commission (TAG) (quotation); Fossett to Barry, June 1, 1864, Box 2B42, J. B. Barry Papers, Center for American History, University of Texas at Austin (BB). Additional detail on Captains M. B. Loyd and R. M. Whiteside can be found in Riley to Loyd, Aug. 7, 1863 & Nicholas to Loyd, Aug. 14, 1863, both from Folder 5, B 401–830, and in Poll Book, Feb. 2, 1863, Folder 5, B 401–830, all from Texas State Troop Records, 1861–1865, Texas State Library & Archives Commission (TST).

8. John Chisum was a major cattle dealer in Texas and the Southwest for almost three decades until his death in 1884. For more information on Chisum, see Harwood P. Hinton, "John Simpson Chisum," *Handbook,* online (accessed Sept. 8, 2006).

9. After a stint in the Texas Rangers that ended in 1864, Charles Goodnight went on to become one of Texas's most popular and legendary cattlemen. He died in 1929. For information on Goodnight, see H. Allen Anderson, "Charles Goodnight," *Handbook,* online (accessed Sept. 8, 2006).

10. For those writers critical of the Rangers' Civil War record, see Rister, "Fort Griffin," *West Texas Historical Association Year Book,* 17; Mayhall, *Indian Wars of Texas,* 125; Fehrenbach, *Lone Star,* 365–8, 523. Authors supportive of the Rangers include Holden, "Frontier Problems and Movements in West Texas, 1846–1900," Ph.D. diss., 85, 104; Smith, *Frontier Defense in the Civil War,* 172; Oates, "Texas Under the Secessionists," *Southwestern Historical Quarterly,* 184; Richardson, *The Frontier of Northwest Texas,* 240; Roth, "Civil War Frontier Defense Challenges in Northwest Texas," *Military History of the West,* 23, 44. Roth claims that the Rangers outperformed federal soldiers stationed in antebellum Texas. Walter Prescott Webb devotes less than a page to the Civil War Texas Rangers. See Webb, *The Texas Rangers,* 219. Like Webb, Robert Utley also has little to say about the Civil War period in his study of the Rangers. Utley defers to David Paul Smith's work. See Utley, *Lone Star Justice,* 133, 324.

11. Van Dorn's General Orders No. 8, May 24, 1861, *The War of the Rebellion: A Compilation of the Official Records of the Union and Confederate Armies,* 70 vols. (Washington, D.C.: Government Printing Office, 1880–1901) (OR), Ser. 1, Vol. 1, 574 (quotation), 575–8; *Mesilla Times,* June 15, 1861. To accurately assess Civil War defense in western Texas, one must compare the position of rebel defensive lines in 1861 to their position in 1865. Any scholarly evaluation must be based upon Colonel Van Dorn's two defensive perimeters, which were officially adopted by Texas and the Confederacy in May 1861. In his study, David Paul Smith omits discussion of Van Dorn's second defensive line, stating that it falls outside the scope of his work. Next, Smith essentially bypasses Van Dorn's

first line of defense, offering instead his own definition of the defensive line for that section of Texas. See Smith, *Frontier Defense in the Civil War*, xiv, 170–1.

12. Walker to Hemphill and Oldham, April 1, 1861, OR, Ser. 1, Vol. 1, 620 (quotation).

13. Smith, *The U.S. Army & the Texas Frontier Economy, 1845–1900*, 3–11, 12 (quotation), 13. This legend that the Rangers successfully defended Texas without help from the federal government is part of the deeply ingrained myth of Texan independence and uniqueness. Texas won its independence from Mexico, was an independent republic (unlike most other states) for ten years, and could take care of itself without help from Uncle Sam. Similar in some respects to western states with a self-reliant streak, Texas has a long and ambivalent relationship with the federal government. On one hand, these states need federal aid; on the other hand, they chafe at federal regulations. The record shows that Texas not only required assistance from the U.S. Army to secure its borders but also needed bailouts from the U.S. Treasury to rescue it from bankruptcy upon admission to the Union and to stabilize its foundering economy during early statehood. The historical realities of this federal assistance, however, run directly counter to Texan identity.

14. Holden, "Frontier Problems," 103.

15. Ibid., 99–100 (quotation). The author uses the terms "Tories" and Unionists" interchangeably. Many Texas Unionists shared Governor Sam Houston's views that secession would be a mistake and that Texas should remain in the Union. Being a Unionist did not mean that one was pro-Northern or an abolitionist. A number of Lone Star Tories were simply anti-secessionist and preferred maintaining the antebellum status quo. Some Unionists were proud Texans but desired no part of the Civil War and preferred to be left alone. Tory-Unionist sentiment was strongest in the frontier counties in North Texas bordering the Red River and in the western Hill Country region. For more on Texas frontier loyalties and attitudes regarding secession, see Marten, *Texas Divided*; Pickering and Falls, *Brush Men and Vigilantes*; Smith, *Frontier Defense in the Civil War*; Buenger, *Secession and the Union in Texas*.

16. For more on this, see Ely, "What To Do About Texas," *New Mexico Historical Review*; Connor, *Texas*, 197; Richardson, *Texas*, 252; ibid., Eighth Edition, Richardson, Anderson, Wintz, and Wallace, 218; Calvert, De León, and Cantrell, *The History of Texas*, 140; Campbell, *Gone to Texas*, 252, 258; Townsend, *The Yankee Invasion of Texas*, 148; Dupree, *Planting the Union Flag in Texas*, 198; Thompson, ed., *New Mexico Territory During the Civil War*; Thompson, "Drama in the Desert," *Password*, 107–26; Hall, "The Formation of Sibley's Brigade and the March to New Mexico," in *Lone Star Blue and Gray*, 149; Wooster, *Texas and Texans in the Civil War*, 42. Thompson, Hall, and Wooster are among the few scholars that

discuss events in Texas's Trans-Pecos after 1862. Record Group 393 (Parts One through Five) at the National Archives contains hundreds of documents detailing Union military occupation and martial law in the Lone Star State west of the Pecos River. The Department of New Mexico garrisoned men at Franklin (El Paso) and San Elizario, Texas, and kept various pickets at Fort Quitman, Hueco Tanks, the Guadalupe Mountains, Pope's Crossing, and Horsehead Crossing (the latter two on the Pecos River).

17. Regarding the collapse of Texas's frontier perimeters and wartime depopulation, the various narratives, explanations, and in some cases, rationalizations discussed here reveal much about enduring strands of Lone Star identity.

18. Hyde to Hebert, Sept. 17, 1861, Archibald Hyde File, Confederate Papers Relating to Citizens or Business Firms, 1861–1865 (Confederate Citizen Files), NA, RG109, Microfilm Series (M) 346 (quotations one and two); Mills, *Forty Years at El Paso, 1858–1898*, 183. Fort Quitman details in Fort Bliss Quartermaster Returns, 1861, Box 401–836, TST. Perhaps Hyde found a receptive audience, for by the end of the year, the military was once again using Fort Quitman. In December 1861, El Paso contractor Simeon Hart delivered 21,000 pounds of flour and 5,000 pounds of corn meal for Sibley's Brigade to the Rio Grande outpost. That same month, James Magoffin (also from El Paso) supplied eighty tons of hay. From December 1861 to May 1862, John Forbes, J. Frank Swank, and Alvino Fernandez worked the Confederate cattle herd at Quitman. See NA, RG109, M346, Confederate Citizen Files for Simeon Hart, J. W. Magoffin, John Forbes, J. Frank Swank, and Alvino Fernandez.

19. U.S. Eighth Census, 1860 (C60), El Paso County, Texas, and Presidio County, Texas, NA, M653, Roll (R) 1293, 65–8 (Las Lympias), 68–71 (Fort Davis), 76–8, 80–1 (Fort Quitman), 78–80 (Camp Rice, Birchville, and Hawkins), 81–4 (Bosque Carmelo), 87 (Fort Stockton and Comanche), 88 (Wild Rose Pass). Also see Ely, "Riding the Butterfield Frontier: Life and Death Along the Butterfield Overland Mail Road in Texas, 1858–1861," Ph.D. diss., 270–2.

20. C60, Kinney County, Texas, NA, M653, R1299, 22 (Fort Clark). In 1860, the Brackett (now Brackettville) community adjacent to Fort Clark had twenty-eight non-military residents. Regarding wartime depopulation at Fort Clark, after 1862, the rebels garrisoned the outpost intermittently. Texas quartermaster files contain no records for the fort after December 1862, and the most of these reports are from 1861. In 1862, the Confederates also abandoned Fort Chadbourne, located on Van Dorn's first defensive line. There are no state records for Chadbourne after 1862, and the bulk of these are from 1861. See Texas State Troop Records, 1861-1865, Texas State Library and Archives Commission. For additional information on Fort Clark, see footnote 55. Even after Texas withdrew its military garrisons from Forts Chadbourne and Clark, Ranger patrols

occasionally camped at these deserted outposts. Regarding Confederate Quartermaster Records on Forts Chadbourne and Clark, see listings for each in NA, RG109, M346, Confederate Citizen Files. Listings for both posts do not go beyond December 1861.

21. Confederate agent Jarvis Hubbell stated that 100 Indians burned Fort Davis in August 1862. Hubbell, former El Paso County Surveyor, along with Edward Hall of Fort Leaton, Texas, and several men were at Fort Davis scavenging any military property "worth removing," just before and immediately after the conflagration. Hubbell's party found a group of sick rebel soldiers at the post and transported all but one of them, for care to Presidio del Norte, Mexico. Before Hubbell and Hall could return for the remaining wounded man, Indian raiders killed him. See Hubbell to Teel, Oct. 13, 1862, Jarvis Hubbell Confederate Citizen File, NA, RG109, M346 (footnote quotation). Union Lieutenant Albert H. French, visiting Fort Davis a month after Hubbell and Hall, reported that the outpost was burned *after* his men passed through in early September 1862 by spies in the employ of another Confederate agent, John Burgess of Presidio del Norte, Mexico. See French to West, Dec. 3, 1862, NA, RG94, Adjutant General's Office (AGO), LR, N446, 1862. See also Shirland to Cutler, Sept. 12, 1862, OR, Ser. 1, Vol. 9, 577–9; Bliss, *The Reminiscences of Major General Zenas R. Bliss*, eds. Smith, Thompson, Wooster, and Pingenot, 233 (quotation). Bliss was in command of Fort Quitman in April 1861 when the rebels took over. He also served at Fort Clark, Fort Stockton, Fort Davis, and Camp Hudson.

22. Fort Davis Quartermaster Returns, 1861, Box 401–837, TST; NA, RG109, M346, Confederate Citizen Files for Sam Smith, James Duff, A. Duclos, F. M. Joiner, Lewis Lee, John Burgess, Archibald Hyde, Jesus de la Garza, Daniel Murphy, Patrick Murphy, Moke & Brother, and John D. Holliday.

23. Fort Stockton Quartermaster Returns, 1861, Box 401–838, TST; Heartsill, *Fourteen Hundred and 91 Days in the Confederate Army*, 52 (Camp Hudson); Wooster, *History of Fort Davis, Texas*, 152-9, 160 (quotation one), 161–2, 163 (quotation two). For 1860 U.S. Army troop numbers for West Texas, see U.S. Senate. *Report of the Secretary of War*. 36th Congress, 2nd Session. 1860. Senate Exec. Doc. No. 1, Vol. 2, Serial 1079, 218–9.

24. Wilson, *When the Texans Came*, 288 (quotation), 291, 311–4.

25. Ibid., 291, 311 (quotation), 312–4.

26. For more on these various invasion plans, see Ely, "Skullduggery at Spencer's Ranch," *Journal of Big Bend Studies*, 23–9; Ely, "What To Do About Texas;" Finch, *Confederate Pathway to the Pacific*, 208–21, 279. In February 1863, James Wiley Magoffin, prominent El Paso County pioneer and secessionist, offered to serve as a supply contractor for a Confederate reinvasion of the southwest. Then in February 1864, he offered his services as a spy in the Trans-Pecos and

Mexico. In recommending Magoffin for the position, Major A.G. Dickinson said that despite Magoffin's age, he was worth twenty men. Dickinson boasted, "I'll warrant we know the movements and intentions of the enemy from the time he reaches El Paso." See Dickinson to Magruder, Feb. 11, 1864, J. W. Magoffin Confederate Citizen File, NA, RG109, M346 (footnote quotation).

27. Skillman left San Antonio for El Paso, Mexico, on October 18, 1862, and returned in late December. Regarding Skillman's wartime service, in January 1862 Texas Governor Francis Lubbock appointed Skillman to raise a regiment of frontier troops for El Paso and Presidio counties. During the first two months of 1862, Skillman (with his brother William) served as an army hay contractor for the Confederate invasion of New Mexico, supplying 150 tons of hay to Fort Bliss, Texas, and Fort Fillmore, New Mexico, for which he received $3,520. In May of the same year, Confederate General H. H. Sibley employed Skillman on a number of occasions to carry the army's mail from Fort Bliss to Fort Thorn, New Mexico, and Alamosa, New Mexico, for a total of $250 in courier fees. See Henry Skillman, Report of Scout to El Paso, contained in Gray to Dickinson, Dec. 31, 1862, Henry Skillman Confederate Citizen File, NA, RG109, M346; William D. Skillman Confederate Citizen File, NA, RG109, M346; Magruder to Cooper, Jan. 8, 1863, NA, RG109, TNMA, LS, Ch. II, Vol. 132; Carleton to Hoffman, June 27, 1864, NA, RG249, Office of the Commissary General of Prisoners, LR, 1864, C729; Special Orders No. 1, Jan. 4, 1862, NA, RG109, Misc. Special Orders, Adjutant General of Texas, 1862-1865, Ch. VIII, Vol. 277, 28. For more on Skillman and events in the Trans-Pecos during the war, see Ely, "Skullduggery at Spencer's Ranch;" Ely, "What To Do About Texas;" Thompson, "Drama in the Desert."

28. Banks to Carleton, Nov. 5, 1863, OR, Ser. 1, Vol. 26, Part I, 788.

29. Ford to Pyron, Jan. 20, 1864, RF, TCM94.1.0784; Ford to Turner, Jan. 22, 1864, OR, Ser. 1, Vol. 53, 952–3; Magruder to Ford, Jan. 29, 1864, NA, RG109, TNMA, LS, Ch. II, Vol. 126 (quotation).

30. Magruder to Ford, Jan. 29, 1864, Feb. 7, 1864, and Kirby Smith to Chief of Texas Cotton Bureau, Jan. 29, 1864, NA, RG109, TNMA, LS, Ch. II, Vol. 126; Merritt to Ford, Feb. 11, 1864, RF, TCM94.1.0707 (impressing horses for Skillman); Ford to Duff, Feb. 9, 1864, RF, TCM94.1.0443 (outfitting Skillman); Ford to Turner (Magruder's office), Feb. 8, 1864, RF, TCM94.1.0919b (quotation). State cartographer A.R. Roessler produced a series of maps from Skillman's scout entitled *Best Route for the Movement of Troops from San Antonio to El Passo [sic] Texas, Being the One Travelled [sic] by the State Geological Corps of Texas in 1860 and by Henry Skillman's Party in March 1864.* See Plats 1004 B and 1004 J, Map Collection. The accompanying narrative journal by Roessler is in folder T1-10-1 at the same archives.

31. Ely, "Skullduggery at Spencer's Ranch"; Magruder to Ford, Jan. 29, 1864, NA, RG109, TNMA, LS, Ch. II, Vol. 126 (quotation); Ford to Alexander, Jan. 24, 1864, RF, TCM94.1.0001; Ford to Riordan, Jan. 24, 1864, RF, TCM94.1.0196; Hutchison to Ford, Jan. 25, 1864, RF, TCM94.1.0124; Ford to Turner, Feb. 8, 1864, RF, TCM94.1.0919a-b; Ford to Turner, Feb. 15, 1864, OR, Ser. 1, Vol. 34, Pt. II, 968; ibid., Edgar to Ford, Feb. 23, 1864, 993. Fort Inge is near Uvalde, TX.

32. Carleton's proposed expedition with Banks never got beyond the planning stages. See Carleton to Halleck, March 20, 1864, OR, Ser. 1, Vol. 34, Pt. II, 671, 672 (quotation), 673. In 1863, Henry Skillman added veteran frontiersman and former stage driver Tom Rife to his spy company. In January of that year, Confederate military authorities placed Rife on temporary detached service from his cavalry unit as part of Skillman's group. The following year, General Magruder and Colonel Ford granted Rife a permanent assignment to the spy company. See John S. Ford, Special Order No. 19, Feb. 6, 1864, John S. Ford Special Order Book, TCM94.1.1096, RF; Thomas Rife, Jan. and Feb. 1864 Company Muster Rolls, March 1865 Regimental Return (detached service records), and Skillman to Ford, Feb. 4, 1864, from Thomas Rife, Confederate Compiled Service Record, NA, RG109, M323. See also, Thomas Rife Confederate Citizen File, NA, RG109, M346. Skillman's superiors kept his group busy throughout 1863. In November 1863, Major Andrew G. Dickinson sent two groups under Tom Rife and Skillman beyond the Pecos River to gather intelligence. See Dickinson to Turner, Nov. 23, 1863, in Andrew G. Dickinson Confederate Compiled Service Record, NA, RG109, M323; Miller to Angerstein, Dec. 13, 1863, and Angerstein to West, Dec. 15, 1863, NA, RG94, AGO, LR, M619, R283.

33. According to one of the survivors, the Spencer's Ranch ambush occurred a quarter of a mile from the Presidio del Norte, Mexico, crossing of the Rio Grande (near the present-day Catholic Church in Presidio, Texas). See statements of Skillman spy company prisoners Jarvis Hubbell, Peter Allen, John Dowling, and Winfield Scott Garner in Carleton to Hoffman, June 27, 1864, NA, RG249, Office of the Commissary General of Prisoners, LR, 1864, C729; Ely, "Skullduggery at Spencer's Ranch," 26-9.

34. Smith, *Frontier Defense*, 150.

35. Diamond to Steele, March 3, 1863, OR, Ser. 1, Vol. 22, Pt. II, 800 (quotation one); Hudson to Dashiell, Feb. 22, 1863, B 401–826, TST (quotation two); ibid., March 8, 1863.

36. Bourland to McCulloch, Dec. 24, 1863, OR, Ser. 1, Vol. 26, Pt. II, 531; Rushing to Lubbock, Aug. 12, 1863, Box 2B42, BB; Hale to Bourland, Jan. 11, 1864, OR, Ser. 1, Vol. 34, Pt. II, 911 (quotation).

37. Barry quoted in Wilbarger, *Indian Depredations in Texas*, 452 (quotation one); Cates, *Pioneer History of Wise County*, 127 (quotation two); Miller, *Pioneering*

North Texas, 70 (quotation three); Wheeler, "Clay County," *Handbook*, online (accessed July 30, 2005). In gauging the exact extent of this depopulation, the researcher must be careful not to compare 1870 federal census figures to those for 1860. One needs to remember that in late 1866 and throughout 1867, the U.S. Army re-garrisoned much of West Texas. The presence of federal troops, therefore, encouraged many settlers to move back to the frontier prior to the 1870 census. For federal re-garrisoning dates in Texas, see Frazer, *Forts of the West*, 139–64.

38. Young County Commissioners Court Minutes, April 10, 1865 (quotation one); Leffler, "Young County," *Handbook*, online (accessed July 30, 2005); McConnell, *The West Texas Frontier*, Vol. II, 148; Orrick to Quayle, Sept. 27, 1864, B 401-387, TAG (quotations two and three). Orrick resigned his captaincy in Jack County soon after abandoning his frontier homestead, and officials accepted his resignation effective Oct. 1, 1864. See Special Orders No. 498, Oct. 18, 1864, NA, RG109, Misc. Special Orders, Adj. Gen. of Texas, 1862–1865, Ch. VIII, Vol. 277, 468.

39. Echoing the point previously discussed in footnote thirteen, a subtext of this anti-depopulation argument is deeply rooted in Lone Star identity, intertwined with myths about "Texan uniqueness" and the Texas Rangers. The historical record shows that Texas, as a republic and a state, could not prevent the Mexican Army or Native Americans from raiding its territory. Ultimately, to secure its borders Texas required the services of the U.S. Army. For more on Texan military forces during the Republic period, see Haynes, *Soldiers of Misfortune*. Even today, the Texas Rangers' prowess remains legendary, as exemplified in a May 2009, Interstate 35 billboard promoting the Texas Ranger Hall of Fame and Museum in Waco. The billboard reads, "One Riot, One Ranger." In other words, it takes only one Ranger to contain an entire riot. According to the Hall of Fame website, "Time and again they [Rangers] proved that one person in the right could triumph over even the greatest odds." Footnote quotation from http://texasranger.org/store/Productpages/AmericaRemembers.htm (accessed May 22, 2009). For more on "forting up," see McConnell, *The West Texas Frontier*, Vol. I, 169, 190, 198; McConnell, *The West Texas Frontier*, Vol. II, 119, 157; Caldwell, *Fort Davis*.

40. McConnell, *The West Texas Frontier*, Vol. II, 124 (quotations one and two). Peter Allen, part of Henry Skillman's rebel spy party traveling from San Antonio to the Trans-Pecos in March 1864, observed, "There are very few people on the frontiers of Texas." See Peter E. Allen statement in Carleton to Hoffman, June 27, 1864, NA, RG249, Office of the Commissary General of Prisoners, LR, 1864, C729 (footnote quotation).

41. Buck Barry account in Wilbarger, *Indian Depredations in Texas*, 452 (quotations one and two); Ford, *Rip Ford's Texas*, 349 (quotation three).

42. Bankhead to Turner, Aug. 16, 1863, OR, Ser. 1, Vol. 53, 890 (quotation).
43. Bourland to McCulloch, Nov. 10, 1863, Box 2B44, BB; Bourland to McCulloch, April 25, 1864, OR, Ser. 1, Vol. 34, Pt. III, 792; See to Barry, Nov. 1, 1863, Box 2B44, BB (quotation one); Throckmorton to Murrah, March 28, 1864, B 301–45, Texas Governor Pendleton Murrah Records, Texas State Library and Archives Commission (PM) (quotation two).
44. McCulloch to Turner, Nov. 1, 1863, OR, Ser. 1, Vol. 26, Pt. II, 378–9; McCulloch to Magruder, Jan. 23, 1864, OR, Ser. 1, Vol. 34, Pt. II, 909 (quotations one and two); McCulloch to Turner, Jan. 6, 1864, OR, Ser. 1, Vol. 53, 924 (quotation three); McCulloch to Turner, April 16, 1864, OR, Ser. 1, Vol. 34, Pt. III, 771-2; McCulloch to Slaughter, May 28, 1864, OR, Ser. 1, Vol. 34, Pt. IV, 635 (quotation four).
45. McCulloch to Kirby Smith, Feb. 5, 1864, OR, Ser. 1, Vol. 34, Pt. II, 945 (quotations one through three); McCulloch to Turner, April 6, 1864, OR, Ser. 1, Vol. 34, Pt. III, 742.
46. Magruder to Kirby Smith, Dec. 24, 1863, OR, Ser. 1, Vol. 26, Pt. II, 529 (quotation one), 530; Magruder to Murrah, April 2, 1864, OR, Ser. 1, Vol. 34, Pt. III, 739 (quotation two).
47. Erath to Culberson, Oct. 4, 1864, B 401–387, TAG; Erath to Murrah, March 20, 1864, B 301–45, PM.
48. Erath to Culberson, June 30, 1864, B 401–387, TAG (quotation one); Callan to Murrah, Feb. 15, 1865, Box 2B41, Frontier Protection Records, Center for American History, University of Texas at Austin (FP) (quotations two and three). In 1852, the U.S. Army established Camp J.E. Johnston, a temporary outpost and predecessor of Fort Chadbourne, on the south bank of the North Concho River. Soldiers abandoned Camp Johnston in October 1852. In 1858 and again in 1867, the U.S. Army stationed troops at Camp Concho, also on the North Concho River in the same vicinity. The Texas Rangers' Camp Concho, however, was at a different location to the southwest on the Middle Concho River near present-day Arden, Texas. Here the Butterfield Overland Road merged with the Upper Emigrant Road from San Antonio and Fredericksburg. At this strategic location, Rangers could monitor wartime traffic on both trails. See Camp Concha [sic] Quartermaster Returns, 1861, Box 401-835, TST. Author field trips to Camp J. E. Johnston and Camp Concho on the North Concho, June 20, 2004, with Patrick Dearen, Joe Allen, and landowners; Feb. 9, 2008, with Garland and Lana Richards, and landowners; Ely, "Riding the Butterfield Frontier," 162–3.
49. Major J. M. Brown report, no date, Folder 18, B 401–827, TST (quotations one and two).
50. Hurman to Walthersdorff, Jan. 24, 1864, RF, TCM94.1.956 (quotation one); Hurman to Walthersdorff, Feb. 17, 1864, RF, TCM94.1.966; Casner to Hurman,

Jan. 24, 1864, RF, TCM94.1.58; Ford to Turner, Jan. 28, 1864, RF, TCM94.1.912 a-b; Walthersdorff to Ford, Jan. 26, 1864, RF, TCM94.1.958 (quotations two and three). According to David Paul Smith, the terms "jayhawker" and "bushwhacker" referred to renegades and disloyal Unionists in Texas. Some of these persons also rode with raiding Indians and committed depredations on the frontier. Smith, *Frontier Defense*, footnote 3, 195–6.

51. Wupperman to Schmitz, Feb. 2, 1865, B 401–387, TAG (quotation); ibid., Robison to Schmitz, Feb. 3, 1865.

52. McAdoo to Culberson, Sept. 15, 1864, B 401–387, TAG (quotation).

53. Holland to Murrah, April 18, 1864, B 301–45, PM (quotations one and two); ibid., Hunter to Murrah, March 31, 1864, (quotation three).

54. Moore, Doss, Holland, and Stengart to Murrah, June 7, 1864, B 401–829, TST (quotations two and three); Brown to Walsh, April 5, 1865, B 401–387, TAG; Special Orders No. 485, July 1, 1864, Misc. Special Orders, Adj. Gen. of Texas, 1862–1865, NA, RG109, Ch. VIII, Vol. 277, 458 (quotation one).

55. Riordan to Ford, Feb. 5, 1864, RF, TCM94.1.0197 (quotation one); Austerman, *Sharps Rifles and Spanish Mules*, 188 (quotation two).

56. McKinney et al. to Murrah, May 2, 1864, B 301–45, PM; ibid., McKinney to Murrah, June 15, 1864 (quotations one and two).

57. Lockhart to Dickinson, May 11, 1864, OR, Ser. 1, Vol. 34, Pt. III, 818 (quotation one); ibid., Edgar to Dickinson, May 11, 1864, 817 (quotation two).

58. McCord to Magruder, May 2, 1864, OR, Ser. 1, Vol. 34, Pt. III, 803 (quotations one and two).

59. *Mesilla Times*, May 17, 1861; ibid., June 8, 1861 (quotation).

60. Mills to Father, Dec. 26, 1862, and Mills to Anson Mills, Sept. 25, 1863, Rex Strickland Papers; Stanfield to Murrah, Dec. 19, 1864, B 301–45, PM (quotations one and two).

61. Barry, *Buck Barry*, 172, 173 (quotation).

62. Fossett to Barry, June 1, 1864, Box 2B42, BB.

63. Texas refugee discussion in Carleton to Bowie, July 6, 1864, Carleton to Thomas, Aug. 6, 1864, Carleton to Fort Marcy, Aug. 7, 1864, all from NA, RG393, Letters Sent, Department of New Mexico, (LSNM), M1072, R3. Spy question raised in Kimmey to Carleton, Dec. 12, 1863, LRNM, Box K 28, 1864; McCulloch to Turner, March 15, 1864, OR, Ser. 1, Vol. 34, Pt. II, 1045.

64. French to Cutler, May 24, 1864, LRNM, M1120, R22 (quotation). Private Bernard Timmins reenlisted in the Veteran Volunteer unit at Franklin, Texas, on Feb. 26, 1864. See Orton, *Records of California Men in the War of the Rebellion*, 708.

65. Sept. 19, 1864 Descriptive List of Texas Deserters, LRNM, M1120, R22; Statements of Henry Riley (quotation one) and Isaac Knight (quotation two),

Examination of Texan Refugees, Oct. 20–22, 1864, NA, RG393, Pt. 1, Dept. of New Mexico, Entry 3161, Misc. LR, 1863–1865.

66. June 10, 1865 List of Texas Refugees, LRNM, M1120, R26; Bowie to Carleton, July 8, 1864, LRNM, M1120, R22.

67. "Comanche County Texas, to California in 1864," in Reed, *Old Time Cattlemen and Other Pioneers of the Anza-Borrego Area*, 3 (quotations one through three); Dean Chenoweth, "Deserter's Diary Tells of Passing Through Here," *San Angelo Standard Times*, Jan. 25, 1970.

68. Reed, "Comanche County Texas, to California in 1864," 4; Chenoweth, "Deserter's Diary;" C60, Titus County, Texas, NA, M653, R1305, 166; C60, Comanche County, Texas, NA, M653, R1289, 253; C60, Denton County, Texas, NA, M653, R1292, 433; United States Ninth Census, 1870 (C70), Titus County, Texas, NA, M593, R1606, 84, 120; C70, San Diego County, California, NA, M593, R78, 526. Llano Estacado Station in Upton County, Texas, is located on the north bank of Centralia Draw, two miles east of the Upton and Reagan county line. Author field trips to Llano Estacado Station, 1998–2006, with Roland Ely, Patrick Dearen, Hal Joyce, Joe Allen, and landowner.

69. Williams, *With the Border Ruffians*, 363, 364 (quotation); Erath to Adjutant General, Feb. 2, 1865, B 401–387, TAG; ibid., Barry to Adjutant General, Jan. 20, 1865.

70. Ibid., (quotation); Callan to Murrah, Feb. 15, 1865, Box 2B41, FP (nine men in federal uniforms arrested).

71. William Franks is among fifteen Texas refugees listed in a July 20, 1864 entry, NA, RG 393, Pt. 1, Dept. of New Mexico, Entry 3214, Provost Marshal, Vol. 121/298 NMEX. See also NA, RG205, Claims Section of the Department of Justice, Cong. Jur. 5622, William C. Franks & Sadie Franks, adm. of James Patterson, tabbed, Box 171, 20W4/21/16/04 (PF); ibid., Record Group 205, Claims Section of the Department of Justice, Cong. Jur. 5623, James Patterson, tabbed, Box 171, 20W4/21/16/04; ibid., RG205, Claims Section of the Department of Justice, Cong. Jur. 10323, William C. Franks, tabbed, Box 301, 20W4/21/19/01. Capt. Thomas L. Roberts enlisted in Co. E, 1st California Infantry, on Aug. 26, 1861, and mustered out on Sept. 13, 1864. See Orton, *Records of California Men*, 354.

72. Carleton to McCleave, July 11, 1865 (quotation), and Carleton to Shoemaker, Sept. 2, 1865, LSNM, M1072, R3.

73. Erath To Culberson, Oct. 4, 1864, B 401–387, TAG; ibid., McAdoo to Culberson, Oct. 20, 1864; Bourland to McCulloch, April 25, 1864, OR, Ser. 1, Vol. 34, Pt. III, 792 (quotation).

74. Bowie to Carleton, June 17, 1864, NA, RG393, LRNM, Box B 259, 1864 (eight cents); NA, RG393, Pt. 1, Dept. of New Mexico, Endorsements Sent, Aug. 23, 1864, Book No. 31 NMEX (22 cents).

75. Kenner, "The Origins of the 'Goodnight' Trail Reconsidered," *Southwestern Historical Quarterly*, 390–4; James Cox, *Historical and Biographical Record of the Cattle Industry and the Cattlemen of Texas and Adjacent Territory*, 478; Haley, *Charles Goodnight*, 120–61; Goodnight, "The Goodnight Trail" manuscript, 3 (quotation one), and "Managing a Trail Herd" manuscript, 1 (quotation two), both manuscripts from J. Evetts Haley Collection; Dearen, *A Cowboy of the Pecos*, 43. In his biography, Goodnight discusses his numerous business dealings with James Patterson and John Chisum but says these all took place after the Civil War. Goodnight also claims that he drove cattle to Fort Sumner before Chisum. Regarding Chisum and other contemporaries of Goodnight, in some of Haley's interviews with Goodnight, conducted during the rancher's later years, it is clear that Goodnight is thinking of posterity and his place in the pantheon of legendary Texas cattlemen. See Haley, *Charles Goodnight*, 203–7, 232–5.

76. Kennedy to Pyron, Feb. 20, 1865, OR, Ser. 1, Vol. 53, 1046 (quotation).

77. Brig. Gen. H. P. Bee, General Order No. 6, Feb. 13, 1863, NA, RG109, TNMA, LR, Entry 110, 1862-1865, Box 1 (banning horses and cattle crossing the Rio Grande from Texas without a permit). Despite Bee's order, the trade with Mexico continued. In August 1864 Confederate Brigadier General P. O. Hebert reaffirmed the ban on Texas cattle crossing into Mexico without special authorization. Hebert's order also proved unenforceable. See General Orders No. 164, Aug. 20, 1864, TNMA, 1864 General Orders File from District Headquarters, RF, TCM94.1.1097. Interestingly, some Texans were also conducting a considerable hog trade with Mexico. Pork buyers in Mexico paid in hard cash (specie), not Confederate paper. Colonel John "Rip" Ford ordered the immediate cessation of this trade and all hogs impressed. See Ford to Turner, Jan. 15, 1864, Ford to Commanding Officer at Eagle Pass, Jan. 20, 1864; Ford to Benavides, Jan. 22, 1864; and Ford to Benavides, Ware, and Giddings, Feb. 4, 1864, John S. Ford Letter Book No. 1, RF, TCM94.1.1101; Ford to Slaughter, Aug. 19, 1864, John S. Ford Letter Book No. 2, RF, TCM94.1.1105. In addition Ford reported a thriving Texas trade with the enemy and Mexico that was occurring between the Nueces River and the Rio Grande. Ordering the arrest of those involved, the colonel observed, "Men who furnish the Yankees are aiding and abetting the enemies of our country, and are committing treason. Such men cannot claim to be our friends." See Ford to Turner, Feb. 8, 1864, Ford to Ware, Feb. 15, 1864, and Ford to Rogers, Feb. 15, 1864 (footnote quotation)—all from John S. Ford Letter Book No. 1, RF, TCM94.1.1101; Callaghan to Hyllested, Feb. 10, 1864, RF, TCM94.1.0023 and Inspector General's Office-Brownsville to Ford, Dec. 4, 1864, RF, TCM94.1.0854.

78. Smith, *From the Cow Camp to the Pulpit*, 88–117; Hinton, "John Simpson Chisum, 1877–1884," *New Mexico Historical Review*, 187; Four author interviews

with Hinton: *The Home Front: Life in Texas During the Civil War* documentary (Fort Worth: www.texashistory.com, 1996), Jan. 27, 2005, March 29, 2005, and Dec. 23, 2005; Letter to Murrah, March 18, 1864, B 301–45, PM (quotation); Cox, *Historical and Biographical Record*, 300–1 (Cox says the Confederate government paid Chisum $40 per head). Additional Chisum information from: Denton County, Texas Tax Rolls 1860–1867, Texas State Library & Archives Commission.

79. McCulloch to Murrah, March 20, 1864, B 301–45, PM (quotation); PF, 69.

80. McCulloch to Murrah, March 20, 1864, B 301–45, PM; ibid., Williams to Murrah, April 2, 1864 (quotation).

81. Smith, *From the Cow Camp,* 88–117, 102; List of Texan Refugees, June 10, 1865, LRNM, M1120, R26.

82. Smith, *From the Cow Camp*, 88–117, 102 (quotation); List of Texan Refugees, June 10, 1865, LRNM, M1120, R26.

83. Smith, *From the Cow Camp*, 102; Dove Creek-Chisum ranch information from J. Evetts Haley interview with Charles Goodnight, Aug. 2, 1928, "Three Goodnight Trails" Manuscript, J. Evetts Haley Collection, 26–7; Kelton, "Battle of Dove Creek," *Handbook*, online (accessed May 26, 2009).

84. Smith, *From the Cow Camp*, 102–5. Smith says his first drive for Patterson was to Fort Yuma, but this is too far a distance. More likely the trip was to El Paso, where Smith's name appears on the June 10, 1865 list of deserters cited earlier.

85. The Texas cattle drives to Fort Sumner continued throughout 1865, after Texas's surrender and still prior to Goodnight and Loving's first drive to New Mexico in the summer of 1866. Robert Wylie began working for Patterson-Franks in June 1865. See Hinton, "Wylie, Robert Kelsey," *Handbook*, online (accessed March 30, 2005). Thomas Murray joined Patterson and Franks in July 1865. See Testimony of Thomas Murray, PF (quotation); ibid., testimony of P.M. Chisum.

86. Gray, *Into the Setting Sun*, 15–6 (quotation one); Cox, *Historical and Biographical Record*, 301; Clarke, *John Simpson Chisum*, 24; "The Casey Family," Letter from Mrs. L. C. Klasner to J. Evetts Haley, March 4, 1933, J. Evetts Haley Collection, (quotation two).

87. Regarding Messrs. Glynn, Patterson, and the old Whitlock Mill near Ft. Stanton, see Smith to Cutler, Dec. 30, 1863, NA, RG393, Pt. 5, LS, Fort Stanton, New Mexico; McCabe to Fort Stanton, NM, Oct. 14, 1864, LRNM, M1120, R26 (quotations one and two). Indians raided livestock from Patterson's Tularosa sawmill in April 1864. See Smith to Commander, Fort Stanton, NM, April 24, 1864, LRNM, M1120, R25. Patterson's sawmill (the old Whitlock Mill) at Tularosa may be the same one that Dr. J. H. Blazer purchased in 1866. Blazer's Mill was later the scene of a bloody gunfight on April 4, 1878, involving Billy the Kid. See Sonnichsen, *Tularosa*, 10, 15; Rickards, *The Gunfight at Blazer's Mill*.

88. Conwell to Carleton, Dec. 3, 1864, NA, RG393, Pt. 1, LRNM, Box C 353, 1864; Special Orders No. 37, June 21, 1864, NA, RG393, Pt. 5, Fort Bliss, Texas, Entry 18, General Orders, Box 9; Barry to Adjutant General, Jan. 20, 1865, B 401–387, TAG.

89. Motheral to Erath, April 17, 1864, B 401–830, TST (quotation two); Bourland to McCulloch, April 13, 1864, OR, Ser. 1, Vol. 34, Pt. III, 773 (quotation one), 774; McCulloch to Slaughter, May 28, 1864, OR, Ser. 1, Vol. 34, Pt. IV, 634–5. Some of the reports misspell J. W. Robbins' name. Robbins served as Jack County Judge from February 1863 until the spring of 1864.

90. Hunter to Murrah, March 20, 1865, B 301–46, PM; ibid., Walker to Murrah, March 16, 1865; Murrah to Walker, March 20, 1865, B 301–47, PM; Walker to Slaughter, Oct. 10, 1864, NA, RG109, TNMA, LS, Ch. II, Vol. 123 (Mexico cattle speculation); Special Orders No. 13, Dec. 19, 1864, NA, RG109, Ch. VIII, Vol. 277, Misc. Special Orders, Adjutant General of Texas, 1862–1865, 478; ibid., Special Orders No. 21, Jan. 19, 1865, 483. Ironically, enemy reports substantiate Major Hunter's claim that John Burgess lied. Carleton's agent in Chihuahua, U.S. Consul Reuben Creel, wrote in November 1864 that "Burgess has lately sent into Texas some of his comrades and they have returned [to Presidio del Norte] with 850 head of fine cattle." Hunter claimed that he sold his entire herd of roughly 800 cattle to Burgess. Burgess, a fervent Lone Star secessionist from the Big Bend, lived at Presidio del Norte and aided Skillman's spy activities. See Burgess to Scurry, March 17, 1863, OR, Ser. 5, Vol. 15, 1065. Creel had several Union agents in the del Norte region, notably Milton Faver and William Hagelseib. See Creel to Carleton, Nov. 10, 1864, LRNM, M1120, R23 (footnote quotation).

91. See footnote 77 for more on these orders. See also Magruder to Boggs, Nov. 8, 1863, NA, RG109, TNMA, LS, Ch. II, Vol. 122 (quotation one); McAdoo to Murrah, Dec. 24, 1864, B 301–46, PM (quotations two and three); ibid., H.A. Mitchell letter, Dec. 12, 1864.

92. Walker to Boggs, Oct. 10, 1864, NA, RG109, TNMA, LS, Ch. II, Vol. 123 (quotation). In January 1864, when General Magruder bankrolled Henry Skillman's spy mission, he sold Texas cotton in Mexico to raise $500 in specie. In order to buy supplies and pay informants, Skillman needed hard cash, as Confederate paper was widely shunned. See Magruder to Kirby Smith, Jan. 29, 1864 and Kirby Smith to Magruder, Jan. 29, 1864, NA, RG109, TNMA, LS, Ch. II, Vol. 126.

93. O.S. Nichols letter to J. Evetts Haley, May 16, 1927, "Trail Trip to Mexico, 1864," J. Evetts Haley Collection, 1–2, 3 (quotations one through three), 4. Nichols received an average of $15 dollars per head, paid in Mexican silver. Mexican officials collected a tax of thirty-five cents per head.

94. Throckmorton to Walsh, Feb. 23, 1865, B 401–387, TAG; Hunter, ed., *The Trail Drivers of Texas*, 372.

95. Throckmorton to Murrah, April 5, 1865, B 301–46, PM (quotations one through three).

96. Reynolds to Culberson, May 5, 1864, B 401–386, TAG (quotation).

97. Texas Historical Commission, *Texas Historic Sites Atlas*, THC Marker No. 5177, Irion County, "Texas Civil War Indian Troubles," online (accessed November 3, 2007) (quotation).

98. Across the state, six road signs erected by counties and the Texas Historical Commission commemorate this well-known Old West cattle route. All of these markers tell the same story, namely, that Charles Goodnight and Oliver Loving laid out this trail in 1866. See Texas Historical Commission, *Texas Historic Sites Atlas*, THC Marker No. 2564, Pecos County, "Horsehead Crossing on the Pecos River," online (accessed November 3, 2007). The remaining Goodnight-Loving Cattle Trail references appear on THC markers #813, 814, 13753, 2565, and 2567.

99. To report an error regarding a state historical marker, the Texas Historical Commission provides an online error link for every marker listed in its *Texas Historic Sites Atlas*, online (accessed November 14, 2007).

CHAPTER 3

1. Author interview with Jesús F. de la Teja, San Marcos, Texas, Dec. 4, 2006; author interview with Robert Wooster, Corpus Christi, Texas, Dec. 5, 2006; author interview with Jerry Thompson, Laredo, Texas, Dec. 5, 2006. This chapter is dedicated to the memory of Joe Primera of Fort Stockton, local historian and friend to many, who passed away in 2008.

2. Flores, "Memory-Place, Meaning, and the Alamo," *American Literary History*, 437 (quotation); De León, *They Called Them Greasers*, 17.

3. Flores, "Memory-Place," 441–2; De León, *They Called Them Greasers*, 77–9; Montejano, *Anglos and Mexicans in the Making of Texas, 1836–1986*, 24, 26–7, 28 (quotation).

4. Flores, "Memory-Place," 441, 442 (quotation); James E. Crisp, "An Incident in San Antonio," *Journal of the West*, 73; Montejano, *Anglos and Mexicans*, 225.

5. Crisp, "An Incident," 73 (quotation); García, *Desert Immigrants*, 1, 4; Montejano, *Anglos and Mexicans*, 104.

6. Referring to Richard White's book, *The Middle Ground*, as discussed in Chapter One; de la Teja Interview; Thompson interview; Wooster interview; Limerick, *The Legacy of Conquest*, 240 (quotations one through three). Historically, the West Texas cities of San Angelo, Midland/Odessa, Amarillo, and Lubbock

are somewhat different in that Anglos have always been the majority population. Today, demographics west of the 100th meridian are rapidly changing,
with increasing Tejano majorities in county after county.

7. United States Eighth Census, 1860 (C60), El Paso County, and Presidio Coun-
ty, Texas (including future Pecos County), Microfilm Series (M) 653, Roll (R)
1293; U.S. Ninth Census, 1870 (C70), Presidio County, Texas (including fu-
ture Pecos County) M593, R1601; C70, El Paso County, Texas, M593, R1583;
U.S. Tenth Census, 1880 (C80), Pecos County, Texas, MT9, R1323; C80, El
Paso County, Texas, MT9, R1301; Twelfth U.S. Census, 1900 (C1900), Pecos
County, Texas, MT623, R1664; C1900, El Paso County, Texas, MT623, R1630;
Wooster, *Frontier Crossroads*, 125, 144; Martínez, *The Chicanos of El Paso*, 18-27;
M. R. González interview, Fort Stockton, Texas, Nov. 17, 2005 (quotation).

8. As cited in footnote 7: C60, Presidio County (including future Pecos County)
and El Paso County; C70, Presidio County (including future Pecos County)
and El Paso County; C80, Pecos and El Paso counties; C1900, Pecos and El
Paso counties; Wooster, *Frontier Crossroads*, 125, 144; Martínez, *The Chicanos
of El Paso*, 18–27; Daggett, *Pecos County History,* Vol. 2, 180–9; Tijerina, *History
of Mexican Americans in Lubbock County, Texas*, 12–3.

9. Pascoe, *What Comes Naturally*, 5–9, 42-3, 63, 243, 311 (quotation); *El Paso Times*,
Oct. 7, 1893, Oct. 8, 1893, Oct. 10, 1893, cited in De León, *Apuntes Tejanos*, Vol. 2,
185-6. In 1942 Abilene, Texas, passed a law banning whites and blacks from having sex or cohabitating. Any such offense was subject to a fine of not more than
$100. It is unclear exactly when the city repealed this law. See Mary McMullen,
"You've Come a Long Way, Baby," *Abilene Reporter-News*, April 12, 1981.

10. Daggett, ed. *Pecos County History*, Vol. 1, 108–10; Pecos County Commissioners Court Minutes, 1875–87; ibid., April 12, 1875; ibid., June 4, 1875; ibid., Sept.
27, 1875; ibid., January Term, 1876.

11. Daggett, *Pecos County*, Vol. 1, 110–7; Pecos County Commissioners Court Minutes 1875–1970; Fort Stockton City Minutes 1910–1955; Thompson, *History of
Marfa and Presidio County, Texas*, Vol. 2, 546.

12. García, *Desert Immigrants*, 160–1; Martínez, *The Chicanos of El Paso*, 18–9; De
León, *San Angeleños*, 28 (quotation). In other parts of West Texas, Mexican
American populations were smaller. Tejanos in Abilene, Midland/Odessa, Lub-
bock, and Amarillo typically had little political representation until after World
War II.

13. González interviews, Fort Stockton, Texas, Nov. 17, 2005 (quotations one and
two), and Oct. 14, 2007. As cited in Chapter One, many of those moving to
the High Plains and Trans-Pecos sections of West Texas after the 1880s were
from East Texas and the South. Southern majorities accrued more rapidly in
the Rolling Plains than in other areas lying west of the 100th meridian. This

demographic shift in West Texas made southern life ways and worldviews one of the region's dominant cultures from the 1890s until the 1980s when the population began changing once again. For more on this southern Anglo migration to West Texas, see Kerr, "Migration into Texas, 1860–1880," *Southwestern Historical Quarterly*, 184–216; Jordan, "A Century and a Half of Ethnic Change in Texas, 1836–1896," *Southwestern Historical Quarterly*, 385–422; Buenger, *The Path to a Modern South*, 148–50.

14. Tijerina, *Tejanos and Texans under the Mexican Flag, 1821–1836*, 137–9; de la Teja interview (quotations one and two).

15. González interviews, Nov. 17, 2005 (quotations one through three), and Oct. 14, 2007; Flores, "The Good Life the Hard Way," Ph.D. diss., 29, 31 (quotation four).

16. Pecos County Commissioners Court Minutes 1875-1918; author interviews with Joe Primera, Fort Stockton, Texas, Nov. 17, 2005, and Oct. 14, 2007; author interview with Pete Terrazas, Fort Stockton, Texas, May 6, 2002; González 2005 interview (quotation). In West Texas the state poll tax limited black and Tejano voting. African Americans could not vote during the first half of the twentieth century in the Democratic primary. Tejanos could vote in the primary in some areas but were kept out in other areas. The white primary was enforced in Lubbock and probably in some other areas of the South Plains and Rolling Plains for blacks.

17. Story from the *Eagle Pass Guide* quoted in the *El Paso Times*, April 11, 1889, cited in De León, *Apuntes Tejanos*, Vol. 2, 160 (quotation one); ibid., 159, citing *El Paso Times*, April 10, 1889 (quotation two); ibid., 174, citing *El Paso Times*, July 24, 1892 (quotation three). Anglo manipulation of the Hispanic vote in El Paso County and Mexico started in the 1850s and continued well after the Civil War. For more on El Paso's Election Ring in the antebellum period, see Ely, "Riding the Western Frontier," Ph.D. diss., 277–83. For more on the post-bellum election ring, see García, *Desert Immigrants*, 155–62.

18. Primera 2005 interview (quotations one and two).

19. González 2005 interview (quotation), Primera 2005 interview.

20. Pecos County Justice of the Peace Inquest Book, Nov. 9, 1912 (quotations one and two); George, *Roundup of Memories*, 181 (quotations three and four); González 2005 interview; Primera 2005 interview.

21. Pecos County Justice of the Peace Inquest Book, Nov. 9, 1912 (quotations one and two); ibid., June 4, 1917 (quotation three); ibid., June 30, 1924 (quotation four); ibid., Jan. 13, 1926 (quotation five); González 2005 interview; Primera 2005 interview.

22. Primera 2005 interview (quotation one); George, *Roundup*, 188 (quotation two); Daggett, *Pecos County*, Vol. 2, 418 (Royal assassination).

23. Stewart and De León, *Not Enough Room*, 29 (quotation); García, *Desert Immigrants*, 5.

24. Terrazas interview (quotation).

25. Pecos County Commissioners Court, January 1914 Term (quotation one); Fort Stockton City Council Minutes for July 28, 1925 (quotation two), April 12, 1927, and April 24, 1928.

26. Flores, "The Good Life," 115–9; *Fort Stockton Pioneer*, April 16, 1908 (Sheffield killing quotation), June 11, 1908 (Polecat quotation), Dec. 3, 1908 (Mexican sheepherder quotations), May 14, 1908 (mad dog quotation).

27. Blight, *Race and Reunion*, 391 (quotation).

28. Martínez, *Mexican-Origin People in the United States*, 65 (quotation one); Montoya, "Chicana/o Desegregation Cases," The University of Dayton School of Law, online (accessed May 20, 2007), (quotation two); Shorr, "Thorns in the Roses," in *Law in the Western United States,* 522–8.

29. White, *Rope and Faggot*, 237–8, 269 (quotations one and two); author interview with Bruce Glasrud, Austin, Texas, March 26, 2009 (quotation three); Glasrud, Carlson, with Kriedler, eds. *Slavery to Integration*, 22 (quotation four); Estes, "An Historical Survey of Lynchings in Oklahoma and Texas," M.A. thesis, 125, 135–40, 141 (1910 Rocksprings lynching), 142–6.

30. Glasrud, *Slavery to Integration*, 22 (quotation one); Steglich, "Population Trends," in *A History of Lubbock*, 445 (quotation two); Timmons, *El Paso*, 188 (quotation three), 188–9 (quotation four).

31. Miller, "Resisting the Ku Klux Klan in El Paso," *Password*, 19–26. Quotation one from Feb. 19, 1923, *Greater El Paso* campaign newspaper reproduced on page 21 of article. See also Christian, *Black Soldiers in Jim Crow Texas, 1899–1917*, 58 (quotation two); Raper, *The Tragedy of Lynching*, 345 (quotations three and four). One glaring exception to El Paso's milder racial climate was a violent confrontation during January 1916. Events related to the Mexican Revolution sparked the outburst, after *Villistas* killed sixteen American mining engineers in Chihuahua. When the bodies arrived in El Paso, local whites went on a bloody rampage. Law enforcement officials quickly suppressed the violence. Mayor Tom Lea worried that if police did not control the angry mob, Anglos would kill every Mexican in the city's barrio. See Timmons, *El Paso*, 221. In addition, there are two documented lynchings for El Paso County, one black and the other white. It is possible that the "white" victim was Hispanic. See Estes, "An Historical Survey," 135–6.

32. González 2007 interview (quotation); Primera 2007 interview; 1891 Toyah incident reported in *El Paso Times*, Nov. 28, 1891, as cited in De León, *Apuntes Tejanos*, Vol. 2, 168; 1906 Toyah case listed in Estes, "An Historical Survey," 140.

33. McFeely, "Afterword," in *Under Sentence of Death*, 320 (quotation one); Brundage, *Lynching in the New South*, 8 (quotation two). Recent lynching studies

recommend that scholars exercise care when citing the Tuskegee Institute and NAACP lynching statistics. In some cases, the victim is categorized as only white or black, with no mention of Hispanic. Period census records often list Mexican Americans as white. As a result, precise minority numbers remain unclear in these Tuskegee/NAACP compilations. In addition, some listed lynchings pertain strictly to frontier law enforcement, such as cattle rustling, and are not race-related. Stewart Tolnay and E. M. Beck also found that these compilations over-counted the actual number of lynchings and contained some duplications and factual errors. For instance, the Tuskegee study put the number of lynchings in Georgia at 517, while Tolnay and Beck found 458. Likewise, for Mississippi, earlier totals listed 568, but Tolnay and Beck discovered 538. While there is no such recent update on the Lone Star State (and one is needed), one might extrapolate such findings for Texas and lower its original total from 489 to 450. See Estes, "An Historical Survey," 125 (Tuskegee numbers), and Tolnay and Beck, *A Festival of Violence*, 273 (revised Georgia and Mississippi figures).

34. Ross, "Lynching," *Handbook*, online (accessed October 29, 2007); Carrigan, *The Making of a Lynching Culture*, 26–9, 175 (quotations one and two), 176-8; Barr, *Black Texans*, 136-7; Estes, "An Historical Survey," 125, 135–46; White, *Rope and Faggot*, 222–69; Raper, *The Tragedy of Lynching*, 319–83, 450–3; Shay, *Judge Lynch . . . His First Hundred Years*, 113–8, 198–206.

35. Carrigan, *The Making of a Lynching Culture*, 175 (quotation), 177, 210 (regarding lynching compilations). Walter White and Frank Shay put the total number of lynchings in Texas at 534 (1882–1927) and 549 (1882–1937), respectively. Given recent scholarship, these numbers seem excessive. The author cites Estes' work, which contains Texas lynching statistics compiled by the Tuskegee Institute and NAACP before World War II, plus an additional incident found in another source, for a statewide total of 489 (which may also be slightly excessive). Despite urging prudence in the use of these compilations, many historians still cite these works and consider them an essential starting point for any research on the topic. For instance, William D. Carrigan incorporates the Tuskegee statistics in his research on Central Texas lynchings but augments them with numerous primary sources. Walter Buenger also cites the Tuskegee study on pages 21 and 271–2 of his work, *The Path to a Modern South*. Until some scholar publishes a new and exhaustive statewide compilation of Texas lynchings, the Tuskegee/NAACP compilations remain an invaluable, albeit imperfect, resource. Also see Brundage, *Lynching in the New South*, 292–4.

36. Wooster interview (quotations one through three).

37. Thompson interview (quotation one); Oscar J. Martínez email to author, July 8, 2007 (quotation two); Arnoldo De León email to author, June 14, 2007 (quotation three).

38. De la Teja interview (quotation one); Roach, "Daniel Webster Wallace," in *Black Cowboys of Texas*, 185 (quotations two and three); ibid., Crimm, "Matthew 'Bones' Hooks: A Pioneer of Honor," 219–41; "The 80 John Wallace Clan: Black Cowboy Rode into County in 1877," *Abilene Reporter-News*, April 5, 1981 (quotation four).

39. González 2005 interview (quotation one); author interview with Clara Duran, Fort Stockton Texas, May 6, 2002 (quotation two); Terrazas interview (quotation three).

40. González 2005 interview (quotations one through four).

41. Duran interview (quotation one); Fort Stockton City Minutes, 1935–1949; García, *Desert Immigrants*, 5–8.

42. García, *Desert Immigrants*, 5–8, 127 (quotation one); Wooster, *Frontier Crossroads*, 125 (quotation two); Tijerina, *History of Mexican Americans in Lubbock County*, 30–1, 41, 50–1; De León, *San Angeleños*, 53, 70–1. For more on race relations in Amarillo, see Todd, *Bones Hooks*, 94–5, 97–100, 104–6, 112–3, 140, 187–8.

43. Downs, ed., *The Future Great City of West Texas, Abilene: 1881-1981*, 9, 44 (quotation); Pritchett, *The Black Community in Abilene*, 10, 17; "Blacks Came Early to Help Form City," *Abilene Reporter-News*, April 5, 1981.

44. Mary McMullen, "You've Come a Long Way, Baby," and "Minorities Say Discrimination Wounds Healing" (quotations one and two), both articles from *Abilene Reporter-News*, April 12, 1981. The Tuskegee Institute compilation includes two lynchings for Abilene (located east of the 100th meridian): a white man in 1909, and a black man in 1922. See Estes, "An Historical Survey," 141, 144.

45. Perales, *Are We Good Neighbors*, 213 (quotation one), 214 (quotation two), 217 (quotation three), 218, 219 (quotation four), 220.

46. Nail, *One Short Sleep Past*, 45 (quotations one and two).

47. Raper, *The Tragedy of Lynching*, 450, 451, (quotation one), 452 (quotation two).

48. Van Nuys, *Americanizing the West*, 31 (quotation one); Roscoe Ady, *West Texas Today*, 5 (quotations two through four). Founded in Fort Worth in late 1918, the West Texas Chamber of Commerce established its headquarters at Stamford, where it remained until 1937, at which time it moved to Abilene. Fort Worth, Stamford, and Abilene are all east of the 100th meridian. In the early years, a number of chamber members were from communities in Texas's shatterbelt region, and other members came from as far east as San Antonio. This mixed membership likely contributed to the mixed identity evidenced in Ady's 1927 piece. See "West Texas Chamber of Commerce," *Handbook*, online (accessed March 17, 2010).

49. *Amarillo, Texas*, 1928, Board of City Development of Amarillo (quotations one and two); McCorkle, *The Panhandle and Plains Region of Texas and Its Possibilities*, Panhandle-Plains Chamber of Commerce, 16–7 (quotation three),

50. Fort Stockton City Council Minutes, Sept. 25, 1928 (street paving); González 2005 interview (quotation).

51. Fort Stockton City Council Minutes, May 15, 1940 (Mexican Boy Scouts); Flores, "The Good Life," 81 (Mexican baseball team); Pecos County Commissioners Court Minutes, February Term 1906 (courthouse dances quotations).

52. Fort Stockton City Council Minutes, May 23, 1939 (Negro burial quotations), June 14, 1938 (Negro settlement quotations).

53. Foster, "Black Lubbock." M.A. thesis, 33–4; Glasrud, "Black Texans, 1900–1930," Ph.D. diss., 148. *San Angelo Standard*, Oct. 13, 1909 (smallpox and 'black devils' quotations), Oct. 14, 1909, Oct. 16, 1909.

54. *San Angelo Standard*, Oct. 13, 1909 (District Attorney quotations, Carruthers' face quotation).

55. *Lubbock Avalanche*, Jan. 20, 1910 (quotations one through three), Oct. 28, 1909, and Nov. 18, 1909 (quotations four and five), as cited on pages 33–4 of Foster's "Black Lubbock." Quotation six is from page 48 of Foster's "Black Lubbock."

56. *Fort Stockton Pioneer*, Nov. 19, 1908 (no Negroes quotation), June 25, 1908 (blackface minstrel quotation). San Angelo was also unappreciative of African American regulars. Several violent confrontations occurred between townspeople and the black troops, including one in early 1881. See Leckie with Leckie, *The Buffalo Soldiers*, 239–40; Dobak and Phillips, *The Black Regulars, 1866–1898*; Bakken, "African-American Military History," in Finkelman, ed., *Encyclopedia of African-American History, 1619-1895*, Vol. 2, 360–71.

57. Pecos County School Board Minutes, Oct. 11, 1915 (Mexican school quotation); Fort Stockton School Board Minutes, July 15, 1918 (satisfactory teacher quotations), August 7, 1919 and Jan. 26, 1923 (Little Mexico quotation); Thompson, *History of Marfa and Presidio County*, Vol. 2, 61; Timmons, *El Paso*, 174; Tijerina, *History of Mexican Americans in Lubbock County*, 27; De León, *San Angeleños*, 31; Carlson, *Amarillo*, 111; Barrett and Oliver, *Odessa*, 116-7.

58. Primera 2005 interview (Mexican school-8th Grade); Fort Stockton School Board Minutes, May 9, 1950 (colored school quotation); Fort Stockton ISD Theresa Mason employment card 1950–1968 (Negro school quotation).

59. Fort Stockton School Board Minutes, April 10, 1956 (George Pina election to board); Daggett, *Pecos County*, Vol. 1, 252 (1972 integration); Primera 2005 interview; González 2005 interview; Terrazas interview (at-large voting quotation). Both San Angelo and Lubbock integrated some their schools as early as 1955. See Doherty, "The Beginnings of Integration in San Angelo ISD," *West Texas Historical Association Year Book*, 80; Steglich, "Population Trends," 440. One of

the last cities in the region to integrate its school district was Odessa, Texas, 100 miles northeast of Fort Stockton, which resisted such efforts until 1982. The city's racial attitudes, representative of the region, are well-documented in the best-selling book by Bissinger, *Friday Night Lights*, xii, 32–3, 58–9, 89–92, 161.

60. Flores, "The Good Life," 89–90, 95–7.
61. González 2005 interview; Pecos County Commissioners Court Minutes, November Term, 1935 (quotations one and two); Flores, "The Good Life," 89–90, 95–7.
62. Flores, "The Good Life," 91 (quotations one through four).
63. Copy of Pecos County Water Improvement District No. 1 Minutes, July 7, 1943, given to author by M. R. González (quotations one and two).
64. González 2005 interview; Flores, "The Good Life," 95–8.
65. González 2005 interview (quotation); Flores, "The Good Life," 95–8.
66. Flores, "The Good Life," 99–102 (Adam Terrazas); González 2005 interview.
67. Flores, "The Good Life," 99–102; González 2005 interview.
68. Ibid.
69. González 2005 interview (quotation one); Terrazas interview (quotation two).
70. González 2005 interview; Terrazas interview; Primera 2005 interview (quotation).

CHAPTER 4

1. Worster, *Under Western Skies*, 22–4, 27, 28 (quotations one and two).
2. White, "Frederick Jackson Turner and Buffalo Bill," in *The Frontier in American Culture*, 15; Smythe, *The Conquest of Arid America*, 42; Smith, *Virgin Land*, 251–2, 253 (quotations one and two); Slotkin, *Gunfighter Nation*, 30 (quotations three through five), 33; Slotkin, *The Fatal Environment*, 39 (quotation six), 215; *Fort Stockton Pioneer*, April 23, 1908 (quotation seven).
3. Smith, *Virgin Land*, 128, 251–3, 255 (quotation one); *Farm Aid*, "About Us," online (accessed June 12, 2007) (quotation two); *Farm Aid*, "Family Farmers," online (accessed June 12, 2007) (quotations three through five).
4. Slotkin, *Gunfighter Nation*, 37 (quotations one and two), 56, 61.
5. Smith, *Virgin Land*, 192, 200.
6. Dearen, *The Last of the Old-Time Cowboys*, 7 (quotations one and two), 9; Dearen, *A Cowboy of the Pecos*, 3 (quotation three), 66; *Fort Stockton Pioneer*, April 23, 1908 (quotation four).
7. *Fort Stockton Pioneer*, May 19, 1911; ibid., March 25, 1909; ibid., April 2, 1909; ibid., May 27, 1909; ibid., April 15, 1909 (quotation).
8. The following works provide an excellent discussion of America's commodification of the environment: Worster, *Rivers of Empire*; Worster, *Under Western*

Skies; Steinberg, *Down to Earth*; Cronon, *Nature's Metropolis*. One of the first and finest environmental histories of Texas's High Plains region is Dan Flores' *Caprock Canyonlands*. See pages 29, 31–2, 38–9, 60–1, 141, 145–6, 156–7 for relevant tie-ins to the present work.

9. Texas Parks and Wildlife Department, "Precipitation in Texas," online (accessed June 11, 2007); Powell, *The Arid Lands*, 12; Smith, *Virgin Land*, 180, 192.

10. Cunfer, *On the Great Plains*, 198-200; author telephone interviews with Farm Service Agency representatives in the following Texas counties: El Paso (June 11, 2007), Tom Green (June 12, 2007), Midland (June 12, 2007), Lubbock (June 12, 2007), Crockett (June 12, 2007), Bailey (June 12, 2007), Gaines (June 12, 2007), and Andrews (June 12, 2007); Ryan and Schifrin, *Midland*, 6–7.

11. Pecos County, Texas, Deed Book, Volume One, May 20, 1876, page 58; H. H. Harrington, Geological Survey of Texas, Department of Agriculture, Insurance, Statistics, and History, *Bulletin No. 2, A Preliminary Report on the Soils and Waters of the Upper Rio Grande and Pecos Valleys in Texas*, 23 (quotation).

12. Texas State Soil and Water Conservation Board, *A Watershed Protection Plan for the Pecos River in Texas, TSSWCB Project #04-11 Draft Report*, 1, 25, 30, 38, 46 (quotations one and two); Baldridge, *A Reminiscence of the Parker H. French Expedition through Texas and Mexico to California in the Spring of 1850*, 21 (quotation three).

13. Texas State Soil and Water Conservation Board, *A Watershed Protection Plan Draft Report*, 38; Bill Leftwich interview, Fort Davis, Texas, June 22, 1992; Charles Hart interview, Fort Stockton, Texas, March 10, 2006 (quotation).

14. *Fort Stockton Pioneer*, May 19, 1911 (quotations one and six); ibid., May 27, 1909 (quotation two); ibid., June 10, 1909 (quotations three through five).

15. *Fort Stockton Pioneer*, Dec. 2, 1909 (quotation); ibid., May 19, 1911; ibid., May 27, 1909; Smythe, *The Conquest of Arid America*, xiii, 335; Worster, *Rivers of Empire*, 7, 11–2.

16. Pecos Valley of Texas Water Users Association, *Petition to the Secretary of the Interior*, C. W. Williams Collection; Jensen, Hatler, Mecke, and Hart, *The Influence of Human Activities on the Waters of the Pecos Basin of Texas #SR-2006-03*, 17 (quotation one), 33 (quotations two and three); Hart, Jensen, Hatler, and Mecke, *Water Issues Facing the Pecos Basin of Texas #3.6.07*, 3.

17. Worster, *Rivers of Empire*, 7, 11–2; Smythe, *The Conquest of Arid America*, 42, 144; Hayter, "Red Bluff Dam and Reservoir," *Handbook*, online (accessed Jan. 26, 2007); Jensen, *The Influence of Human Activities*, 21.

18. Jensen, *The Influence of Human Activities*, 2, 7, 8, 10; Texas State Soil and Water Conservation Board, *A Watershed Protection Plan Draft Report*, 22; Hart interview; Texas Parks and Wildlife Department, "Golden Alga Responsible for Fish Kill on the Pecos River," News Release, March 26, 2007.

19. Texas AgriLife Research, Texas Water Resources Institute, *A Watershed Protection Plan for the Pecos River in Texas,* October 2008 (Final Report); Hart interview; Miyamoto, Yuan, and Anand, "TR-291 2006, Reconnaissance Survey of Salt Sources and Loading into the Pecos River," "TR-292 2006, Influence of Tributaries on Salinity of Amistad International Reservoir," and "TR-298 2007, Water Balance, Salt Loading, and Salinity Control Options of Red Bluff Reservoir, Texas" (Technical Reports), online (accessed June 24, 2010); Jensen, *The Influence of Human Activities,* 1, 2, 7.

20. Jim Ed Miller, Pecos, Texas, phone interview, Oct. 20, 2007 (quotations one and two); Hart, *Water Issues,* 1; Jensen, *The Influence of Human Activities,* 2; Texas State Soil and Water Conservation Board, *A Watershed Protection Plan,* 32.

21. Texas Board of Water Engineers, *Bulletin 6106, Vol. 1, Geology and Ground-Water Resources of Pecos County, Texas,* 43–9; Texas Water Development Board, *Report 294, Surveys of Irrigation in Texas: 1958, 1964, 1969, 1974, 1979, and 1984,* 218; Miller interview (quotation).

22. Condra, Lacewell, Hardin, Lindsey, and Whitson, *An Economic Feasibility Study of Irrigated Crop Production in the Pecos Valley of Texas,* Texas Water Resources Institute, 1–11; Miller interview.

23. Texas Board of Water Engineers, *Bulletin 6106,* 35–6, 43–9, 58–61, 70–2, 97; Condra, *An Economic Feasibility Study,* 1–5, 6 (quotation one), 7–11, 34–6, 42–3, 76–9, 86–7, 96–9; Texas Water Commission, *Bulletin 6214, Vol. 1, Geology and Ground-Water Resources of Reeves County, Texas,* 1, 5, 48, 56; 2006 Pecos County irrigated acreage statistics from Texas Farm Bureau, Reeves-Pecos County Office, Fort Stockton, Texas; 1964 and 2002 Reeves County irrigated acreage statistics from Dr. Mike Foster, Texas A&M Agricultural Research Station at Pecos, Texas (Foster phone interview on June 28, 2007); Texas Water Development Board, *Report 294,* 218; Miller interview; Hart interview (quotation two).

24. Bill Moody interview, Fort Stockton, Texas, May 6, 2002 (quotation); Hart interview; Mike Mecke, Fort Stockton, Texas, phone interview, March 6, 2006; Hart, *Water Issues,* 2–3.

25. Tom Beard interview, Alpine, Texas, March 14, 2006 (quotation one); Robert J. Kinucan interview, Alpine, Texas, March 14, 2006 (quotation two).

26. Texas Water Development Board, *Region E-Far West Texas Regional Water Plan,* 5–39; ibid., *2007 Regional Water Plan;* Farm Service Agency representative interview, El Paso County, Texas, June 11, 2007; Skeet Jones interview, Mentone, Texas, March 12, 2006 (quotation two); Miller interview (quotations one and three); Norwine, Giardino, and Krishnamurthy, *Water for Texas,* 65–73, 229–56; Longo and Yoskowitz, eds., *Water on the Great Plains,* 12–4, 125–36.

27. *San Angelo Standard,* Special Edition, Oct. 4, 1884; Justice and Leffler, "Pecos County," *Handbook,* online (accessed April 22, 2006); *The Western Range,* U.S.

Senate Document No. 199, Letter from the Secretary of Agriculture, 74th Congress, 2nd Session, 16, 125 (sheep ranching); *Fort Stockton Pioneer*, April 23, 1908 (quotation). Regarding sheep ranching in Texas, the best work to date on this subject is Carlson's *Texas Woollybacks*. Although this study has much useful information on the history of the sheep industry in Texas, it does not discuss the overstocking and overgrazing of West Texas's grasslands.

28. The six studies are Bentley, *Cattle Ranges of the Southwest*; Smith, *Grazing Problems in the Southwest and How to Meet Them*; Barnes, *Western Grazing Grounds and Forest Ranges*; Barnes, *The Story of the Range*; *The Western Range*, U.S. Senate Document No. 199, Letter from the Secretary of Agriculture, 74th Congress, 2nd Session; Clawson, *The Western Range Livestock Industry*. Quotation citations: Bentley, *Cattle Ranges*, 6-7 (quotation one), 8-9 (additional information); *San Angelo Standard*, Special Edition, Oct. 4, 1884; Barrett and Oliver, *Odessa*, 39 (quotation two).

29. Bentley, *Cattle Ranges*, 8–9, 11; Dearen, *A Cowboy of the Pecos*, 3 (quotation), 188, 195; Atherton, *The Cattle Kings*, 164–5; "Range rush" concept from comments made by Todd M. Kerstetter to author in May 2006.

30. Bentley, *Cattle Ranges*, 7–8, 9 (quotation one), 10, 12, 13 (quotation two); Smith, *Grazing Problems*, 7–10; Wilkinson, "Cattle Raising on the Plains," *Harper's Magazine*, 791; Dale, *The Range Cattle Industry*, 5, 32–3, 130–1, 184–5. On page 191 of his 1930 work, Dale notes, "The time has clearly come when inefficient and haphazard business methods in the ranching industry can no longer hope to succeed. Careful, scientific study should be given to utilization, conservation and restoration of ranges . . . and [to] the carrying capacity of pasture lands."

31. Secretary of Agriculture, *The Western Range*, 9 (quotation), 16, 48, 68, 89, 93, 109; Bentley, *Cattle Ranges*, 7-9; Smith, *Grazing Problems*, 7–10; 1934 pictures of dead cattle on Pecos River, J. Evetts Haley Collection. There is some controversy regarding the Secretary of Agriculture's 1936 report, *The Western Range*, and whether this data has a "New Deal" agenda. See Clawson, *The Western Range Livestock Industry*, 60–1. The 1898–1950 studies by federal officials, range management specialists, and agricultural agents included in this study along with county and state data, however, support *The Western Range*'s conclusions regarding cattle ranching in Texas.

32. Rives, *Soil Survey of Pecos County, Texas*, 1–10, 24, 26; Johnson, *The Natural Regions of Texas*, 117; Secretary of Agriculture, *The Western Range*, 9–14; Sheridan, *Desertification of the United States*, Council on Environmental Quality, 3.

33. Box, "Range Deterioration in West Texas," *Southwestern Historical Quarterly*, 37. On page 45 of the same article, Professor Box says that chronic overgrazing by West Texas cattlemen "raped the range in thirty years." See also *Soil Survey of Reeves County, Texas*, 38 (quotation one); *Soil Survey of El Paso County, Texas*, 34; Marks, *Three-Mile and Sulfur Draw Watershed Project, Hudspeth*

and Culberson Counties, Texas, Final Environmental Impact Statement, 30, 33; Schkade, Clark, and Pieper, *Midland-Odessa,* 21 (quotation two).

34. Smith, *Grazing Problems,* 13–4.

35. Clawson, *The Western Range Livestock Industry,* 60–1; Schmidly, *Texas Natural History,* 385–6, 392 (quotation one); Secretary of Agriculture, *The Western Range,* 9 (quotation two), 182; Powell, *Grasses of the Trans-Pecos and Adjacent Areas,* 17–25. Will C. Barnes, Chief of Grazing, U.S. Forest Service, says that nineteenth-century livestock raisers gave no thought to the future. Barnes notes, "It was a clear case of 'first come first served and the devil take the hindmost.'" See Barnes, *The Story of the Range,* 8 (footnote quotation).

36. Brush infestation issues covered in Hamilton, McGinty, Ueckert, Hanselka, and Lee, eds., *Brush Management,* 102; Powell, *Grasses of the Trans-Pecos,* 17–25; Kinucan interview; Hart interview.

37. Hamilton, *Brush Management,* 158; Wilcox, Dugas, Owens, Ueckert, Hart, eds., *Shrub Control and Water Yield on Texas Rangelands,* Texas Agricultural Experiment Station Research Report 05-1, 8; Hart interview; Kinucan interview.

38. Kinucan interview (quotations one and two); Beard interview (quotations three and four). For more on rangeland management, see Donahue, *The Western Rangeland Revisited.* For more on wildlife conservation and hunting, see Jacoby, *Crimes Against Nature;* Warren, *The Hunter's Game;* Reiger, *America's Sportsmen and the Origins of Conservation.*

39. Kinucan interview; Beard interview (quotation). For good examples of sound range management practices, see Holechek, Pieper, and Herbel, *Range Management,* 17–8, 178–90, 193–208; Vallentine, *Grazing Management,* 14–22, 294–8, 302–12, 321–38.

40. Author telephone interviews with Farm Service Agency representatives in the following Texas counties: El Paso (June 11, 2007), Tom Green (June 12, 2007), Midland (June 12, 2007), Lubbock (June 12, 2007), Crockett (June 12, 2007), Bailey (June 12, 2007), Gaines (June 12, 2007), and Andrews (June 12, 2007).

41. Cunfer, *On the Great Plains,* 200 (quotation one), 199 (quotations two and three). Cunfer's study, along with Green's *Land of the Underground Rain,* remain the best works on irrigated farming in Texas's High Plains region. See also Kate Galbraith, "How Bad is the Ogallala Aquifer's Decline in Texas?" June 17, 2010, *The Texas Tribune.* Galbraith cites the 2007 TWDB State Water Plan, which projects that irrigation pumping will lower the aquifer fifty-two percent by the year 2060. She also cites a December 2008 Texas Tech report by K. R. Mulligan predicting a marked decline in regional pivot irrigation by 2030.

42. Texas Water Development Board, *Region E-Far West Texas Regional Water Plan,* 5–39; ibid., *2007 Regional Water Plans* for Region A-Texas Panhandle, and

Region F-Pecos Basin; author telephone interviews with Farm Service Agency representatives in the following Texas counties: El Paso (June 11, 2007), Tom Green (June 12, 2007), Midland (June 12, 2007), Lubbock (June 12, 2007), Crockett (June 12, 2007), Bailey (June 12, 2007), Gaines (June 12, 2007), and Andrews (June 12, 2007); Foster interview; Mecke interview; Hart interview; Beard interview.

43. The U.S. Army founded Fort Stockton in 1859. The military required steady supplies of beef for its soldiers and ranchers soon moved into the area to fill government contracts for cattle. Jones interview (quotation). It should be noted that one of the bright spots in the ranching story are the continuing efforts by the USDA, Texas's Agricultural Extension Service, and Texas's ranch management schools to promote proper rangeland conservation and restoration practices.

CHAPTER 5

1. Cashion, *The New Frontier*, 6 (quotations one through three). As Hal Rothman points out, one major problem that occurs when a community augments its natural identity is that in appropriating a new tourist persona, i.e., an Old West mystique, the city becomes somewhat artificial. To attract additional tourist revenue, some communities today create a heritage that sells, trading some of their genuine core characteristics for those "more appealing" to visitors. Many cities have adopted an Old West or western persona. Thanks to movies, television, art, and literature, the Old West remains very popular with both American and foreign tourists. One worrisome consequence of cities appropriating a new identity for visitors is that these communities eventually come to believe their reinvented heritage and forget authentic elements of their past. Rothman shows that while a city may attract more tourist dollars with its augmented identity, it has ultimately made a "Devil's Bargain." See Rothman, *Devil's Bargains*, 17–28.

2. Woodward, *The Burden of Southern History*, 19; Campbell, *An Empire for Slavery*, 1 (quotation). In an effort to attract increased tourist revenue, Abilene, Texas, like Fort Worth, has branded itself as an Old West destination. One prominent Abilene attraction, *Frontier Texas*, boasts that it is "where the Old West comes to life." (From *Frontier Texas* billboard on Interstate 20 near Abilene, Texas, March 19, 2010, footnote quotation one). Abilene, which receives twenty-four inches of rainfall annually, lies seventy miles east of Texas's aridity break line. Abilene historian Katharyn Duff says, "The rain [in Abilene] might not be as plentiful as everybody wanted, but it was five or six inches more than regions such as the trans-Pecos [*sic*] received. It was the critical margin that determines

if a land can support enriching diversification [i.e., farming]." Abilene is more western environmentally and culturally than Fort Worth. In Texas, however, the American West begins in neither Fort Worth nor Abilene, but beyond the 100th meridian at the twenty-inch rainfall line between Sweetwater and Colorado City. See Duff, *Abilene ... On Catclaw Creek: A Profile of a West Texas Town*, 88 (footnote quotation two).

3. Spratt, *The Road to Spindletop*, 85 (quotations one through four), 86 (quotation five).
4. Buenger, "The Story of Texas?," *Southwestern Historical Quarterly*, 489 (quotation).
5. Flores review of *Inherit the Alamo*, in *Southern Humanities Review*, 68–70, as paraphrased in Crisp, "An Incident in San Antonio," *Journal of the West*, 73 (quotations one and two).
6. Cantrell, "The Bones of Stephen F. Austin," *Southwestern Historical Quarterly*, 177 (quotations one through four), 178 (quotation five).
7. Buenger, *The Path to a Modern South*, xviii (quotation).
8. Cashion, "What's the Matter with Texas?" *Montana, The Magazine of Western History*, 2–15; Richardson and Rister, *The Greater Southwest*, 13–4 (quotation).
9. Limerick, *Something in the Soil*, 23 (her definition of the West); "The Burdens of Western American History" in Limerick, *The Legacy of Conquest*, 322–49.
10. These central New West issues are clearly stated in the following works: Center of the American West, University of Colorado at Boulder, *Atlas of the New West*; Limerick, Milner, and Rankin, eds., *Trails Toward a New Western History*; Limerick, *Something in the Soil*, 23–6. Many of these same western issues were first raised by Webb in "The American West: Perpetual Mirage," *Harper's Magazine*, 25, 30.
11. Ely, "Bedlam at Belknap," *West Texas Historical Association Year Book*, 82–6, 91–3, 97–8; Ely, "Riding the Western Frontier," M.A. thesis, 124–35, 143–4. One of the few issues that Texas does not have in common with the rest of the West is the matter of public and private lands. Much of the land in the West is under federal control; whereas in Texas, private individuals and the state own most of the acreage. Texas kept its lands as per its annexation agreement when it joined the Union in 1846.
12. Ely, "Riding the Western Frontier," 9–10; Hafen, *The Overland Mail, 1849–1869*, 15–6; White, *It's Your Misfortune and None of My Own*, 57–9, 128.
13. Ely, "Riding the Western Frontier," 10; Smith, *The U.S. Army & the Texas Frontier Economy*, 11–3; Wooster, *Frontier Crossroads*, 141; Wooster, March 3, 2006, Presidential Address, Texas State Historical Association Annual Banquet, Austin, Texas (quotation).
14. Author interview with Tom Beard, Alpine, Texas, March 14, 2006 (water mining, water syndicates, regional water districts); Blumenthal, "Angry Texans

demanding halt to water deal," in *Texans for Public Justice*, www.tpj.org, Dec. 11, 2003 (state water mining); Matt Jenkins, "Mixing Oil and Water in the Lone Star State," in Paonia, Colorado, *High Country News*, Nov. 24, 2003 (Proposed GLO sale to Rio Nuevo); Lynn Walker, "Pickens sends landowners letters," in *Wichita Falls Times Record News*, April 30, 2008 (water pipeline controversy); Elliott Blackburn, "Pickens-led water, power project stirs concerns," in the *Lubbock Avalanche-Journal*, May 15, 2008 (opposition to water harvesting of Ogallala Aquifer); Elliott Blackburn, "Pickens' wind project finds rough sailing," in the *Lubbock Avalanche-Journal*, Oct. 29, 2008 (water harvesting and water transmission lines to urban areas); Sterry Butcher, "Tom Craddick-Clayton Williams bill, Officials rally against proposed water district," in Marfa, Texas, *Big Bend Sentinel*, June 1, 2009; "An Act for Clayton to Follow," Editorial in Terlingua, Texas, *Big Bend Gazette*, April 30, 2009; Betsy Blaney, "Former Texas candidate suing water district," *The Associated Press*, Jan. 27, 2010 (quotation).

15. West, "Trails and Footprints," in *The Future of the Southern Plains*, 18; Beard interview (Future of West Texas, depopulation), author interview with Charles Hart, Fort Stockton, Texas, March 10, 2006 (Future of West Texas, depopulation); author telephone interview with Mike Mecke, Fort Stockton, Texas, March 6, 2006 (Future of West Texas, depopulation); author interview with Robert J. Kinucan, Alpine, Texas, March 14, 2006 (Future of West Texas, depopulation); Diana Davids Hinton interview, Midland, Texas, Oct. 18, 2007. Conservative estimates by some experts regarding oil depletion are 2100; however, average estimates are that this will occur by 2050–2075.

16. See Chapter Four, "'The Garden of Eden' and the 'Cowman's Paradise;'" Beard interview (changing economy); Kinucan interview (changing economy). Todd M. Kerstetter comments to author in 2007 (quotation).

17. Betsy Blaney, "Former Oil Town Eyes Radioactive Waste," *Associated Press*, May 2, 2005; Janet Elliott, "State Regulators OK West Texas nuclear waste dump," *Houston Chronicle*, May 21, 2008; Betsy Blaney, "Andrews being asked for more waste site funds," *Associated Press* story in the *Lubbock Avalanche-Journal*, May 7, 2009; Betsy Blaney, "Commission to redraw rules for Andrews waste site," *Lubbock Avalanche-Journal*, June 15, 2010; Smyrl, "Texas Low-Level Radioactive Waste Disposal Authority," *Handbook*, online (accessed July 12, 2007); "Environmental Justice Case Study: The Struggle for Sierra Blanca, Texas Against A Low-Level Nuclear Waste Site," Environmental Justice Initiative, School of Natural Resources and Environment, University of Michigan-Ann Arbor, www.michedu/ (accessed online, May 26, 2009).

18. See Chapter Four, "'The Garden of Eden' and the 'Cowman's Paradise;'" Beard interview (changing economy); Kinucan interview (changing economy); author visits to region, 1976–2009.

19. Ibid., including Beard interview (quotation).

20. Wishart, ed., *Encyclopedia of the Great Plains*, 613, 616.
21. Carlson, *Amarillo*, 1–2, 229 (quotation one); Dunn, "Agriculture Builds a City," in *A History of Lubbock*, 240 (quotation two); Graves, "Lubbock, An Epitome of Urbanization," *West Texas Historical Association Year Book*, 6.
22. Wishart, *Encyclopedia of the Great Plains*, 374 (quotation), 375.
23. Weber, *Myth and the History of the Hispanic Southwest*, 134 (quotations one and two).
24. Montejano, *Anglos and Mexicans in the Making of Texas, 1836–1986*, 224, 225 (quotation).
25. Author conversation with Jesús F. de la Teja about Texas Essential Knowledge and Skills (TEKS) Social Studies Standards, April 29, 2010, San Marcos, TX; Texas Secretary of State, *Texas Register*, April 16, 2010, Texas Education Agency, 19 TAC, Chapter 113, TEKS Social Studies Standards and Amendments, online (accessed April 29, 2010); James C. McKinley, Jr., "Texas Conservatives Seek Deeper Stamp on Texts," March 10, 2010, *New York Times* (quotation).
26. Texas Education Agency, Online News Release, May 21, 2010, "State Board of Education Gives Final Okay to Social Studies Standards," online (accessed June 12, 2010); James C. McKinley, Jr., "Texas Approves Curriculum Revised by Conservatives," March 12, 2010, *New York Times* (quotations one and two); Traci Shurley, "State Board member walks out in frustration over social studies proposals," March 11, 2010, *Fort Worth Star-Telegram* (quotations three and four).

BIBLIOGRAPHY

MANUSCRIPTS AND ARCHIVAL COLLECTIONS

Adjutant General's Office. Letters Received, 1862–1865, Record Group 94, National Archives, Washington, D.C.

Barry, J. B. "Buck" Papers. Center for American History, University of Texas at Austin.

Burgess, John. Confederate Citizen File, Confederate Papers Relating to Citizens or Business Firms, 1861–1865, Record Group 109, National Archives, Washington, D.C.

City Council Minutes. Fort Stockton, Texas.

Commissioners Court Minutes. Pecos County, Texas.

Commissioners Court Minutes, Young County, Texas.

Deed Records. El Paso County, Texas.

Deed Records. Pecos County, Texas.

Deed Records. Presidio County, Texas.

De la Garza, Jesús. Confederate Citizen File, Confederate Papers Relating to Citizens or Business Firms, 1861–1865, Record Group 109, National Archives, Washington, D.C.

Denton County, Texas. Tax Rolls 1860–1867, Texas State Library and Archives Commission.

Department of Justice Claims Section. William C. Franks and Sadie Franks, admin. of James Patterson, Record Group 205, National Archives, Washington, D.C.

Department of New Mexico. Letters Received, 1862–1865, Record Group 393, National Archives, Washington, D.C.

Department of New Mexico. Letters Sent, 1862–1865, Record Group 393, National Archives, Washington, D.C.

Department of New Mexico. Provost Marshal, Record Group 393, National Archives, Washington, D.C.

Department of Texas. Letters Received, 1862–1863, Record Group 109, National Archives, Washington, D.C.

Dickinson, Andrew G. Confederate Compiled Service Record, Record Group 109, National Archives, Washington, D.C.

District of Texas, New Mexico, and Arizona. Letters Sent, 1863–1865, Record Group 109, National Archives, Washington, D.C.

Duclos, A. Confederate Citizen File, Confederate Papers Relating to Citizens or Business Firms, 1861–1865, Record Group 109, National Archives, Washington, D.C.

Duff, James. Confederate Citizen File, Confederate Papers Relating to Citizens or Business Firms, 1861–1865, Record Group 109, National Archives, Washington, D.C.

Fernandez, Alvino. Confederate Citizen File, Confederate Papers Relating to Citizens or Business Firms, 1861–1865, Record Group 109, National Archives, Washington, D.C.

Forbes, John. Confederate Citizen File, Confederate Papers Relating to Citizens or Business Firms, 1861–1865, Record Group 109, National Archives, Washington, D.C.

Ford, John "Rip." Papers. UDC Collection, Haley Library, Midland, Texas.

Fort Stockton Independent School District Records.

Frontier Protection Records. Center for American History, University of Texas at Austin.

Goodnight, Charles. Interviews. J. Evetts Haley Collection, Haley Library, Midland, Texas.

Hart, Simeon. Confederate Citizen File, Confederate Papers Relating to Citizens or Business Firms, 1861–1865, Record Group 109, National Archives, Washington, D.C.

Holliday, John D. Confederate Citizen File, Confederate Papers Relating to Citizens or Business Firms, 1861–1865, Record Group 109, National Archives, Washington, D.C.

Hubbell, Jarvis. Confederate Citizen File, Confederate Papers Relating to Citizens or Business Firms, 1861–1865, Record Group 109, National Archives, Washington, D.C.

Hyde, Archibald. Confederate Citizen File, Confederate Papers Relating to Citizens or Business Firms, 1861–1865, Record Group 109, National Archives, Washington, D.C.

Inquest Book. Pecos County, Texas.

Joiner, F. M. Confederate Citizen File, Confederate Papers Relating to Citizens or Business Firms, 1861–1865, Record Group 109, National Archives, Washington, D.C.

"La Grange Company Journal." M0082, Department of Special Collections, Stanford University Libraries.

Lee, Lewis. Confederate Citizen File, Confederate Papers Relating to Citizens or Business Firms, 1861–1865, Record Group 109, National Archives, Washington, D.C.

Lubbock, Francis. Papers. Texas Governors Papers, Texas State Library and Archives Commission.

Magoffin, J. W. Confederate Citizen File, Confederate Papers Relating to Citizens or Business Firms, 1861–1865, Record Group 109, National Archives, Washington, D.C.

Misc. Special Orders. Adjutant General of Texas, 1862–1865, Record Group 109, National Archives, Washington, D.C.

Moke and Brother. Confederate Citizen File, Confederate Papers Relating to Citizens or Business Firms, 1861–1865, Record Group 109, National Archives, Washington, D.C.

Murphy, Daniel. Confederate Citizen File, Confederate Papers Relating to Citizens or Business Firms, 1861–1865, Record Group 109, National Archives, Washington, D.C.

Murphy, Patrick. Confederate Citizen File, Confederate Papers Relating to Citizens or Business Firms, 1861–1865, Record Group 109, National Archives, Washington, D.C.

Murrah, Pendleton. Papers. Texas Governors Papers, Texas State Library and Archives Commission.

Nichols, O. S. "Trail Trip to Mexico, 1864" Letter. J. Evetts Haley Collection, Haley Library, Midland, Texas.

Office of the Commissary General of Prisoners. Letters Received, 1864, Record Group 249, National Archives, Washington, D.C.

Pease, Elisha M. Papers. Austin History Center, Austin, Texas.

Pecos Valley of Texas Water Users Association. *Petition to the Secretary of the Interior: The Pecos River Project in Texas.* Pecos, TX, 1916.

Powell, J. W. *Eleventh Annual Report of the Director of the United States Geological Survey, Part II: Irrigation.* Washington, D.C.: Government Printing Office, 1891.

Rife, Thomas. Confederate Compiled Service Record, Record Group 109, National Archives, Washington, D.C.

Rife, Thomas. Confederate Citizen File, Confederate Papers Relating to Citizens or Business Firms, 1861–1865, Record Group 109, National Archives, Washington, D.C.

Roessler, A. R. *Best Route for the Movement of Troops from San Antonio to El Paso [sic] Texas, Being the One Travelled [sic] by the State Geological Corps of Texas in 1860 and by Henry Skillman's Party in March 1864.* Map Collection, Texas State Archives and Library Commission.

——— Journal. Texas State Library and Archives Commission.

Skillman, Henry and William D. Confederate Citizen File, Confederate Papers Relating to Citizens or Business Firms, 1861–1865, Record Group 109, National Archives, Washington, D.C.

Smith, Sam. Confederate Citizen File, Confederate Papers Relating to Citizens or Business Firms, 1861–1865, Record Group 109, National Archives, Washington, D.C.

Strickland, Rex. Papers. Special Collections Library, University of Texas at El Paso.

Swank, J. Frank. Confederate Citizen File, Confederate Papers Relating to Citizens or Business Firms, 1861–1865, Record Group 109, National Archives, Washington, D.C.

Texas Adjutant General's Department Records, 1861–1865. Texas State Library and Archives Commission.

Texas State Troop Records, 1861–1865. Texas State Library and Archives Commission.

U.S. Secretary of War. U.S. Bureau of Topographical Engineers, *Reports of Reconnaissances in Texas & New Mexico.* Washington, D.C.: Government Printing Office, 1850.

U.S. Senate. *Report of the Secretary of War.* 36th Congress, 2nd Session. 1860. Senate Exec. Doc. No. 1, Vol. 2.

United States Eighth Census (1860). National Archives, Washington, D.C.
Comanche County, Texas
Denton County, Texas
El Paso County, Texas
Kinney County, Texas
Maverick County, Texas
Presidio County, Texas
Titus County, Texas
Uvalde County, Texas

United States Eighth Census Slave Schedules (1860). National Archives, Washington, D.C.
El Paso County, Texas
Maverick County, Texas
Presidio County, Texas
Uvalde County, Texas

United States Ninth Census (1870). National Archives, Washington, D.C.
El Paso County, Texas
Presidio County, Texas

San Diego County, California
Titus County, Texas
United States Tenth Census (1880). National Archives, Washington, D.C.
    El Paso County, Texas
    Pecos County, Texas
    Presidio County, Texas
United States Twelfth Census (1900). National Archives, Washington, D.C.
    El Paso County, Texas
    Pecos County, Texas
Water Improvement District No. 1 Minutes. Pecos County, Texas.
Weed, L.N. "Overland Journey to California in 1849." William Robertson Coe Collection, WA MSS 517, Beinecke Rare Book and Manuscript Library, Yale University Libraries.

AUTHOR INTERVIEWS

Beard, Tom. Alpine, Texas, March 14, 2006
de la Teja, Jesús F. San Marcos, Texas, Dec. 4, 2006, and April 29, 2010
Duran, Clara. Fort Stockton, Texas, May 6, 2002
Foster, Mike. Pecos, Texas, June 28, 2007
Glasrud, Bruce. Austin, Texas, March 26, 2009
González, M. R. Fort Stockton, Texas, Nov. 17, 2005, and Oct. 14, 2007
Hart, Charles. Fort Stockton, Texas, March 10, 2006
Hinton, Diana Davids. Midland, Texas, Oct. 18, 2007
Hinton, Harwood P. Austin, Texas, Jan. 27, 2005, March 29, 2005, and Dec. 23, 2005
Jones, Skeet Lee. Mentone, Texas, March 12, 2006
Kinucan, Robert J. Alpine, Texas, March 14, 2006
Leftwich, Bill. Fort Davis, Texas, June 22, 1992
Mecke, Mike. Fort Stockton, Texas, March 6, 2006
Miller, Jim Ed. Pecos, Texas, Oct. 20, 2007
Moody, Bill. Fort Stockton, Texas, May 6, 2002
Primera, Joe. Fort Stockton, Texas, Nov. 17, 2005, and Oct. 14, 2007
Terrazas, Pete. Fort Stockton, Texas, May 6, 2002
Texas Farm Service Agency agent. Andrews County, June 12, 2007
———. Bailey County, June 12, 2007
———. Crockett County, June 12, 2007
———. Ector County, June 12, 2007
———. El Paso County, June 11, 2007
———. Gaines County, June 12, 2007
———. Lubbock County, June 12, 2007
———. Midland County, June 12, 2007

BIBLIOGRAPHY

————. Tom Green County, June 12, 2007

Thompson, Jerry D. Laredo, Texas, Dec. 5, 2006

Wooster, Robert. Corpus Christi, Texas, Dec. 5, 2006

PRIMARY SOURCES

Baldridge, Michael. *A Reminiscence of the Parker H. French Expedition through Texas and Mexico to California in the Spring of 1850.* Los Angeles: Scraps of California IV, 1959.

Barry, James Buckner. *Buck Barry: Texas Ranger and Frontiersman.* Edited by James K. Greer. Lincoln: University of Nebraska Press, 1976.

Baylor, George Wythe. *Into the Far Wild Country: True Tales of the Old Southwest.* Edited by Jerry D. Thompson. El Paso: Texas Western Press, 1996.

Bentley, H. L. *Cattle Ranges of the Southwest: A History of the Exhaustion of the Pasturage and Suggestions for its Restoration.* Washington, D.C.: Government Printing Office, 1898.

Bliss, Zenas R. *The Reminiscences of Major General Zenas R. Bliss, 1854–1876: From the Texas Frontier to the Civil War and Back Again.* Edited by Thomas T. Smith, Jerry D. Thompson, Robert Wooster, and Ben Pingenot. Austin: Texas State Historical Association, 2007.

Condra, Gary D., Ronald D. Lacewell, Daniel C. Hardin, Kenneth Lindsey, and Robert E. Whitson. *An Economic Feasibility Study of Irrigated Crop Production in the Pecos Valley of Texas.* Texas Water Resources Institute. College Station: Texas A&M University, 1979.

Cox, James. *Historical and Biographical Record of the Cattle Industry and the Cattlemen of Texas and Adjacent Territory.* New York: Antiquarian Press, 1959.

Ford, John Salmon. *Rip Ford's Texas.* Edited by Stephen B. Oates. Austin: University of Texas Press, 1963.

Haley, J. Evetts. *Charles Goodnight: Cowman and Plainsman.* Norman: University of Oklahoma Press, 1989.

Harrington, H. H. Geological Survey of Texas, Department of Agriculture, Insurance, Statistics, and History. *Bulletin No. 2, A Preliminary Report on the Soils and Waters of the Upper Rio Grande and Pecos Valleys in Texas.* Austin: State Printing Office, 1890.

Hart, Charlie, Ric Jensen, Will Hatler, and Mike Mecke. *Water Issues Facing the Pecos Basin of Texas #3.6.07.* San Marcos, TX: Texas Water Resources Institute, 2007.

Heartsill, W. W. *Fourteen Hundred and 91 Days in the Confederate Army.* Edited by Bell Irvin Wiley. Jackson, TN: McCowat-Mercer Press, 1954.

Hunter, Marvin J., ed. *The Trail Drivers of Texas.* San Antonio: Jackson Printing Company, 1920.

Jensen, Ric, Will Hatler, Mike Mecke, and Charles Hart. *The Influence of Human Activities on the Waters of the Pecos Basin of Texas #SR-2006–03.* San Marcos, TX: Texas Water Resources Institute, 2007.

Marks, George C. *Three-Mile and Sulfur Draw Watershed Project, Hudspeth and Culberson Counties, Texas, Final Environmental Impact Statement.* Temple, TX: U.S. Department of Agriculture, Soil Conservation Service, December, 1975.

Mills, W. W. *Forty Years at El Paso, 1858–1898.* Edited by Rex Strickland. El Paso: Carl Hertzog, 1962.

Murdock, H., Steve White, Md. Nazrul Hoque, Beverly Pecotte, Xiuhong You, and Jennifer Balkan. "The Texas Challenge in the Twenty-First Century: Implications of Population Change for the Future of Texas." Department of Rural Sociology. College Station: Texas A&M University, December 2002.

Orton, Richard H. *Records of California Men in the War of the Rebellion, 1861–1867.* Salem, MA: Higginson Book Company, 1998.

Reed, Lester. *Old Time Cattlemen and Other Pioneers of the Anza-Borrego Area.* Borrego Springs, CA: Anza-Borrego Desert Natural History Association, 1986.

Rives, Jerry L. *Soil Survey of Pecos County, Texas.* U.S. Government Printing Office: USDA Soil Conservation Service, May 1980.

Sheridan, David. *Desertification of the United States.* Council on Environmental Quality 1981. Washington, D.C.: Government Printing Office, 1981.

Smith, Jared G. *Grazing Problems in the Southwest and How to Meet Them.* Washington: U.S. Government Printing Office, 1899.

Smith, Sidney W. *From the Cow Camp to the Pulpit: Being Twenty-Five Years Experience of a Texas Evangelist.* Cincinnati: The Christian Leader Corporation, 1927.

Soil Survey of El Paso County, Texas. U.S. Government Printing Office: USDA Soil Conservation Service in cooperation with Texas Agricultural Extension Experiment Station, November 1971.

Soil Survey of Reeves County, Texas. U.S. Government Printing Office: USDA Soil Conservation Service in cooperation with Texas Agricultural Extension Experiment Station, June 1980.

Sumpter, Jesse. *Paso Del Águila: A Chronicle of Frontier Days on the Texas Border.* Edited by Ben E. Pingenot. Austin: Encino Press, 1969.

Texas AgriLife Research, Texas Water Resources Institute. *A Watershed Protection Plan for the Pecos River in Texas.* Final Report, October 2008.

Texas Board of Water Engineers. *Bulletin 6106, Vol. 1, Geology and Ground-Water Resources of Pecos County, Texas.* Austin: State of Texas, 1961.

Texas Farm Bureau, Reeves-Pecos County Office, Fort Stockton, Texas. 2006 Irrigated Acreage Statistics for Pecos County, Texas.

Texas Library and Historical Commission. *Journal of the Secession Convention of Texas, 1861.* Edited by Ernest William Winkler. Austin: Austin Printing Company, 1912.

Texas Parks and Wildlife Department. "Golden Alga Responsible for Fish Kill on the Pecos River." News Release, March 26, 2007.

Texas State Soil and Water Conservation Board. *A Watershed Protection Plan for the Pecos River in Texas, TSSWCB Project #04–11 Draft Report.* Austin: Texas State Soil and Water Conservation Board, 2007.

Texas Water Commission. *Bulletin 6214, Vol. 1, Geology and Ground-Water Resources of Reeves County, Texas.* Austin: State of Texas, 1972.

Texas Water Development Board. *Report 294, Surveys of Irrigation in Texas: 1958, 1964, 1969, 1974, 1979, and 1984.* Austin: State of Texas, 1986.

———. *Far West Texas Regional Water Plan.* Austin: State of Texas, 2001.

———. *Regional Water Plans.* Austin: State of Texas, 2007.

Thompson, Jerry D., ed. *New Mexico Territory During the Civil War: Wallen and Evans Inspection Reports, 1862–1863.* Albuquerque: University of New Mexico Press, 2008.

U.S. Secretary of Agriculture. *The Western Range.* U.S. Senate Document No. 199, 74th Congress, 2nd Session. Washington, D.C.: Government Printing Office, 1936.

The War of the Rebellion: A Compilation of the Official Records of the Union and Confederate Armies. Washington, D.C.: U.S. Government Printing Office, 1880–1901.

Wilbarger, J. W. *Indian Depredations in Texas.* Austin: Hutchings Printing House, 1889.

Wilcox, Bradford P., William A. Dugas, M. Keith Owens, Darrell N. Ueckert, Charles R. Hart, eds. *Shrub Control and Water Yield on Texas Rangelands: Current State of Knowledge, 2005.* Texas Agricultural Experiment Station Research Report 05–1. College Station: Texas A&M University, 2005.

Wilkinson, Frank. "Cattle Raising on the Plains." *Harper's Magazine* (April 1886).

Williams, R. H. *With the Border Ruffians: Memories of the Far West, 1852–1868.* New York: E. P. Dutton and Company, 1907.

Wilson, John P. *When the Texans Came: Missing Records from the Civil War in the Southwest, 1861–1862.* Albuquerque: University of New Mexico Press, 2001.

NEWSPAPERS

Associated Press
Abilene Reporter-News
Big Bend Gazette
Big Bend Sentinel
El Paso Times
Fort Stockton Pioneer
Fort Worth Record-Telegram
Fort Worth Star-Telegram

High Country News
Houston Chronicle
Lubbock Avalanche-Journal
Mesilla Times
New York Times
San Angelo Standard Times
San Antonio Alamo-Express
Texas Tribune
Wichita Falls Times Record News

SECONDARY SOURCES

Ady, Roscoe. *West Texas Today.* West Texas Chamber of Commerce (October 1927).

Amarillo, Texas. Board of City Development of Amarillo (1928).

Almaguer, Tomás. *Racial Fault Lines: The Origins of White Supremacy in California.* Berkeley: University of California Press, 1994.

Archambeau, Ernest R. "The First Federal Census in the Panhandle—1880." *Panhandle-Plains Historical Review* 23 (1950).

Atherton, Lewis. *The Cattle Kings.* Lincoln: University of Nebraska, 1972.

Austerman, Wayne R. *Sharps Rifles and Spanish Mules: The San Antonio-El Paso Mail, 1851–1881.* College Station: Texas A&M Press, 1985.

Bakken, Gordon Morris. "The Courts, The Legal Profession, and the Development of Law in Early California." In John F. Burns and Richard J. Orsi, eds. *Taming the Elephant: Politics, Government, and Law in Pioneer California.* Berkeley: University of California Press, 2003.

———. "African-American Military History." In Paul Finkelman, ed. *Encyclopedia of African-American History, 1619–1895.* New York: Oxford University Press, 2006.

Barnes, Will C. *Western Grazing Grounds and Forest Ranges.* Chicago: The Breeder's Gazette, 1913.

———. *The Story of the Range.* Washington: U.S. Government Printing Office, 1926.

Barr, Alwyn. *Black Texans: A History of African Americans in Texas, 1528–1995.* Second Edition. Norman: University of Oklahoma Press, 1996.

Barrett, Velma and Hazel Oliver. *Odessa: City of Dreams, A Miracle of the Texas Prairies.* San Antonio: The Naylor Company, 1952.

Baum, Dale. *The Shattering of Texas Unionism: Politics in the Lone Star State During the Civil War Era.* Baton Rouge: Louisiana State University Press, 1998.

Biesele, Rudolph Leopold. *The History of German Settlements in Texas, 1831–1861.* Privately printed by Author, second printing, 1964.

Bissinger, H. G. *Friday Night Lights: A Town, A Team, And A Dream.* New York: Da Capo Press, 2004.

Blight, David W. *Race and Reunion: The Civil War in American Memory*. Cambridge, MA: The Belknap Press of Harvard University Press, 2001.

Box, Thadis W. "Range Deterioration in West Texas." *Southwestern Historical Quarterly* 71 (July 1967).

Brundage, W. Fitzhugh. *Lynching in the New South: Georgia and Virginia, 1880–1930*. Urbana: University of Illinois Press, 1993.

Buenger, Walter L. *Secession and the Union in Texas*. Austin: University of Texas Press, 1984.

———. *The Path to a Modern South: Northeast Texas Between Reconstruction and the Great Depression*. Austin: University of Texas Press, 2001.

———. "The Story of Texas? The Texas State History Museum and Forgetting and Remembering the Past." *Southwestern Historical Quarterly* 105 (January 2002).

Caldwell, Clifton. *Fort Davis: A Family Frontier Fort*. Albany, TX: Clear Fork Press, 1986.

Calvert, Robert A., Arnoldo De León, and Gregg Cantrell. *The History of Texas*. Third Edition. Wheeling, IL: Harlan Davidson, Inc., 2002.

Campbell, Randolph B. *A Southern Community in Crisis: Harrison County, Texas, 1850–1880*. Austin: Texas State Historical Association, 1983.

———. *An Empire for Slavery: The Peculiar Institution in Texas, 1821–1865*. Baton Rouge: Louisiana State University Press, 1989.

———. *Gone to Texas: A History of the Lone Star State*. New York: Oxford Press, 2003.

———. "Entangled Stories of the Lone Star State." In Gregg Cantrell and Elizabeth Hayes Turner, eds. *Lone Star Pasts: Memory and History in Texas*. College Station: Texas A&M University Press, 2007.

Cantrell, Gregg. "The Bones of Stephen F. Austin: History and Memory in Progressive-Era Texas." *Southwestern Historical Quarterly* 108 (October 2004).

Carlson, Paul H. *Texas Woollybacks: The Range Sheep and Goat Industry*. College Station: Texas A&M University Press, 1982.

———. *Amarillo: The Story of a Western Town*. Lubbock: Texas Tech University Press, 2006.

Carrigan, William D. *The Making of a Lynching Culture: Violence and Vigilantism in Central Texas, 1836–1916*. Urbana: University of Illinois, 2006.

Cashion, Ty. "What's The Matter With Texas?" *Montana, The Magazine of Western History* 55 (Winter 2005).

———. *The New Frontier: A Contemporary History of Fort Worth and Tarrant County*. San Antonio: Historical Publishing Network, 2006.

Cates, Cliff D. *Pioneer History of Wise County*. St. Louis: Nixon-Jones, 1907.

Center of the American West. University of Colorado at Boulder. *Atlas of the New West*. New York: W.W. Norton & Company, 1997.

Christian, Garna L. *Black Soldiers in Jim Crow Texas, 1899–1917*. College Station: Texas A&M University Press, 1995.

Clark, Elizabeth A. *History, Theory, Text: Historians and the Linguistic Turn*. Cambridge, MA: Harvard University Press, 2004.

Clarke, Mary Whatley. *John Simpson Chisum: Jinglebob King of the Pecos*. Austin: Eakin Press, 1984.

Clawson, Marion. *The Western Range Livestock Industry*. New York: McGraw-Hill Book Company, Inc., 1950.

Connor, Seymour V. *Texas: A History*. Arlington Heights, IL: AMH Publishing Corporation, 1971.

Crane, R. C. "The West Texas Agricultural and Mechanical College Movement and the Founding of Texas Technological College." *West Texas Historical Association Year Book* 7 (1931).

Crimm, Ana Carolina Castillo. "Matthew 'Bones' Hooks: A Pioneer of Honor." In Sara R. Massey, ed. *Black Cowboys of Texas*. College Station: Texas A&M University Press, 2000.

Crisp, James E. "An Incident in San Antonio: The Contested Iconology of Davey Crockett's Death at the Alamo." *Journal of the West* 40 (Spring 2001).

Cronon, William. *Nature's Metropolis: Chicago and the Great West*. New York: W.W. Norton & Company, 1991.

Cunfer, Geoff. *On the Great Plains: Agriculture and Environment*. College Station: Texas A&M University Press, 2005.

Daggett, Marsha Lea., ed. *Pecos County History*. Canyon, TX: Staked Plains Press, 1984.

Dale, Edward Everett. *The Range Cattle Industry*. Norman: University of Oklahoma Press, 1930.

Dearen, Patrick. *A Cowboy of the Pecos*. Plano: Republic of Texas Press, 1997.

———. *The Last of the Old-Time Cowboys*. Plano: Republic of Texas Press, 1998.

De León, Arnoldo. *Apuntes Tejanos*. Texas State Historical Association. Ann Arbor, MI: University Microfilms International, 1978.

———. *The Tejano Community: 1836–1900*. Albuquerque: University of New Mexico Press, 1982.

———. *They Called Them Greasers: Anglo Attitudes toward Mexicans in Texas, 1821–1900*. Austin: University of Texas Press, 1983.

———. *San Angeleños: Mexican Americans in San Angelo, Texas*. San Angelo: Fort Concho Museum Press, 1985.

Dobak, William A., and Thomas D. Phillips. *Black Regulars, 1866–1898*. Norman: University of Oklahoma Press, 2001.

Doherty, Gregory A. "The Beginning of Integration in San Angelo ISD." *West Texas Historical Association Year Book* 69 (1993).

Donahue, Debra L. *The Western Rangeland Revisited*. Norman: University of Oklahoma Press, 2000.

Downs, Fane, ed. *The Future Great City of West Texas, Abilene: 1881 1981*. Abilene: Rupert N. Richardson Press, 1981.

Duff, Katharyn. *Abilene . . . On Catclaw Creek: A Profile of a West Texas Town*. Abilene, TX: The Reporter Publishing Co., 1969.

Dunn, Roy Sylvan. "Agriculture Builds a City." In Lawrence L. Graves, ed. *A History of Lubbock*. Part Two. Lubbock: West Texas Museum Association, 1960.

Dupree, Stephen A. *Planting the Union Flag in Texas, The Campaigns of Major General Nathanial P. Banks in the West*. College Station: Texas A&M University Press, 2008.

Ely, Glen Sample. "Bedlam at Belknap: Frontier Lawlessness on the Butterfield Overland Mail Line." *West Texas Historical Association Year Book* 82 (2006).

———. "Gone from Texas and Trading with the Enemy: New Perspectives on Civil War West Texas." *Southwestern Historical Quarterly* 110 (April 2007).

———. "Skullduggery at Spencer's Ranch: Civil War Intrigue in West Texas." Sul Ross State University. *Journal of Big Bend Studies* 21 (2009).

———. "What to Do About Texas? Texas and the Department of New Mexico in the Civil War." *New Mexico Historical Review* 85 (Fall 2010).

Ely, Glen Sample, and W. S. Benson. *The Home Front: Life in Texas During the Civil War*. Video documentary. Fort Worth, TX: www.texashistory.com, 1996.

Fehrenbach, T. R. *Lone Star: A History of Texas and the Texans*. New York: The Macmillan Company, 1968.

Finch, L. Boyd. *Confederate Pathway to the Pacific: Major Sherod Hunter and Arizona Territory, C.S.A.* Tucson: The Arizona Historical Society, 1996.

Flores, Dan. *Caprock Canyonlands*. Austin: University of Texas Press, 1990.

Flores, Richard R. "Memory-Place, Meaning, and the Alamo." *American Literary History* 10 (Autumn 1998).

Francaviglia, Richard V. *The Cast Iron Forest: A Natural and Cultural History of the North American Cross Timbers*. Austin: University of Texas Press, 2000.

Frazer, Robert W. *Forts of the West*. Norman: University of Oklahoma Press, 1988.

García, Mario T. *Desert Immigrants: The Mexicans of El Paso, 1880–1920*. New Haven: Yale University Press, 1981.

George, Olan M. *Roundup of Memories*. Seagraves, TX: Pioneer Book Publishers, 1987.

Glasrud, Bruce A. and Paul H. Carlson, with Tai D. Kriedler, eds. *Slavery to Integration: Black Americans in West Texas*. Abilene, TX: State House Press, 2007.

Gournay, Luke. *Texas Boundaries: Evolution of the State's Counties*. College Station: Texas A&M University Press, 1995.

Graham, Don, James W. Lee, and William T. Pilkington, eds. *The Texas Literary Tradition: Fiction, Folklore, History*. Austin: University of Texas, 1983.

Graves, Lawrence L. "Lubbock, An Epitome of Urbanization." *West Texas Historical Association Year Book* 36 (1960).

Gray, Beatrice Grady. *Into the Setting Sun: A History of Coleman County*. Santa Anna, TX, 1936.

Green, Donald E. *Land of the Underground Rain: Irrigation on the Texas High Plains, 1910–1970*. Austin: University of Texas Press, 1973.

Hafen, Le Roy R. *The Overland Mail, 1849–1869: Promoter of Settlement, Precursor of Railroads*. Cleveland: The Arthur H. Clark Company, 1926.

Hall, Martin Hardwick. "The Formation of Sibley's Brigade and the March to New Mexico." In Ralph A. Wooster, ed. *Lone Star Blue and Gray: Essays on Texas in the Civil War*. Austin: Texas State Historical Association, 1995.

Hämäläinen, Pekka. *The Comanche Empire*. New Haven: Yale University Press, 2008.

Hamilton, Wayne T., Allan McGinty, Darrell N. Ueckert, C. Wayne Hanselka, and Michelle R. Lee, eds. *Brush Management: Past, Present, Future*. College Station: Texas A&M University Press, 2004.

Haynes, Sam W. *Soldiers of Misfortune: The Somervell and Mier Expeditions*. Austin: University of Texas Press, 1990.

Hine, Robert, and John Mack Faragher. *The American West: A New Interpretive History*. New Haven: Yale University Press, 2000.

Hinton, Harwood P. "John Simpson Chisum, 1877–1884." *New Mexico Historical Review* 31 (July 1956).

Holden, William Curry. *Alkali Trails*. Dallas: The Southwest Press, 1930.

Holechek, Jerry L., Rex D. Pieper, and Carlton H. Herbel. *Range Management: Principles and Practices*. Second Edition. Englewood Cliffs, NJ: Prentice-Hall, Inc., 1995.

Jacoby, Karl. *Crimes Against Nature: Squatters, Poachers, Thieves and the Hidden History of Conservation*. Berkeley: University of California Press, 2001.

Jordan, Terry G. *German Seed in Texas Soil: Immigrant Farmers in Nineteenth-Century Texas*. Austin: University of Texas Press, 1966.

Jordan Terry G., with John L. Bean, Jr., and William M. Holmes. *Texas*. Boulder, CO: Westview Press, Inc., 1984.

Jordan, Terry G. "A Century and a Half of Ethnic Change in Texas, 1836–1896." *Southwestern Historical Quarterly* 89 (April 1986).

Johnson, Elmer H. *The Natural Regions of Texas*. Austin: University of Texas, 1931.

Johnson, Susan Lee. *Roaring Camp: The Social World of the California Gold Rush*. New York: W.W. Norton & Company, 2000.

Kenner, Charles. "The Origins of the 'Goodnight' Trail Reconsidered." *Southwestern Historical Quarterly* 77 (January 1974).

Kerr, Homer L. "Migration into Texas, 1860–1880." *Southwestern Historical Quarterly* 70 (October 1966).

Knox, Ellis O. "Racial Integration in the Public Schools of Arizona, Kansas, and New Mexico." *The Journal of Negro Education* 23 (Summer 1954).

Lack, Paul D. "In the Long Shadow of Eugene C. Barker. The Revolution and Republic." In Walter L. Buenger and Robert A. Calvert, eds. *Texas through Time: Evolving Interpretations.* College Station: Texas A&M University Press, 1991.

Lamar, Howard Roberts. *The Far Southwest, 1846–1912: A Territorial History.* New Haven: Yale University Press, 1966.

———. *Dakota Territory, 1861–1889: A Study of Frontier Politics.* Fargo: Institute for Regional Studies, North Dakota State University, 1997.

La Vere, David. *Life Among the Texas Indians: The WPA Narratives.* College Station: Texas A&M University Press, 1998.

———. *The Texas Indians.* College Station: Texas A&M University Press, 2004.

Leckie, William H., and Shirley A. Leckie. *The Buffalo Soldiers.* Revised Edition. Norman: University of Oklahoma Press, 2003.

Limerick, Patricia Nelson. *The Legacy of Conquest: The Unbroken Past of the American West.* New York: W.W. Norton and Company, 1987.

———. *Something in the Soil: Legacies and Reckonings in the New West.* New York: W. W. Norton and Company, 2000.

Limerick, Patricia Nelson, Clyde A. Milner II, and Charles E. Rankin, eds. *Trails Toward a New Western History.* Lawrence: University of Kansas Press, 1991.

Longo, Peter J. and David W. Yoskowitz, eds. *Water on the Great Plains: Issues and Policies.* Lubbock: Texas Tech University Press, 2002.

Marten, James. *Texas Divided: Loyalty and Dissent in the Lone Star State, 1856–1874.* Lexington: University Press of Kentucky, 1990.

Martínez, Oscar J. *The Chicanos of El Paso: An Assessment of Progress.* El Paso: Texas Western Press, 1980.

———. *Mexican-Origin People in the United States: A Topical History.* Tucson: University of Arizona Press, 2001.

Mayhall, Mildred P. *Indian Wars of Texas.* Waco, TX: Texian Press, 1965.

McConnell, Joseph Carroll. *The West Texas Frontier.* Vol. I. Jacksboro, TX: Gazette Print, 1933.

———. *The West Texas Frontier.* Vol. II. Palo Pinto: Texas Legal Bank & Book Co., 1939.

McConnell, Weston Joseph. *Social Cleavages in Texas: A Study of the Proposed Division of the State.* New York: Columbia University, 1925.

McCorkle, Ray B. *The Panhandle and Plains Region of Texas and Its Possibilities.* Panhandle-Plains Chamber of Commerce (1920).

McFeely, William S. "Afterword." In W. Fitzhugh Brundage, ed. *Under Sentence of Death: Lynching in the South.* Chapel Hill: The University of North Carolina Press, 1997.

Meinig, D. W. *Imperial Texas: An Interpretive Essay in Cultural Geography.* Austin: University of Texas Press, 1969.

Menchaca, Martha. *The Mexican Outsiders: A Community History of Marginalization and Discrimination in California.* Austin: University of Texas Press, 1995.

Miller, Carol Price. "Resisting the Ku Klux Klan in El Paso." El Paso County Historical Society. *Password* 54 (Spring 2009).

Miller, W. Henry. *Pioneering North Texas.* San Antonio: The Naylor Company, 1953.

Milner, Clyde A., Carol A. O'Connor, and Martha A. Sandweiss, eds. *The Oxford History of the American West.* New York: Oxford University Press, 1994.

Montejano, David. *Anglos and Mexicans in the Making of Texas, 1836–1986.* Austin: University of Texas Press, 1987.

Nail, David L. *One Short Sleep Past: A Profile of Amarillo in the Thirties.* Canyon, TX: Staked Plains Press, 1973.

Newcomb, W. W. *The Indians of Texas: From Prehistoric to Modern Times.* Austin: University of Texas Press, 1961.

Norwine, Jim, John R. Giardino, and Sushma Krishnamurthy. *Water for Texas.* College Station: Texas A&M University Press, 2005.

Oates, Stephen B. "Texas Under the Secessionists." *Southwestern Historical Quarterly* 67 (October 1963).

Pascoe, Peggy. *What Comes Naturally: Miscegenation Law and the Making of Race in America.* New York: Oxford University Press, 2009.

Perales, Alonso S. *Are We Good Neighbors?* San Antonio: Artes Graficas, 1948.

Pickering, David, and Judy Falls. *Brush Men and Vigilantes: Civil War Dissent in Texas.* College Station: Texas A&M University Press, 1999.

Powell, A. Michael. *Grasses of the Trans-Pecos and Adjacent Areas.* Austin: University of Texas Press, 1994.

Powell, John Wesley. *The Arid Lands.* Edited by Wallace Stegner. Lincoln: University of Nebraska Press, 2004.

Pritchett, Jewell G. *The Black Community in Abilene.* Abilene, TX: Pritchett Publications, 1984.

Raper, Arthur F. *The Tragedy of Lynching.* New York: Dover Publications, Inc., 1970.

Reiger, John F. *America's Sportsmen and the Origins of Conservation.* Third Edition. Corvallis, OR: Oregon State University Press, 2001.

Reynolds, Donald E. *Editors Make War: Southern Newspapers in the Secession Crisis.* Nashville: Vanderbilt University Press, 1970.

———. *Texas Terror: the Slave Insurrection Panic of 1860 and the Secession of the Lower South.* Baton Rouge: Louisiana State University Press, 2007.

Richardson, Rupert Norval, and Adrian Anderson, Cary D. Wintz, Ernest Wallace. *Texas: The Lone Star State.* 8th Edition. Upper Saddle River, NJ: Prentice-Hall Inc., 2001.

Richardson, Rupert Norval, and Carl Coke Rister. *The Greater Southwest.* Glendale, CA: The Arthur H. Clark Company, 1935.

Richardson, Rupert Norval. *Texas: The Lone Star State.* New York: Prentice-Hall, Inc., 1943.

———. *The Frontier of Northwest Texas: 1846–1876.* Glendale, CA: Arthur H. Clark Company, 1963.

Rickards, Colin. *The Gunfight at Blazer's Mill.* El Paso: Texas Western Press, 1974.

Rister, Carl C. "Fort Griffin." *West Texas Historical Association Year Book* 1 (1925).

Roach, Joyce Gibson. "Daniel Webster Wallace: A West Texas Cattleman." In Sara R. Massey, ed. *Black Cowboys of Texas.* College Station: Texas A&M University Press, 2000.

Roth, Jeffrey M. "Civil War Frontier Defense Challenges in Northwest Texas." *Military History of the West* 30 (Spring 2000).

Rothman, Hal K. *Devil's Bargains: Tourism in the Twentieth-Century American West.* Lawrence: University Press of Kansas, 1998.

Ryan, Robert H., and Leonard G. Schifrin. *Midland: The Economic Future of a Texas Oil Center.* Austin: Bureau of Business Research, University of Texas, 1959.

Schkade, L. L., Charles T. Clark, and Charles A. Pieper. *Midland-Odessa: An Analysis of the Economic Base for Urban Development.* Austin: Bureau of Business Research, University of Texas, 1965.

Schmidly, David J. *Texas Natural History: A Century of Change.* Lubbock: Texas Tech University Press, 2002.

Sewell, William H. *Logics of History: Social Theory and Social Transformation.* Chicago: University of Chicago Press, 2005.

Shay, Frank. *Judge Lynch . . . His First Hundred Years.* New York: Ives Washburn, Inc., 1938.

Shorr, Howard. "Thorns in the Roses: Race Relations and the Brookside Plunge Controversy in Pasadena, California, 1914–1947." In Gordon Morris Bakken, ed. *Law in the Western United States.* Norman: University of Oklahoma Press, 2000.

Slotkin, Richard. *Gunfighter Nation: The Myth of the Frontier in Twentieth-Century America.* Norman: University of Oklahoma Press, 1998.

———. *The Fatal Environment: The Myth of the Frontier in the Age of Industrialization, 1800–1890.* Norman: University of Oklahoma Press, 1998.

Smith, David Paul. *Frontier Defense in the Civil War: Texas' Rangers and Rebels.* College Station: Texas A&M University Press, 1992.

Smith, Henry Nash. *Virgin Land: The American West as Symbol and Myth.* Cambridge, MA: Harvard University Press, 1970.

Smith, Thomas T. *The U.S. Army & the Texas Frontier Economy, 1845–1900.* College Station: Texas A&M University Press, 1999.

Smythe, William E. *The Conquest of Arid America.* Norwood, MA: Norwood Press, 1905.

Sonnichsen, C. L. *The Mescalero Apaches*. Norman: University of Oklahoma Press, 1958.

———. *Tularosa: Last of the Frontier West*. New York: Devin-Adair Company, 1963.

Spratt, John Stricklin. *The Road to Spindletop: Economic Changes in Texas, 1875–1901*. Austin: University of Texas Press, 1983.

Steglich, Winfred G. "Population Trends." In Lawrence L. Graves, ed. *A History of Lubbock*. Part Three. Lubbock: West Texas Museum Association, 1961.

Stegmaier, Mark J. "'An Imaginary Negro in an Impossible Place?' The Issue of New Mexico Statehood in the Secession Crisis, 1860–1861." *New Mexico Historical Review* 84 (Spring 2009).

Steinberg, Ted. *Down to Earth: Nature's Role in American History*. New York: Oxford University Press, 2002.

Stewart, Kenneth L., and Arnoldo De León. *Not Enough Room: Mexicans, Anglos, and Socioeconomic Change in Texas, 1850–1900*. Albuquerque: University of New Mexico Press, 1993.

Strickland, Rex W. *The Turner Thesis and the Dry World*. El Paso: Texas Western Press, 1960.

Thompson, Cecilia. *History of Marfa and Presidio County, Texas: 1535–1946*. Austin: Nortex Press, 1985.

Thompson, Jerry D. "Drama in the Desert: The Hunt for Henry Skillman in the Trans-Pecos, 1862–1864." El Paso County Historical Society. *Password* 37 (Fall 1992).

Tijerina, Andrés A. *History of Mexican Americans in Lubbock County, Texas*. Lubbock: Texas Tech Press, 1979.

———. *Tejanos and Texans under the Mexican Flag, 1821–1836*. College Station: Texas A&M University Press, 1994.

Tiling, Moritz. *History of the German Element in Texas, From 1820–1850*. Houston: Author printing, 1913.

Timmons, W. H. *El Paso: A Borderlands History*. El Paso: Texas Western Press, 1990.

Todd, Bruce G. *Bones Hooks: Pioneer Negro Cowboy*. Gretna, LA: Pelican Publishing Company, Inc., 2005.

Tolnay Stewart E., and E. M. Beck. *A Festival of Violence: An Analysis of Southern Lynchings, 1882–1930*. Urbana: University of Illinois Press, 1995.

Townsend, Stephen A. *The Yankee Invasion of Texas*. College Station: Texas A&M University Press, 2006.

Utley, Robert M. *Lone Star Justice: The First Century of the Texas Rangers*. New York: Oxford University Press, 2002.

Vallentine, John F. *Grazing Management*. San Diego: Academic Press, Inc., 1990.

Vandiver, Frank E. *The Southwest: South or West*. College Station: Texas A&M University Press, 1975.

Van Nuys, Frank. *Americanizing the West: Race, Immigrants, and Citizenship, 1890–1930*. Lawrence: University Press of Kansas, 2002.

Wallace, Ernest. *The Howling of the Coyotes: Reconstruction Efforts to Divide Texas*. College Station: Texas A&M University Press, 1979.

———. *Ranald S. Mackenzie on the Texas Frontier*. College Station: Texas A&M University Press, 1993.

Wallace, Ernest, and E. Adamson Hoebel. *The Comanches: Lords of the South Plains*. Norman: University of Oklahoma Press, 1952.

Warren, Louis S. *The Hunter's Game: Poachers and Conservationists in Twentieth-Century America*. New Haven: Yale University Press, 1997.

Webb, Walter Prescott. *The Great Plains*. Boston: Ginn and Company, 1931.

———. *The Texas Rangers: A Century of Frontier Defense*. Boston & New York: Houghton Mifflin Company, 1935.

———. "The American West, Perpetual Mirage." *Harper's Magazine* (May 1957).

Weber, David J. *The Mexican Frontier, 1821–1846: The American Southwest Under Mexico*. Albuquerque: University of New Mexico Press, 1982.

———. *Myth and the History of the Hispanic Southwest*. Albuquerque: University of New Mexico Press, 1988.

West, Elliott. "Trails and Footprints: The Past of the Future Southern Plains." In Sherry L. Smith, ed., *The Future of the Southern Plains*. Norman: University of Oklahoma Press, 2003.

White, Richard. *It's Your Misfortune and None of My Own: A New History of the American West*. Norman: University of Oklahoma Press, 1991.

———. *The Middle Ground: Indians, Empires, and Republics in the Great Lakes Region, 1650–1815*. Cambridge: Cambridge University Press, 1991.

———. "Frederick Jackson Turner and Buffalo Bill." In James R. Grossman, ed. *The Frontier in American Culture*. Berkeley: University of California Press, 1994.

White, Walter. *Rope and Faggot: A Biography of Judge Lynch*. New York: Alfred A. Knopf, 1929.

Wishart, David J., ed. *Encyclopedia of the Great Plains*. Lincoln: University of Nebraska Press, 2004.

Woodward, C. Vann. *The Burden of Southern History*. Revised Edition. Baton Rouge: Louisiana State University Press, 1968.

Wooster, Ralph A. *Texas and Texans in the Civil War*. Austin: Eakin Press, 1995.

Wooster, Robert. *Frontier Crossroads: Fort Davis and the West*. College Station: Texas A&M University Press, 2006.

———. *History of Fort Davis, Texas*. Santa Fe: Southwest Cultural Resources Center, National Park Service, 1990.

Worster, Donald. *Rivers of Empire: Water, Aridity, and the Growth of the American West*. New York: Pantheon Books, 1985.

———. *Under Western Skies: Nature and History in the American West.* New York: Oxford University Press, 1992.

PAPERS AND PRESENTATIONS

Humphries, Holle. "Conceiving a Texan West: What Art Tells Us about Regionalism." Texas State Historical Association Annual Meeting. Austin, Texas, March 4, 2006.

———. "Public Monument Sculpture in West Texas: Honoring the Historical Heritage of Regional Values." West Texas Historical Association Annual Meeting. Lubbock, Texas, March 31, 2006.

Wooster, Robert. Presidential Address. Texas State Historical Association Annual Banquet. Austin, Texas, March 3, 2006.

THESES AND DISSERTATIONS

Ely, Glen Sample. "Riding the Western Frontier: Antebellum Encounters Aboard The Butterfield Overland Mail." M.A. thesis, Texas Christian University, August 2005.

———. "Riding the Butterfield Frontier: Life and Death Along the Butterfield Overland Mail Road in Texas, 1858–1861." Ph.D. diss., Texas Christian University, 2008.

Estes, Mary Elizabeth. "An Historical Survey of Lynchings in Oklahoma and Texas." M.A. thesis, University of Oklahoma, 1942.

Flores, Maria Eva. "The Good Life the Hard Way: The Mexican American Community of Fort Stockton, Texas, 1930–1945." Ph.D. diss., Arizona State University, 2000.

Foster, Robert L. "Black Lubbock: A History of Negroes in Lubbock, Texas, to 1940." M.A. thesis, Texas Tech University, 1974.

Glasrud, Bruce Alden. "Black Texans, 1900–1930: A History." Ph.D. diss., Texas Tech University, 1969.

Holden, William Curry. "Frontier Problems and Movements in West Texas, 1846–1900." Ph.D. diss., University of Texas at Austin, 1928.

Ramirez, Manuel Bernardo. "El Pasoans: Life and Society in Mexican El Paso, 1920–1945." Ph.D. diss., University of Mississippi, 2000.

ONLINE

Anderson, H. Allen. "Charles Goodnight." *Handbook of Texas Online.* www.tsha.utexas.edu/handbook/online/articles/GG/fgo11.html (accessed Sept. 8, 2006).

Arizona State University Libraries. "Chicanos in Arizona." www.asu.edu/lib/ar
chives/chicaz.html (accessed July 2, 2007).

The Arizona Republic. "A History of African-Americans in Arizona." www.azcen
tral.com/culturesaz/afroam/afrohistory.html (accessed July 2, 2007).

"Battle of the Nueces." *Handbook of Texas Online.* www.tshaonline.org/handbook/
online/articles/NN/qfn1.html (accessed May 23, 2009).

Blaney, Betsy. "Former Oil Town Eyes Radioactive Waste." May 2, 2005. www.msnbc
.msn.com/id/7709778/ (accessed July 12, 2007).

Blumenthal, Ralph. "Angry Texans demanding halt to water deal." *Texans for Public
Justice.* Dec. 11, 2003. www.tpj.org.

Bowman, Kristi L. "The New Face of School Segregation." *Duke Law Journal.* www
.law.duke.edu/shell/cite.pl?50+Duke+L.+J.+1751 (accessed July 2, 2007).

Byrkit, James W. "Land, Sky, and People: The Southwest Defined." *Journal of the
Southwest* 34 (Autumn 1992). http://digital.library.arizona.edu/jsw/3403/index
.html (accessed July 7, 2007).

Carey, H. C. *Map of Mexico, 1822 National Atlas.* David Rumsey Collection. www
.davidrumsey.com/ (accessed June 9, 2006).

"Environmental Justice Case Study: The Struggle for Sierra Blanca, Texas Against a
Low-Level Nuclear Waste Site." Environmental Justice Initiative. School of Natural Resources and Environment, University of Michigan-Ann Arbor. www.mi
chedu (accessed May 26, 2009).

Farm Aid. "About Us." www.farmaid.org/site/c.qlI5IhNVJsE/b.2723609/k.C8F1/Ab
out_Us.htm (accessed June 12, 2007).

———. "Family Farmers." www.farmaid.org/site/c.qlI5IhNVJsEb.2750749/k.89E0/
Family_Farmers.htm (accessed June 12, 2007).

Finley, Anthony. *Mexico, 1831 World Atlas.* David Rumsey Collection. www.davidrum
sey.com/ (accessed June 9, 2006).

Graves, Lawrence L. "Texas Tech University." *Handbook of Texas Online.* www.tsha
.utexas.edu/handbook/online/articles/TT/kct32.html (accessed November 12,
2007).

Hamilton, Nancy. "University of Texas at El Paso." *Handbook of Texas Online.* www
.tsha.utexas.edu/handbook/online/articles/UU/kcu11.html (accessed November
12, 2007).

Hayter, Delmar J. "Red Bluff Dam and Reservoir." *Handbook of Texas Online.* www
.tsha.utexas.edu/handbook/online/articles/RR/rur2.html (accessed January 26,
2007).

Hinton, Harwood P. "John Simpson Chisum." *Handbook of Texas Online.* www.tsha
.utexas.edu/handbook/online/articles/CC/fch33.html (accessed Sept. 8, 2006).

———. "Wylie, Robert Kelsey." *Handbook of Texas Online.* www.tsha.utexas.edu/
handbook/online/articles/view/WW/fwy7.html (accessed March 30, 2005).

"Journal of William P. Huff of an Overland Trip from Richmond, Fort Bend County,
Texas, to Mariposa in Southern California in the Years 1849 and 1850." http://

web.archive.org/web/19961126103709/http://sunsite.berkeley.edu/MaderaM ethod/zhuff_diary.html (accessed April 24, 2007). Copyright, David Ewing Stewart.

Justice, Glenn, and John Leffler. "Pecos County." *Handbook of Texas Online.* www.tsha. utexas.edu/handbook/online/articles/PP/hcp5.html (accessed April 22, 2006).

Kelton, Elmer. "Battle of Dove Creek." *Handbook of Texas Online.* www.tshaonline .org/handbook/online/articles/DD/btd1.html (accessed May 26, 2009).

Kleiner, Diana J. "Fort Worth Star-Telegram." *Handbook of Texas Online.* www.tsha online.org/handbook/online/articles/FF/eef4.html (accessed June 2, 2009).

Leffler, John. "Young County." *Handbook of Texas Online.* www.tsha.utexas.edu/ handbook/online/articles/YY/hcy2.html (accessed July 30, 2005).

McCaslin, Richard B. "Great Hanging at Gainesville." *Handbook of Texas Online.* www.tshaonline.org/handbook/online/articles/GG/jig1.html (accessed May 23, 2009).

Miyamoto, S., Fasong Yuan, and Shilpa Anand. Texas AgriLife Research, Texas Water Resources Institute. "TR-291, 2006, Reconnaissance Survey of Salt Sources and Loading into the Pecos River." *Pecos River Basin Assessment Program.* Technical Reports. www.pecosbasin.tamu.edu/project_documents.php (accessed June 11, 2007).

——.Texas AgriLife Research, Texas Water Resources Institute. "TR-292, 2006, Influence of Tributaries on Salinity of Amistad International Reservoir." *Pecos River Basin Assessment Program.* Technical Reports. www.pecosbasin.tamu.edu/project_doc uments.php (accessed June 11, 2007).

——. Texas AgriLife Research, Texas Water Resources Institute. "TR-298, 2007, Water Balance, Salt Loading, and Salinity Control Options of Red Bluff Reservoir, Texas." *Pecos River Basin Assessment Program.* Technical Reports. www.pe cosbasin.tamu.edu/project_documents.php (accessed June 11, 2007).

Montoya, Margaret E. "Chicana/o Desegregation Cases." *The University of Dayton School of Law.* www.academic.udayton.edu/RACE/04NEEDS/affirm16.htm (accessed May 20, 2007).

The Official Site of Texas Tourism. Office of the Governor, Economic Development and Tourism. "Texas: It's Like a Whole Other Country." www.traveltexas.com/ Index. aspx (accessed July 12, 2007).

Ross, John R. "Lynching." *Handbook of Texas Online.* www.tsha.utexas.edu/hand book/online/articles/LL/jgl1.html (accessed October 29, 2007).

Ruiz, Vicki L. "South by Southwest: Mexican Americans and Segregated Schooling, 1900–1950." *Organization of American Historians.* www.oah.org/pubs/magazine/ deseg/ruiz.html (accessed June 18, 2006).

Salter, Ruben, Jr. "In the Steps of Esteban: Tucson's African American Heritage." *University of Arizona.* http://parentseyes.arizona.edu/esteban/bios_med-legal_sal ter.html (accessed June 18, 2006).

Smyrl, Vivian Elizabeth. "Texas Low-Level Radioactive Waste Disposal Authority." *Handbook of Texas Online.* www.tsha.utexas.edu/handbook/online/articles/TT/metur.html (accessed July 12, 2007).

Sparling, Wesley E. "Texas Frontier Centennial." *Handbook of Texas Online.* www.tshaonline.org/handbook/online/articles/TT/lkt3.html (accessed June 2, 2009).

Tanner, Henry S. *Map of the United States of Mexico, June 1826.* David Rumsey Collection. www.davidrumsey.com/ (accessed June 9, 2006).

———. *Mexico and Guatemala, 1836 World Atlas.* David Rumsey Collection. www.davidrumsey.com/ (accessed June 9, 2006).

Texas Education Agency. Online News Release. May 21, 2010. "State Board of Education Gives Final Okay to Social Studies Standards." www.tea.state.tx.us/index4.aspx?id=2147484354 (accessed June 12, 2010).

Texas Historical Commission. *Texas Historic Sites Atlas.* http://atlas.thc.state.tx.us/shell-county.htm (accessed November 14, 2007).

Texas Parks and Wildlife Department. "Precipitation in Texas." www.tpwd.state.tx.us/landwater/land/maps/gis/map_downloads/images/pwd_mp_e0100_1070e_6.gif (accessed June 11, 2007).

Texas Ranger Hall of Fame and Museum. www.texasranger.org/store/Productpages/AmericaRemembers. htm (accessed May 12, 2009.)

Texas Secretary of State. *Texas Register.* April 16, 2010. Texas Education Agency. 19 TAC, Chapter 113, TEKS Social Studies Standards and Amendments. www.sos.state.tx.us/texreg/ (accessed April 29, 2010).

Texas State Data Center and Office of the State Demographer. Thematic Maps. "1990 U.S. Population Density-Black Persons." www.txsdc.utsa.edu/download/pdf/txcensus/black.jpg (accessed July 22, 2008).

U.S. Census Bureau. "Harrison County, TX 2000 QuickFacts." www.quickfacts.census.gov/qfd/states/48/ 48203.html (accessed July 22, 2008**).**

———. "Pecos County, Texas." www.census.gov/population/cencounts/tx190090.txt (accessed April 22, 2006).

———. "Texas Quick Facts." www.quickfacts.census.gov/qfd/states/48000.html (accessed on July 1, 2007).

———. "Texas County Selection Map." www.quickfacts.census.gov/qfd/maps/texas_map.html (accessed on July 1, 2007).

"West Texas Chamber of Commerce." *Handbook of Texas Online.* www.tshaonline.org/handbook/online/articles/WW/daw1.html (accessed March 17, 2010).

Wheeler, Clark. "Clay County." *Handbook of Texas Online.* www.tsha.utexas.edu/handbook/online/articles/CC/hcc12.html (accessed July 30, 2005).

Wooster, Ralph A. "Civil War." *Handbook of Texas Online.* www.tshaonline.org/handbook/online/articles/CC/qdc2.html (accessed May 23, 2009).

www.citytowninfo.com/places/texas (accessed Nov. 12, 2009).

INDEX

Martínez, Oscar, 84, 87
Mason, Theresa, 94
Matthews, M. W., 70
Maxey, Bell, 53
Mays, Reuben, 45
McAdoo, John, 49, 55–56, 62, 70–71
McCord, J. E., 57–58
McCulloch, Henry, 65
McFeely, William D., 86
McKinney, C. C., 57
Meinig, D. W., 31
Mexican Americans. *See* Tejanos
Mexican War [Texas War of Independence], 76–77
Midland, TX, 8, 90
Miller, Jim Ed, 107–8, 110
Mills, W. W., 58
monuments
    historical markers, xvi, 30–31
    as source of information, 73–74
Morrow, Samuel, 59
Murchison, John, 18–20
Murphy, Daniel, 45
Murphy, Patrick, 45
Murrah, Pendleton, 53–54, 63–65
Murray, Thomas, 67–68
mythologizing Texas, 6, 131
    escapism and, 129
    historical markers and, 73–74
    origins of "Goodnight-Loving Cattle
        Trail" and, 63
    of racism, 76
    of ranching, 119
    and yeoman farmer as American ideal,
        100, 106

Nail, David L., 90
Native Americans
    as defining component of the West, 124
    environment and cultures of, 16–17
    frontier security and raiding by, 45,
        50–52

natural resources, 23, 80, 126
    See also land as resource; water
        resources
Neff, Pat, 33
New Mexico, 29, 30, 46–48
nuclear waste storage, 127

Odessa,TX, 8, 94, 125
Ogallala Aquifer, 16, 108, 118, 128, 166n41
oil and gas resources, 23
Orrick, E. M., 51
Ozona, TX, 90

Pascoe, Peggy, 78
Patterson, James, 61, 67, 69
Pease, E. M., 32
Perales, Alonso, 22
Peter, Emory, 68–69
Pickens, T. Boone, 126
politics
    fraudulent elections, 29, 81–82
    poll taxes and disenfranchisement, 81
    race relations as political issue, 85–86
    Tejanos as elected officials, 79, 94–95
Powell, John Wesley, 16, 102
precipitation
    droughts, 11, 15–16, 103, 107, 111, 113–15,
        118
    twenty-inch rainfall break line, 11, *13, 14,*
        102–3, 121
Primera, Joe, 81–82, 98
Progressive Era
    irrigated farming and the, 101–2
    race relations during, 23, 77, 84, 87, 88,
        91
    and redefinition of Texas state identity,
        123
    social and cultural changes during, 77

Quayle, William, 49

ABOUT THE AUTHOR

Glen Sample Ely's documentaries have appeared on PBS, the History Channel, and the Discovery Channel. His scholarly work has appeared in journals such as *Southwestern Historical Quarterly* and the *New Mexico Historical Review.* A Ph.D. graduate of Texas Christian University, he lives in Fort Worth, Texas.
   www.texashistory.com

Alwyn Barr, one of Texas's most prolific historians, is retired from the department of History at Texas Tech University.